HEGEL AND SPINOZA

---

diaeresis

HEGEL AND SPINOZA

Substance and Negativity

Gregor Moder

Foreword by Mladen Dolar

Northwestern University Press
Evanston, Illinois

Northwestern University Press
www.nupress.northwestern.edu

Printed in the United States of America

10 9 8 7 6 5 4 3 2 1

Library of Congress Cataloging-in-Publication Data

Names: Moder, Gregor, 1979– author. | Dolar, Mladen, writer of foreword.
Title: Hegel and Spinoza : substance and negativity / Gregor Moder.
Other titles: Hegel in Spinoza. English | Diaeresis.
Description: Evanston, Illinois : Northwestern University Press, 2017. | Series: Diaeresis | Based in part on Hegel in Spinoza : substanca in negativnost. Ljubljana : Društvo za teoretsko psihoanalizo, 2009; translated from Slovenian by the author—Email from publisher.
Identifiers: LCCN 2017016865 | ISBN 9780810135420 (cloth : alk. paper) | ISBN 9780810135413 (pbk. : alk. paper) | ISBN 9780810135437 (e-book)
Subjects: LCSH: Hegel, Georg Wilhelm Friedrich, 1770–1831. | Spinoza, Benedictus de, 1632–1677. | Negativity (Philosophy) | Substance (Philosophy)
Classification: LCC B2949.N4 M6313 2017 | DDC 193—dc23
LC record available at https://lccn.loc.gov/2017016865

Contents

Acknowledgments

This book would not have been possible without the incessant inspiration I received from conversations with many colleagues and friends. I am indebted to, among many others, Andrew Cole, Mirt Komel, Pierre Macherey, Catherine Malabou, Jamila M. H. Mascat, Robert Pfaller, Slavoj Žižek, and Alenka Zupančič; to the international community at the former Jan van Eyck Academy in Maastricht, the Netherlands, as well as to the group of friends of German Idealism gathered at the Aufhebung Association in Ljubljana, Slovenia; and above all to Mladen Dolar, who carefully read and generously commented on earlier drafts. I learned a great deal from all of them. The majority of the research for this project was funded by University of Ljubljana, for which I am eternally grateful. And finally, I would like to thank everyone who helped in preparing the manuscript for publication, to Adrian Johnston, Todd McGowan, and Slavoj Žižek; and to Nathan MacBrien, who led me through the process with great kindness and absolute professionalism.

Foreword: Hegel or Spinoza? Yes, Please!

Mladen Dolar

At a famous spot in the lectures on the history of philosophy Hegel emphatically proclaimed: "Either Spinozism or no philosophy at all" (*Entweder Spinozismus oder keine Philosophie*).[1] It is true that Hegel, in the picturesque dramaturgy of his lectures given to an enthralled audience, never missed a chance to praise or scold, often exaggerating in the heat of the moment, yet he nonetheless never said anything quite like this about anyone else. If one truly wants to be a philosopher then one has to be a Spinozist; one must embrace Spinoza's courage and audacity of thinking; one has to espouse the speculative stance of the unity of thinking and being. More than that, one has to engage with thinking which is at the same time a production of being and not merely a reflection of something supposedly existing before and outside of thought. Not only engaging with the absolute, but also producing the absolute. Spinoza is thus presented as the touchstone of any modern thought, the decisive entry into philosophy and the prospect of its highest reach. And yet within the same dramaturgical move typical of the lectures, this high praise is transformed into a sharp criticism over the course of only a few sentences: the audacious journey got stuck already at the very first step; Spinoza's substance, so courageously proposed in the beginning, is stuck in its rigidity, remaining within the boundaries of understanding (*Verstand*), unable to reach the realm of reason (*Vernunft*). It is bereft of all movement and change because it lacks the inner driving force of negativity: Understanding deals with determinations that do not contradict each other. Negation is simple determinateness. Negation of negation, however, is contradiction, it negates the negation; thus it is affirmation, but at the same time also negation as such. This contradiction is something that understanding cannot endure; it pertains to reason. This is the point that is lacking in Spinoza, this is his shortcoming.[2]

For Hegel, negativity is precisely the speculative lever that enables us to think the life of the absolute; it is the way by which every substantial determination necessarily passes over into its other and thereby loses itself; it loses its self-identity, it negates itself, it progresses through the persistent movement of self-referential negation, "negation of negation."

But through this process negativity nevertheless remains the inner principle of the life of the absolute; the absolute is not something free of negativity, but something produced by negativity. For Hegel, substantiality is that which preserves itself through negation; not something that would persist in its positivity and identity beyond the vagaries of change and beyond the process of what Hegel has called, in an excellent word, self-othering, *Sichanderswerden.* This is precisely why, for Hegel, "everything depends on grasping and expressing the True not merely as *substance* (i.e., as persistence of something positive and identical) but also equally as *subject* (i.e., as a process of incessant losing oneself and producing oneself only through this loss)." This is the standpoint of reason, while Spinoza, in Hegel's view, got stuck in the impasses of understanding. As opposed to this, Spinoza famously maintained: "Each thing, insofar as it is in itself, endeavors to persist in its own being,"[3] and: "No thing can be destroyed, except by a cause external to itself."[4] No entity is endowed with negativity in itself; it is driven by the pure persistence of conatus, negation can only come from outside. Thus it seems that Hegel's reading of Spinoza presents us with two emphatic alternatives: either Spinozism or loss of any philosophical standpoint worthy of this name—it is only through Spinozism that the substance and the absolute can be taken seriously; but then this leads to another emphatic choice: either the Spinozist substance that cannot embrace negativity, a substance that is not and cannot become a subject, or the proposition that "substance is subject." Either conatus or self-othering.

This famous page from Hegel's lectures condenses the gist of the problem, boiling it down to two crucial concepts, that of substance and that of negativity. The entire tradition which in one way or another took its cue from Hegel and followed his line of thought, even if in a very critical way, the tradition guided by dialectics as the paradigm of thought, thereby adopted, in one way or another, Hegel's judgment of Spinoza, albeit adding to it more refined historical specifications. On the other hand, an entire tradition that wanted to break free from the clutches of Hegelian dialectics and sought other ways of thinking, found its privileged foothold precisely in Spinoza. Spinoza was the anti-Hegel; he read and criticized Hegel already in advance, foreseeing and avoiding the traps of negativity. Following this argument, the Hegelian medicine for the rigidity of Spinozist substance was itself the source of a severe disease: the negation, along with the negation of negation, the contradiction, sublation, and so on, are ultimately nothing but an integral part of the Hegelian teleological process, whose true result is not the preservation and affirmation of negativity, but precisely its abolishment, a stratagem leading to a reestablishment of identity, the suspension of heterogeneity on the path toward the Hegelian absolute knowledge. As opposed to this, Spinoza was presented as the model of thinking the affirmative production of differences, avoiding the traps of Hegelian negativity while at the same time retaining its speculative charge.

In the background of so much of contemporary thought one can therefore posit an emphatic alternative: either Hegel or Spinoza. Partisans of the one side see in the other side a paradigmatic blunder, even though both sides also speak respectfully of one another and point out the greatness of their adversary. But in this conflict, no one can claim the neutral ground and simply attribute to the sides their proper places, seeing in them two great monuments of thought pertaining to the past. Both sides engage and obligate, and so it is impossible to take a neutral distance, praising their merits and scolding their flaws with an impartial gaze. There is no neutral judgment; we are always on a conceptual battleground, caught in the crossfire.

Hegel and Spinoza have been thus, explicitly or implicitly, cast in the roles of two contradicting paradigms over which contemporary philosophical battles are being fought in many essential respects. One can easily list some names, with on the one side the Frankfurt School, the bulk of Marxism, Kojève and his legacy, Sartre, Lacan, Badiou, and so on, and on the other side Althusser and his school, and most prominently Deleuze (who famously proposed the slogan *oublier Hegel*, let's "forget Hegel," forget that this unfortunate calamity ever happened). It is nevertheless surprising that there exist so few investigations that would carefully and judiciously confront these two paradigms and reflect on the possible productivity of their encounter. The scarce scholarship that would undertake such a heroic enterprise—the most prominent author by far is Pierre Macherey, whose famous book carries the emphatic title *Hegel or Spinoza*[5]—is largely imbued with ardent partisanship of the one side against the other, extolling the one and deprecating the other.

Against this backdrop, this book by Gregor Moder presents a most refreshing novelty for which I cannot find a match in current philosophical literature. It succeeds in performing something remarkably difficult, to the point of being almost impossible: it attempts to faithfully follow the one and the other, both Hegel and Spinoza, through the key stages of their respective thoughts; it considers attentively their fundamental theoretical decisions and solutions and weighs their far-reaching implications. Gregor Moder passionately defends the one and the other against a series of standard objections, addressed from the one side to the other over the last two centuries; he carefully avoids the major drawback in this discussion, namely that the one side takes the other as a straw man and attacks a stereotype or a caricature rather than engaging with thought. He maintains both threads of thought simultaneously as far as it is possible without discarding one and simply espousing the other, without taking sides in advance. Yet he does not do this *sine ira et studio,* from the neutral or impartial perspective of a scholar of the history of philosophy, passing judgments and giving each their own; rather, he does it with the utmost engagement in the matter, absolutely aware at each moment that there is no neutral perspective, that the battlefield constitutes the native ground of thought, that one cannot evade conceptual antagonism, and that the task of thinking consists in relentlessly producing new conceptual weapons, opening up new points of view, and never submitting to rash solutions or habitual images.

Note on Sources and Abbreviations

Throughout the book, works by Spinoza are cited from the following publication: Baruch de Spinoza, *Spinoza: Complete Works,* translated by Samuel Shirley et al. (Indianapolis, Ind.: Hackett, 2002). The title of the work in question is provided in abbreviated form: *E* refers to the *Ethics, TIE* to the *Treatise on the Emendation of the Intellect, TTP* to the *Theological-Political Treatise, TP* to *Political Treatise,* and *EPS* to his letters (1 to 84). In the case of the *Ethics,* the reference is further specified to help the reader find the appropriate part (I to V), proposition (P), definition (Def), axiom (A), corollary (Cor), scholium (Sch), or appendix (Apx). *E*IIP7Sch therefore refers to the scholium to proposition 7 of part II of the *Ethics.*

Works by Hegel are cited from an existing English translation wherever possible. In some cases German text is additionally provided; the most common edition is used, Suhrkamp's *Gesamte Werkausgabe: Werke,* volumes 1–20, edited by Eva Moldenhauer and Karl Markus Michel (Frankfurt am Main: Suhrkamp, 1986). The reference to this work is abbreviated as *TWA,* followed by the volume and page numbers.

HEGEL AND SPINOZA

Introduction

Hegel and Spinoza: The Question of Reading

For Hegel, Spinoza's philosophy presented an irresistibly attractive and at the same time relentlessly provocative system of thought. If we were to list Hegel's main incentives, that is to say, his necessary interlocutors, his favorite adversaries, we would be forced to put Spinoza's philosophy near the very top, perhaps even directly below Hegel's polemics with Kant and other famous German Idealists. The reasons for this are, in part, purely extrinsic, or "historical." In the eighteenth and nineteenth centuries, Spinoza was essential reading for German intellectuals. He was read by Goethe and Herder, who recognized in his system the pantheism of a continuously developing universal force of life. When romanticism sought to conjoin the question of subjectivity to a vitalistic Whole in order to lay the grounds for its project of nature as an expressive totality, as cosmic subjectivity, it drew its inspiration precisely from Spinozism.[1] Before Hegel, Spinoza was discussed by other classic figures of German Idealism such as Kant, Schelling, and Fichte, and perhaps there is not too much exaggeration in the statement that they could not have developed their philosophical systems without the reflection in the mirror of Spinozism.[2] If it is true that Hegel's position was, in his early period, generally speaking a Spinozist one,[3] then this was only possible because at that time in intellectual Germany a generalized image of Spinozism—for instance, in the form of a romantic pantheism, a living cosmos, and organic unity—was simply an image that demanded immediate engagement, either in its favor or against it.

But why was the figure of Spinoza so dramatically important in the development of German Idealism? How did this inflammatory thinker of nature without a transcendent deity, passionately excommunicated by Jews, hated and ridiculed by Christians, avoided by all, and submerged in relative obscurity suddenly rise to become a topic of general discussion and to a certain extent even a model philosopher, a philosopher as such? The answer, for the most part, lies in a long-lasting controversy among prominent intellectuals which is known as the *Pantheismusstreit* or *Spinozismusstreit* (pantheism- or Spinozism-controversy). The spark that started the controversy was a scandal among the intellectual elite of the time, a scandal that involved strong personal convictions, breach of trust, and a tragic death. It started in 1785 when Friedrich Heinrich Jacobi, at that time a peripheral but socially quite active figure, published his letters to a renowned thinker of the Enlightenment, Moses Mendelssohn, complete with his commentary, under the title of *Ueber die Lehre des Spinoza, in Briefen an den Herrn Moses Mendelssohn* (translated as *Concerning the Doctrine of Spinoza in Letters to Herr Moses Mendelssohn*). This publication pushed Spinozism, as well as Jacobi, onto center stage.

The exchange of letters between Jacobi and Mendelssohn started off with the question of whether Lessing, one of the legendary personalities of the German and indeed the European Enlightenment, was a Spinozist or not. Upon learning that Mendelssohn was preparing a publication on Lessing, Jacobi wrote to him and reported that during his visit to Lessing, the latter declared himself a Spinozist. At the time this was an incendiary claim, since being a Spinozist meant as much as being a radical atheist. But the discussion quickly transcended this particular question and evolved to tackle some of the prominent questions of the day, principally the relationship between understanding and faith. Mendelssohn, who was quite upset by Jacobi's publication of their correspondence, feverishly worked day and night to produce a response. When it was finished, he took the manuscript personally to the publisher on one cold January night, got dramatically sick, and subsequently died; some of Jacobi's critics blamed him for Mendelssohn's death.[4]

The controversy sparked by this exchange came to involve the entire intellectual elite, from Herder to Hamman, Reinhold, and Kant. In general terms, what was at stake was the divide between the Enlightenment on the one hand and the Sturm und Drang and romantic movements on the other hand; the relationship between knowing and believing; and between understanding and feeling. One of the key objections to the Enlightenment, raised by the Sturm and Drang movement and by pietism, claimed that in its criticism of traditional authorities and prejudices in the name of the universal understanding it was oblivious to the fact that its own universal position was also possible only in its specific cultural and historical context, and that understanding thus became the very authority that suppresses freedom.[5]

But Jacobi went even further. He claimed that the position of understanding alone, if followed to its extreme consequences, leads to determinism and fatalism and is therefore fundamentally immoral. For him, Spinozism was the most radical, yet at the same time the most consequential form of a rational system. This is why he claimed that a philosophy based on understanding is necessarily a form of Spinozism. Hence the alternative: either one is a philosopher, and therefore a Spinozist, or one has to reject Spinozism, rejecting with it the principle of discursive understanding and philosophy.[6] The reach of the knowledge that one could attain by means of understanding and philosophy was too short for Jacobi. According to him, they cannot *grasp* the core of the truth and are limited to posing true statements. The core of the truth remains in all cases something immediate and unanalyzable, something that can only be grasped by intuition or faith. Any true knowledge must therefore be grounded in faith; and understanding is grounded in intuition. We can use these theses by Jacobi as a negative background upon which we may formulate the fundamental challenges of German Idealism: how to secure and defend the ethical place of freedom within the framework of philosophy as "Spinozism"; or in another context: does knowledge require an external guarantee—such as faith or intuition—or is it, to the contrary, guaranteed as knowledge intrinsically, and perhaps capable of producing its own foundation? This is why we can say that the German Idealists embraced Spinozism as an exemplary philosophical system, while trying to reject and supersede it at the same time.[7]

But it was not only for these general and accidental reasons that Hegel was interested in rejecting and admiring Spinoza; there were also specific and for his own philosophy quite essential reasons. On the one hand, Hegel claimed Spinoza was the peak of modern philosophy, even the only possible beginning in philosophy, and he even went so far as to claim that there is no philosophy save as Spinozism.[8] On the other hand, most of Hegel's reproaches to Spinoza can be summed up as the reproach that the very philosophy which enables the possibility of philosophy as such is at the same time stuck in its beginning: it never progressed from its starting point, it never developed its own positions. Since this philosophy was incapable of thinking contradiction, Hegel often viewed it as a Parmenidean or identity principle, according to which only being is, while nonbeing is not; he regarded it as a living fossil for supposedly reintroducing a non-Christian, "Oriental" philosophy of light and the principle of *ex nihilo nihil fit* (nothing can come out of nothing) in philosophy. Hegel himself emphatically affirmed Christian metaphysics and its principle of *creatio ex nihilo* (creation out of nothing).[9]

Hegel's reproach of immobility or rigidity in Spinoza can be analyzed in three different yet closely related ways. Firstly, Hegel claims that the Spinozist substance is incapable of transforming itself or organically growing—which is in obvious contrast to interpretations circulating in German romanticism and preromanticism. To put it in Hegel's decisive formulation, it is a substance that is not yet substance *and* subject. In this respect, Spinozism is a variation of the "*pantheism* of the Eleatics,"[10] and its substance is immobile in exactly the same way that the being of the

Eleatics is immobile: it is a pure abstract affirmation and immediacy, and it involves no movement or contradiction. Secondly, Spinoza's geometric principle of demonstration, *more geometrico*, is the method of demonstration in mathematics, which was dismissed by Hegel as well as by other German Idealists, since such a method cannot grasp the self-developing nature and the organic movement of the absolute. In this sense, the rigidity of the substance is closely related to the rigidity of its method of explication.[11] Thirdly, Spinozism nevertheless already formulated the most brilliant dialectical concepts, such as, for instance, *causa sui* (cause of itself) and the principle of *omnis determinatio est negatio* (all determination is negation), but it failed to develop them to their utmost consequences. It stuck at the beginning. According to Hegel, in the definition of *causa sui* Spinoza already formulated the "indifference of being and nothingness"; in this concept he already grasped the fundamental speculative idea of self-mediation—for the cause of itself produces itself as its effect and therefore as something other than itself—but apparently failed to apply these principles to the absolute substance, for otherwise it would not have been immobile.[12]

What kind of reading is Hegel's reading of the philosophy of Spinoza? It would be much too naive—if not completely wrong—to say that he picked out some Spinozist concepts and productively implemented them in his own philosophy while discarding others as deficient. In fact, Hegel never read any of the philosophers in the history of philosophy in this fashion. Moreover, he never read any phenomenon of the spirit—be it artistic, religious, philosophical, or political—in this fashion. Hegel's reading of a text is completely different from what we usually understand as reliable historical reading; it is never a reading that diligently collects and weighs its sources, references, summaries, and reports, comparing one against the other, and carefully choosing the most adequate explanation in the pursuit of compiling a transparent oversight of the whole with the explicit ambition of producing an impartial view of the matter at hand.

In a way, Hegel's reading is "nonhistorical" and "unreliable"; that is to say, it is most certainly a reading that takes us away from the immediate letter of the text and its historical context, often in an unashamed and quite apparent attempt at developing Hegel's own philosophical theses. And yet it does not do so by picking out useful positions and concepts, and separating them from others. On the contrary, the Hegelian reading always admits that the text it is reading is a necessary expression of the spirit and that it is therefore in itself already in truth—and not just a more or less fortunate collection of successful and unsuccessful claims. It is a reading that does not measure its text to an external guideline, but insists on an immanent explanation. A text is therefore always already *in truth*; but at the same time, its truth is never a complete, absolute, or *entire truth*. As an affirmative expression of the spirit, a text is always an expression of the absolute, and yet as an affirmative and determinate expression it is also always already its negation. It is as if the truth expressed in the text, through this very expression, already became something other than it was, therefore demanding a new expression.

A text as an expression of the spirit already implies something that cannot be grasped in its immediate form; it implies something unexpressed. If one was to call on the Aristotelian distinction between actuality and potentiality, then one could say that the text implies an unexpressed potentiality in its very actuality; the texture of the text, so to speak, is never a smooth one. But we can never simply separate the "actual" from the "potential," as if they were two independent threads; they can be discerned only in retrospect. Aristotle used the distinction between actual and potential to explain movement or change—and perhaps we can say that the text we are reading, for Hegel, is much like a body in motion: it is certainly there, before us, as something true, but at the same time it is not fully there yet; something still needs to happen to it, it must still get somewhere. This is why the Hegelian reading does not weigh its text, picking out its useful parts and discarding the rest. It rather seeks to *repeat* the text in its truth; and by repeating its truth it reveals its potentiality, its dynamism. One could say that the Hegelian reading is a *productive repetition of the truth* of the text it is reading.[13]

So, what kind of reading is Hegel's reading of Spinoza? We can formulate the question that interested Hegel in Spinoza as the question of whether it is possible to think contradiction or movement on the level of the absolute substance, or, to borrow from the title of one of Slavoj Žižek's books on Christianity, whether it is possible to think the absolute as a *fragile* absolute.[14] More precisely: how can one read and explicate Spinozism in order to successfully produce such a concept of the absolute? What Hegel found in Spinoza was the idea that only what exists, exists, and that the substance is one and universal, but at the same time also the idea that any particular determination is already a negation of that primordial unity. What Hegel thought was lacking in the work of Spinoza was not something that was completely absent from that philosophy and had to be artificially added to it, from its outside; rather, it was something that was certainly there, written in the first line of the first part of Spinoza's major work, the *Ethics*, in the definition of the *causa sui*. Hegel's speculative reading does not take Spinozism as its adversary, but strictly speaking as an integral part of its own position.[15] To state again, what Hegel lacked in Spinoza was not a certain positive content, but rather a form of insistence and consequentiality: had Spinoza comprehended the cause in itself as self-determination of the universal substance, and according to the principle of *omnis determinatio est negatio* as self-negation of the absolute, he would already have had an explicit formulation of the negation of negation, a concept of a productive contradiction, and therefore a concept of an absolute in motion.

Hegel's question about Spinoza's philosophy could therefore be understood as a question of movement, specifically of movement or contradiction of the beginning, of the primordial. In other words, it is a question of dynamism internal to being itself, and at the same time a question of why it was necessary for Spinozism, as far as the question of movement of the primordial is concerned, to get stuck at the beginning, at the first sentence, and why it was unable to move from this beginning. To use a recursive formula: why was it necessary for the Spinozist absolute to appear as immobile to Spinozism itself, when it already appeared for the Hegelian reading as an absolute with inner dynamism; that is, as an absolute which on the one hand, for Spinozism itself, was immobile, an identity absolute, whereas on the other hand, for the Hegelian reading, it was already an absolute of contradiction, an absolute in movement?

Lost in Translation

Before submerging deeper into Hegel's reading of Spinoza, let me schematically point out some of the principal objections to this reading and the concerns regarding it that were traditionally raised. First of all, the understanding of Spinozism as pantheism—be it Eleatic or romanticist—is not entirely justified. Gueroult demonstrated, and his argument was taken up by many other commentators, that in Spinozism the point was not so much that the whole (or the universe) is called God, but that everything that exists exists "in" God.[16] The more proper designation would therefore be pan-en-theism.

Two, Hegel's reproach to the mathematical method of demonstration, claiming that it was inept for demonstrating a philosophical truth—an argument that he constantly repeated throughout his body of work—was, in principle, also Spinoza's reproach.[17]

Three, the definition of the cause of itself, praised by Hegel as the moment of absolute knowledge and explained as the fundamental, principal determination of Spinoza's system, does not really play, in Spinoza, the role of an absolute beginning from which everything else stems and evolves. Moreover, being the cause of itself is but a property of the substance, merely explicating the substance; if we understand it as defining or determining the substance, we have already submitted the essence of God to his power and therefore fallen into the matrix of theological finalism.[18]

Four, Spinozism is not organized either as a philosophy of the absolute beginning nor as a philosophy of the beginning with the absolute—at least not in the *Ethics.* Deleuze pointed out the difference between the *Short Treatise on God, Man and His Wellbeing,* which indeed begins with God, and the *Ethics,* where the argument does *not* start with God and aims rather at being able to rise to God as quickly as we can.[19]

Five, there are many details that suggest that Hegel's treatment of Spinoza was either less than thorough or even a deliberate attempt at forcing Spinozism to fit into a neatly arranged space that Hegel cleared for it in the grand scheme of the development of the spirit throughout the history of philosophy. An overwhelming example of this procedure, for Macherey, was Hegel's reduction of the infinity of attributes in Spinoza's system to only two attributes of extension and thought (and explaining those as basically Eleatic being and thinking), a reduction that apparently serves no other purpose than to place Spinoza immediately after Descartes in the logical-historical sequence of philosophy.[20]

But, six, none of the other aspects of Hegel's reading of Spinoza was quite as far-reaching as the notorious principle of *omnis determinatio est negatio.* This principle was not Hegel's invention, and Hegel was not the first to try to explain the entirety of Spinoza's system from this principle. The idea that to determine is to negate reached Hegel in relation to Spinoza through Jacobi.[21] What is astonishing about this principle is, to put it quite simply, that Spinoza never used it as a guiding principle of his philosophy. The sentence was floating around in the air even before Jacobi, but it was this infamous polemicist that gave it the form of an ontological principle according to which all actually existing (that is, determinate) things are marked by an intrinsic decadence or nonbeing (that is, by negation).[22]

But if we follow Macherey's thorough and elaborate analysis, Hegel's specific take on this principle is even more fascinating. The reason why Hegel was so enthusiastic about this "Spinozist" principle is that he read it inversely: as if all negation is determination, that is, as if a negation of an entity is in fact a productive procedure of (positive) determination.[23] The Hegelian gesture with regard to Spinozism can then be summed up as follows: had Spinoza comprehended "his" principle as a speculative principle, that is, as a principle of potentiality, then his system of absolutely infinite substance and finite modes would never have been just a system of ontological degradation, of simple negation, but rather a system of the negation of negation, of productive negation. This may all sound well, except for one simple flaw—the principle of ontological degradation is not a Spinozist principle at all!

If Hegel's reading of Spinozism was fundamentally dependent on the principle which differentiates between an undetermined, perfect absolute on the one hand and a sequence of gradual determinations, differentiations, and ontological dilutions or degradations on the other hand, then it is obvious that Hegel understood the system of the substance, attributes, and the modes as a typical emanationist system.[24] But while Spinoza was indeed inspired by the vast Neoplatonic tradition of the emanationist causality, Deleuze emphasized that he produced within it an important immanentist twist. Both emanative cause and immanent cause remain in themselves when producing their effect—but they differ in that with immanentist causality, the effect also "remains in" its cause. This distinction has enormous consequences for the entire system, because the immanent cause knows no ontological hierarchy, and since the effect was never "cast out" or "sent out" and never "fell out" of its cause, it also does not need to teleologically "return" to its cause.[25]

The perplexity of Hegel's reading of Spinoza's philosophy relies mainly on the fact that he was attracted by concepts and principles—for instance, the definition of *causa sui* as the beginning of philosophy with a contradiction between the cause and the effect at work in the absolute substance, *omnis determinatio est negatio* as the first step toward a concept of productive negation—that were without any doubt tremendously important for Hegel, but seem to have only a tangential relation to Spinoza. And as if this were not enough, some of Hegel's reproaches to Spinoza do not only seem unjustified, but also unreasonable to the extent that they unnecessarily see an adversary where there is in fact an ally. The most obvious example of this is the question of the method. Spinoza's famous example of working iron from the *Treatise on the Emendation of the Intellect* is an attack on Descartes's method of clear and distinct perception: if one accepts the premise that in order to work iron, one must first acquire a proper working tool, a hammer, then one must necessarily also accept the following premise that in order to produce that working tool, the hammer, one must first acquire another hammer and other tools, and so on ad infinitum.[26] Spinoza's definition of the adequate idea in the *Ethics* spells out quite clearly that it is an idea "which, insofar as it is considered in itself without relation to its object has all the properties, that is, intrinsic characteristics, of a true idea."[27] Spinoza's concept of "method" therefore demands an intrinsic relation to truth, which is precisely what Hegel's "Introduction" to the *Phenomenology of Spirit* was so brilliantly arguing for in its criticism of the Kantian demand that one must first discuss the limits of knowledge before even attempting to reach the truth.[28] All of this seems to suggest that what Hegel was so enthusiastic about and at the same time annoyed by in Spinozism was . . . Hegel himself. Or, as Macherey put it, it seems that Spinoza served Hegel as some sort of mirror surface upon which his own ideas were reflected.

And perhaps Macherey's remark can indeed go for the image of Spinoza in German Idealism in general: they needed it precisely as the image against which they were able to formulate their own philosophical positions.[29] But perhaps something similar can be said about the image of Hegel in what we could call the French materialism of the twentieth century. In Althusser, to immediately take the example of a thinker that we will often come back to, we can detect not only the generalizing tendency to reduce Hegel to a collection of dry wisdom, but also the failure to perceive the proximity of some of his own philosophical endeavors to those of Hegel. Additionally, it is important to note that in opposing Hegel, Althusser leaned heavily on the philosophy of Spinoza.

In particular, let us take a look at Althusser's well-known interpretation of the so-called materialist inversion of Hegelian dialectics. What is at stake for Althusser is not simply to take binary oppositions like matter/idea, practice/theory, economy/ideology, and then overturn their order of primacy. For Althusser, it does not suffice to invert the stream of causality, so to speak, and claim that instead of the primacy of theory one should argue for the primacy of practice; or that the system of economic production is not dependent on the dominant state maxim (mercantilism, liberalism, etc.), but vice versa, so that the dominant state ideology is dependent on the relations of economic production. The inversion of Hegelianism that must take place, for Althusser, is therefore not just an inversion of the direction in which determination works within idealism, but a much more ambitious step: he demands no less than an outright disownment of the hierarchical ontological-causal model of determination. Such a model was characteristic of the metaphysical systems of Neoplatonism, and Althusser strongly argued for the Spinozist principle of—to apply the Deleuzean reading through Duns Scotus—the univocity of being.[30]

This principle is the key to understanding Althusser's theses, where theory is not the opposite of practice but rather such and such theoretical practice; where the ideology of the state is not the opposite of the system of economic production but rather such and such ideological production. This already determines the image of Hegel rejected by Althusser: it is the image of Hegel as an inversion of Neoplatonism. Macherey—a student of Althusser's and coauthor of the famous *Reading "Capital"*—spells it out: "What Hegel proposes is simply to reverse this [Neoplatonic] order, by placing the Whole at the end of the process and by arranging its determinations as moments that progressively lead there."[31] What Althusserians saw in Hegel was essentially the embodiment of both theology and teleology, coupled with the inverse ontological model of systems of emanative causality, where instead of the falling from the absolute and the subsequent return to it we have the process of sublation as a persistent advance toward it. This is why the infamous concept of absolute knowledge was explained as a mythical point of convergence of knowledge and truth, exhibiting the fundamental fallacy of the idealist theory of knowledge, its confusion of the object of knowledge and the real object, which allows it to keep "silently pondering the religious fantasies of epiphany and parousia."[32]

One must note that Althusser and his students were hardly the only French school that saw teleology and theology working hand in hand throughout Hegel. Derrida pointed out that Lacan, Althusser, Foucault, Deleuze, Sartre, Merleau-Ponty, Lévinas, and many others went through a case of an "organized allergy . . . towards the Hegelian dialectic," each with their own specific theoretical background and entry point.[33] This all started with the legendary lectures of Koyré and Kojève, whose readings of Hegel massively influenced generations of scholars and thinkers. Catherine Malabou points out that Kojève's reading of absolute knowledge as the End of Time, which lay the foundation for the idea of absolute knowledge as a convergence of all oppositions, was itself heavily influenced by Heidegger's explanation of absolute knowledge as Parousia, and by his claim that primary time, for Hegel, was past time.[34] One could claim, then, that a large portion of the French rejection of Hegel is based on Heidegger's critique of Hegelianism as onto-theological metaphysics.

Of course, within the construction of his *Phenomenology of Spirit*, Hegel *did* place the chapter on absolute knowledge immediately after the chapter on revealed religion; in fact, as the logical conclusion of that chapter. The spirit of revealed religion is *for itself* still separated from its object, even though the two are clearly one *in itself*. Consciousness is still not reconciled or united with essence. Hegel writes: "Its own reconciliation therefore enters its consciousness as something *distant*, as something in the distant *future*."[35] This is Hegel's own formulation of the necessity for the advent of absolute knowledge. The reference to Parousia as the future reconciliation is quite apparent. And yet the knowledge at stake in absolute knowledge is not knowledge of some mystical-religious truth. In absolute knowledge, consciousness does not learn anything new; no new content is reached. Absolute knowledge is not the mythical elimination of the difference between subject and object, between truth and knowledge; it is not the Holy Grail of cognition, it is not the prophesized moment of immediate and final truth where concrete words express concrete being. Rather, absolute knowledge is an empty point. It is precisely the concept of the fundamental irreconcilability in the heart of truth itself. To use a recursive phrasing proposed by Mladen Dolar: the truth is nothing but the hiatus between truth and knowledge.[36] Absolute knowledge is the place of this void, and this void is what produces the *effect* of Parousia.

Perhaps we could say that absolute knowledge works like a *punctuation mark* at the end of a sentence. The punctuation itself has no content; it is simply a formal decision that the process is at an end. This way it refers the reader back to the sentence itself, producing the *effect of the meaning* that was in the sentence all along.

Punctuation marks—full stops, commas, semicolons, and so on—clearly belong to the field of writing. Since there is no sound for them, it may seem, at first glance, that they are imposed on natural, organic spoken language. However, it is common linguistic knowledge that such "artificial" imposition is in fact characteristic of "natural" language itself. We know from everyday experience that certain silences produce meaning just as well as words; we are all aware and constantly use the dramatic pause; we know that silence is golden, and so on; that is to say, we know that punctuation marks belong to language as such, whether it is written or spoken. Moreover, as was pointed out by Saussure a long time ago, what signs are signifying is not defined by their positive or affirmative content, "but negatively by their relations with the other terms of the system," and therefore "their most precise characteristic is in being what the others are not."[37]

Derrida pushed this argument even further and claimed that writing is not a secondary representation of immediate, natural, or organic speech, that it is not a later deformation of the authentic voice, but that it even has a specific advantage over the spoken word. The negativity of writing, precisely its necessary delay and deformation, is in fact inscribed in the essence of language itself. Derrida writes: "If 'writing' signifies inscription and especially the durable institution of a sign . . . , writing in general covers the entire field of linguistic signs. In that field a certain sort of instituted signifiers may then appear, 'graphic' in the narrow and derivative sense of the word, ordered by a certain relationship with other instituted—hence 'written,' even if they are 'phonic'—signifiers. The very idea of institution . . . of the sign is unthinkable before the possibility of writing and outside of its horizon."[38]

The negativity of language, pointed out by Saussure and Derrida, implies that the punctuation mark is, in fact, the primordial phenomenon of language. That artificial and purely formal cut of the punctuation mark, imposed on the affirmative texture of organic language, is in fact its innermost possibility, its proper character. Now, how is this connected to the problem of absolute knowledge? The point is that absolute knowledge operates precisely in such a double function. On the one hand, it works as the full stop at the end of a sentence, as the point of the promised End Judgment; but on the other hand, this End Judgment turns out to be purely void and dimensionless, nothing more than a formal point revealing to us that any positive, affirmative content of an End Judgment is always an *effect* or a *product* of its process. This formal gesture of a punctuation mark is radically foreign to Spinoza and contemporary incarnations of Spinozism. It is precisely this simple gesture that Hegel found, *in nuce*, lacking in Spinoza: what Spinoza said was already everything that needed to be said; all that was still missing was the punctuation mark at the end of the sentence.

Residual Questions

To sum up the problematic of reception, one could make the general observation that the relationship between Hegelianism and Spinozism is often a relationship of mutual fascination with one self, a kind of mutual intellectual masturbation. It seems that Hegel, and to some extent this goes for German Idealism in general, recognized in Spinoza a powerful image, one that helped him formulate his own project better, but also one that had discouragingly little to do with Spinoza's philosophy itself. At the same time, one could claim that the French Spinozists—with Althusser and Deleuze carrying the banner—recognized in Hegel a caricature of a theologian and a finalist which they gleefully hated and denounced, but failed to see the common ground that bound their projects to that of Hegel.

However, this mutually failed relationship which determines much of the contemporary debate within materialism nevertheless pivots around some basic themes.[39] While on the one hand Hegel read Spinozism as a system of emanative causality and ontological degradation, Althusserians, on the other hand, read Hegelian dialectics as an inversion of the emanationist system. Hegel claimed that Spinozism is fundamentally an example of what he called Oriental determinism, an example of abstract negativism where everything determined is simply negative, where all singularity is dissolved in the absolute substance—and where there cannot be any concept of the freedom of the subject. But similarly, Hegel was reproached for presenting a mechanical finalism where the movement of thought is reduced to a straightforward transition through rigidly outlined stages of development and where there is never a place for true surprise, since everything leads to a predictable conclusion, to the mythic point of Parousia. And after all, even the Althusserian theory of ideological interpellation was criticized by Lacanians as basically a functionalist theory, since it can only "explain its proper success, but not how and why it does not work,"[40] since it fails to account for the traumatic residue of its process, a kind of a leftover that "*far from hindering the full submission of the subject to the ideological command, is the very condition of it.*"[41]

These objections—determinism, mechanical teleology, functionalism—overlook the fact that neither Hegelians nor Spinozists subscribe to a hierarchical concept of causality, and that they do not understand transformation or movement within the order of the actual in Cartesian terms of a spontaneous thinking substance—which influences mechanical operations of the extended substance by intervening from outside of it. Both Hegelians and Spinozists, in their own specific terms and concepts, argue for a substance capable of organizing its own transformation. How exactly is such a self-determination demonstrated, on what grounds is it argued for, and what specific concepts and strategies are employed—this remains an open question and lies at the core of the problematic that we will address as the problematic of Hegel and Spinoza. In its own way, the problematic of reception once again points to the question of movement within the absolute, to the question of the contradictory status of beginning and to the question of an irreducible dynamism, hidden in the positive landscape of a text. The residual questions that will guide our inquiry as our basic thematic points are as follow. Firstly, the question of teleology, especially in its relationship to causality. Secondly, the question of the relationship between the absolute and the determined, where Hegel and Spinoza formulated solutions that sometimes seem to their adversaries as only minor adjustments of the classical metaphysical causal model of Neoplatonists, but in fact completely remove that model. And thirdly, the question of the limit that precedes what lays beyond.

1

Hegel's Logic of Pure Being and Spinoza

In the Beginning Was the Missed Opportunity to Keep Quiet

What does the beginning of Hegel's logic have to do with Eastern Europe, specifically with Vilnius, Lithuania? In the buildup to the U.S.-led invasion of Iraq in 2003, Secretary of State Colin Powell made an infamous address to the Security Council of the United Nations. He argued persuasively, if not quite irrefutably, in support of the invasion, citing intelligence reports of weapons of mass destruction in the hands of the ruthless dictator Saddam Hussein. He urged the Security Council to support the invasion—or else become irrelevant. The very next day, on February 6, 2003, no less than ten countries from Eastern Europe signed what came to be known as the Vilnius letter, throwing their full and unquestioning support behind the United States and forming a block against France and Germany within Europe. On February 17, President Jacques Chirac of France commented on the Vilnius group, calling their move "infantile" and "reckless" and uttered, not even hiding his indignation, these immortal words: "Eastern Europe missed a good opportunity to keep quiet."

One may argue that Chirac was basically correct in treating the Vilnius group as a group of countries very eager to submit to the master—which they clearly were, many political analysts pointing out that the letter finding Powell's speech at Security Council meeting absolutely convincing must have been drafted and agreed upon days, if not weeks before that speech was even delivered—but Chirac was even more correct in coining, or at least in propagating, the beautiful phrase which deserves our full attention. It is a brilliant philosophical proposition and we will treat it as such. We must therefore leave Powell and Chirac to their own destinies and address the philosophical question implied in Chirac's spontaneous gibe. Our general aim here is to argue that the beginning of Hegel's logic is nothing if not a missed opportunity to keep quiet.

We can analyze Chirac's statement as a philosophical sentence in two fundamentally different ways that can, as I hope to demonstrate, shed some light on two alternative readings of Hegel's logic of pure being.

The first way is to understand silence as a privileged state of philosophy, where to speak means to break the silence, and to utter words is to commit violence against silence. To an extent, this meaning is implied in the importance of silence that Boethius ascribed to the true philosopher: "I would have known [you were a philosopher], had you kept your silence."[1] In this perspective, formulating distinct, determined propositions is already a kind of failure—because truth in the emphatic sense is precisely what lies beyond such finite claims.

This may sound strange to those who consider truth to be a property of propositions, such as, for example, the famous proposition by Bertrand Russell asserting that there is a cat on a mat. The concept of truth that is at stake in our example is clearly very different from Russell's; in fact, we can formulate it as precisely that which cannot be grasped within a proposition, as that which cannot be uttered in an affirmative sentence. In the history of Western thought, this concept of truth was perhaps most clearly argued for in the tradition of negative or apophatic theology. According to infamous authors such as Proclus, God cannot be grasped directly with the means of finite human understanding, and so the best way to approach him is by way of negation (*via negationis*), by speaking only in terms of what God is not. The truth (of God) remains utterly unutterable, even unthinkable.

But there is another way to understand Chirac's statement philosophically, and I argue that it describes the proper Hegelian position. First of all, on the level of the propositional form, "to miss an opportunity to keep quiet" is a double negation, a negation of negation. Curiously enough, saying that "Eastern Europe missed an opportunity to keep quiet" does not at all mean the same thing as saying that "Eastern Europe has spoken." Already at the level of pure formalism we have an example of two negatives that don't make an affirmative. This gives us the first hint of Hegel's concept of the negation of negation which cannot be reduced to simple affirmation. But the more important point of this perspective—one that really separates it from the perspective of apophatic theology—is the different status it ascribes to silence. In Hegel's logic, silence is not a privileged philosophical state, it is not the mark of the true philosopher, but rather an impossibility. The point is not that there is some unutterable kernel of truth that necessarily escapes the formulations of human language and remains beyond it, but rather that such an unutterable truth is what is *produced* in the realm of language, through language, and in fact, through the procedure that we may call that of "uttering the unutterable."

We could name this perspective—the Hegelian perspective—the perspective of production, the perspective which takes as its prerequisite condition the procedure of double negation. In contemporary thought, this perspective is perhaps most productively exploited in the field of Lacanian psychoanalysis. In his seminar on female sexuality, Lacan employs a double negative and states that the impossibility is that which "doesn't stop not being written."[2] Inasmuch as it is productive, one may be inclined to call this perspective affirmative, but it must be noted that this concept of production cannot be reduced to pure or naive or simple affirmation, just as it does not confine itself to the overcautious perspective of apophatic theology.

Regarding Jacques Chirac's philosophical sentence, we can therefore, in fact, distinguish three positions. Firstly, there is pure affirmation, the claim that propositions must have a discernible positive content in order to be admitted as true or false. "The cat is on the mat" is true if it relates to "the cat" which is "on" "the mat." This position doesn't reflect on why it is useful or rational or pertinent to the situation to think about cats-on-the-mats, and thus remains completely outside of the point Chirac and Powell were, respectively, trying to make. Secondly, we have the position of *via negationis*. Apophatic theology, to take this example, claims that negative propositions about God can be informative, or hold truth, *even though they cannot be rephrased in an affirmative form.* This means that while we cannot directly attribute infinity to God (for our concepts of infinity are but human concepts), we can still deny that God is finite. And finally, there is negation of negation, productive negation, where the claim is that a proposition does not attempt to describe what is true and inevitably fails, but that truth is something that is produced in the very proposition that failed to grasp it. This final position is that of Hegel's logic of pure being. What I find so beautiful about it is that it combines both the Russellian as well as the apophatic understanding of truth, while overcoming their shortcomings at the same time.

Being, Pure Being—Without Further Determination

If one skips all the prefaces and the introductions and the preliminary notes about how to begin in science—which, in all honesty, is not necessarily the most advisable choice—then Hegel's *Science of Logic* begins with the logic of pure being. The fundamental, and for Hegel most essential thesis is that being is the same as nothing, "pure indeterminateness and emptiness."[3] If there is anything that we can intuit about it, then it is an empty intuition; we are intuiting pure nothing. It is hard to declare anything about pure being and pure nothing. As soon as we give them a determination or definition, they have already evaded us in their purity. All that we can say about them is that there is nothing that we can say about them, that they are empty and without determination.

At this point, Hegel could simply have fallen silent. He could have upheld the Wittgensteinian principle that whereof one cannot speak, thereof one should be silent. His logic would end before it even started and would never have taken place. But alas, at that decisive moment in the history of Western thought, Hegel missed a great opportunity to keep quiet. The fundamental impossibility—the impossibility to speak determinately about pure being and pure nothing—constitutes the beginning proper of Hegel's logic. Logic begins by admitting its failing, by declaring its own incapacity to speak, and by doing so it nevertheless finds its own voice.

The first proposition of Hegel's logic is the principle of becoming, which means the becoming-nothing of being and the becoming-being of nothing. As is immediately clear from Hegel's remarks to the very brief passages on being, nothing, and becoming in *Science of Logic*, this principle is so fundamental that it echoes titanic historical and philosophical oppositions between the Orient and Christianity, between the Eleatics and Heraclitus. The logic of being takes the Heraclitean side and explains the principle that "everything flows" as the claim that everything is becoming.[4] It strongly opposes the principle of *ex nihilo nihil fit*, characteristic of what Hegel calls "identity systems," such as "the abstract *pantheism* of the Eleatics and essentially also . . . that of Spinoza." For Hegel, identity systems are in contradiction with Christian metaphysics because of their "opposition to *becoming* in general and hence also to the creation of the world out of nothing."[5]

However, we should not understand the oppositions between Christianity and the Orient and between Heraclitus and the Eleatics as an agonistic opposition, even though Hegel himself seems to suggest this. The point is rather that the identity systems tell us something true about themselves—but at the same time this truth is external to them. Their truth is precisely the Christian or Heraclitean becoming. This is why identity systems are internal to the principle of becoming; they constitute its part. An identity system can only insist on its claims, while a system of becoming comprehends both the identity system *and* its truth. The principle of becoming is therefore not a symmetric opponent of the principle of identity; it is not even a completely different principle. It is the identity principle itself, grasped together with its truth. In this sense, it is self-referential. But what is it that refers to itself in this principle? Nothing, pure nothing. The principle of becoming is therefore the principle of self-referential negativity.

The philosophical stance that the logic of pure being takes can also be phrased like this: if a system of thought fully subscribes to the principle that nothing comes out of nothing, then that system itself will come to nothing. Such a system cannot comprehend becoming, which is nevertheless its truth, and since it is incapable of thinking becoming, its operation of thought also cannot partake in becoming. What we are dealing with here is apparently a certain correspondence between being and thinking. In the general sense, this is characteristic of Hegel's logic *tout court*; the science of logic is the science of what is actual, and hence the development of logic is the development of the actual. This position seems to completely contradict the Kantian separation of human knowledge and the thing in itself, or to put it in different terms, it seems to contradict the distinction between epistemology and ontology, or yet in different terms, the Althusserian distinction between the real object and the object of cognition; in general, it seems to contradict the separation between the object and the subject.

And yet, Hegel's position is not adequately formulated if we simply replace the distinction between being and thinking with their sameness and claim that thinking is immediately the same as being or that human knowledge is the immediate development of the thing itself or that the subject is always already in a union with an object. There is a correspondence between thinking and being, but not immediate sameness, such as one could perhaps attribute to Parmenides. Perhaps the relationship between being and thinking in Hegel can be said to be crossed with the relationship between being and nothing.

To Think or Not to Think?

Being and nothing are the same—but what does their sameness actually mean? It doesn't mean that the *content* of their determinations is the same, since they don't have any; they are also not the same judging from their external *formal* determination, namely that they are both without determination. And their sameness is also not simply a transformation of the emptiness of their content into the emptiness of their formality, such as in the proposition "thinking pure being is the same as not thinking." In fact, the opposite is true: there is an enormous difference between not-thinking and thinking pure nothing or pure being; in the end, what is at stake is the difference between to think and not to think. What we can say about being and nothing can therefore not be said about thinking and not-thinking; at least not at the same time. Furthermore, pure being and pure nothing can only be expressed in the same way because not to think is not the same as to actually think. Only if we do *think* pure being and pure nothing can they appear as the same and at the same time as absolutely different.

The principle of the identity system, according to which nothing comes out of nothing, implies that it is impossible to think nothing, or that every thought is necessarily a thought of something which is not nothing. This allows the identity system to claim that if we think nothing, we are not thinking at all. However, the Hegelian point is that the truth of this sentence already constitutes the first logical proposition, the proposition of the sameness of being and nothing. The *truth* of the principle of identity is what this principle enunciates unknowingly and even in spite of itself; this is why the truth of this principle appears to this principle as its externality or otherness. This does not mean that the truth of the identity principle is something that we must attach to it from the outside; such is, in essence, the claim of the principle of becoming. While the truth of the identity principle is external to that principle itself, the principle of becoming includes not only the truth of the principle of identity, but also that principle itself. And furthermore, from the perspective of becoming, the principle of identity appears in its logical necessity; the truth of the principle of identity retroactively provides the grounding to the very principle it produced as its truth. From the perspective of becoming, the truth of identity is immanent to the identity principle itself. Perhaps we could borrow the concept of symptomal reading from Althusserian epistemology and claim that the principle of becoming is a symptomal reading of the principle of identity.[6]

Pure being and pure nothing are the same in the sense that nothing determinate can be said about them and that one cannot introduce a distinction at this level—any distinction would imply a determination and would therefore not treat being and nothing as pure. But as soon as we get to what Hegel called "their truth," that is, as soon as they are declared and made manifest, we are already in becoming where "*each* immediately *vanishes in its opposite*" and where they are the same and absolutely different at the same time.[7] Following Dieter Henrich's analysis of the beginning of Hegel's logic, we could claim that the sameness of being and nothing is neither, firstly, the sameness of their object or content (for they have none), nor, secondly, the sameness of their formal determination as empty of determinations (for this would already imply understanding them as existence [Dasein]), nor, thirdly, the indifference of objectivity and formality (when it doesn't matter whether one *thinks* being and nothing or not, it is impossible to say anything at all; in order to claim the sameness of being and nothing one must, first of all, think them).[8]

The sameness of being and nothing, their truth, can only be expressed in thought, where they appear as not only the same, but also as absolutely different. In other words, the sameness of being and thinking is only possible if we assume the difference between to think and not to think. This does not mean that the difference only appears in thought, while in themselves, being and nothing are the same! To claim this would mean already to presuppose a simple distinction between thinking (as the formal givenness of thought) and being (as the content or the object of thinking), a distinction that would already assume too much determination. We should rather understand thinking as the very difference that separates between the pure sameness and absolute distinction. The truth of being and nothing, their movement into the sameness and absolute difference is thinking as the self-referential difference. Thinking is not some rival of being; it doesn't oppose it, and it is not even completely different from it; rather, it is being itself, together with its self-referential nature: it is the self-referential negativity.

The Objection

What I suggest is a reading of the logic of pure being taking place at a crossroads where on the one hand, where there is no thought, being and nothing are the same, but on the other hand, where thought emerges, being and nothing are the same *and* absolutely different at the same time. But one may wonder what exactly entitles us to separate between thinking and not-thinking in the first place? Could we not take pure thinking (which is not the same as determinate thinking, that is, thinking of something determined) and pair it with pure not-thinking (which is not the same as determinate not-thinking, if by this term we understand the absence of thinking of something determined), thus producing a couple that follows the very same pattern of the Hegelian couple of being and nothing? Isn't it clear that—at least from the Hegelian standpoint—pure thinking is the same as pure not-thinking? And furthermore, by introducing the distinction between thinking and not-thinking and claiming that thinking is the very difference between thinking and not-thinking, have we not simply relocated the self-referential difference that we can find at the result of the logic of pure being back to its beginning, so that the immediate indeterminateness appears as something reflected and therefore as something mediated and in itself redoubled? To explain the logic of pure being with the aid of the difference between thinking and not-thinking, have we not forced categories of the logic of reflection onto the logic of pure being?

This objection to the proposed reading is twofold; or perhaps, these are two separate objections. Firstly, the objection claims that the sameness of being and nothing already implies the sameness of thinking and not-thinking; or that the latter couple is explained in the same way as the former. The primordial sameness admits no distinction and therefore nothing can be immanently deduced from it; it is like the perfect, seamless monolith without any fracture or crack in which one could set one's foot and take a stand; as soon as there is any determination or distinction, one simply slides off that monolith, taking the determination down with one. Secondly, the objection claims that the proposed reading of the logic of pure being forgets that pure being is a rigid, immovable, monolithic barrier, which is to say that nothing can be deduced from it and that it leads nowhere—the proposed reading forgets the purity of pure being itself.

The first general response to these two objections is that they tell us something interesting about the relationship between the logic of being and the logic of reflection. It seems that this relationship is another variation of the relationship that Hegel formulates between the Orient and Christianity or between the Eleatics and Heraclitus. If we can understand the logic of being as a monolith that amounts to nothing, then perhaps the logic of reflection is that same monolith together with the claim that it amounts to nothing. The second general response is that I do in fact propose a reading of the logic of pure being not as a monolith without any cracks or fractures, but rather as the immediate unity of the monolith and the crack; to put it in different terms, the monolith is perfectly seamless precisely because it is nothing but the crack.

Logic of Pure Being, Ontology of Pure Thought

Let us look closer now at the objection that one should not distinguish between thinking and what I propose we call not-thinking. Perhaps we could already reject this objection in advance, for what is logic supposed to be if not precisely thinking? Is it not obvious that if there is no thinking, there can also be no logic? We can ask ourselves that famous question, "to be or not to be," but there can be no question about "to think or not to think." René Descartes put this in the most dramatic terms when he argued that even an all-powerful demon could not make us doubt whether we are really thinking or not—for even such doubts would constitute a form of thinking. By taking up this argument we are making a very clear choice in favor of thinking; a choice which nevertheless poses the question of how exactly does one separate logic from not-thinking, because if this was indeed so clear and self-evident, why would Descartes need to conjure up his demon in order to make it clear in the first place?

It seems these are our basic alternatives: either logic takes thinking simply as something given, as something one cannot call into question and can only humbly accept, as inheritance or gift, and one moves in logic by a force which is external to logic and superior to it; or the primordial separation of thinking from not-thinking is part of the beginning of logic, so that at the very beginning, logic must indeed think its own non-beginning, its own not-thinking. To put it in terms that echo Hegel's critique of Jacobi even more explicitly: we should either think the beginning of logic as something that constitutes a part of logic and is included in it, or we should consider the beginning of logic as a result of an act of external force that should be inspected by a superior science of the origin. The question of faith and knowledge becomes, in the *Science of Logic*, the question of an absolute beginning. It is the question of whether or not we should count the beginning to that of which it is a beginning; and it is one of the most entertaining questions of the entire philosophical tradition.

It may seem that Hegel's answer to this question is clear and simple. Who doesn't know that Hegel's central critique of Kant was that he was trying to discuss cognition outside of the science itself?

> But to want to clarify the nature of cognition *prior* to science is to demand that it should be discussed *outside* science, and *outside* science this cannot be done, at least not in the scientific manner which alone is the issue here.[9]

Likewise, in *Phenomenology of Spirit,* Hegel famously argued that a Kantian preliminary reflection about the limits of our cognition—namely the "anxiety about falling into error" and the "mistrust of science which itself is untroubled by those scruples and simply . . . gets down to cognizing"—presupposes a separation of cognition from the absolute and from the truth itself and therefore constitutes the error itself. Hegel concludes that this "fear of error thus reveals itself to be more likely the fear of the truth."[10]

Thus it would seem that Hegel's position on the question of beginning is in fact identical to Spinoza's position which was advocated by Althusser and his school and is perhaps best explained with the phrase *habemus enim ideam veram,* "for we do have a true idea."[11] As Althusser pointed out, the emphasis is on the word *enim*: the question of the justification of our knowledge is subordinate to the fact that we do possess the knowledge.[12]

It would appear that the only possible conclusion is that, for Hegel, the beginning of science is included in the science itself, that the starting point of science is that we do, in fact, think, that thinking is not the same as not-thinking, and that—as Hegel himself wrote: "A beginning is *logical* in that it is to be made in the element of a free, self-contained thought, *in pure knowledge*."[13]

And yet, the claim that thinking is some sort of self-referential negativity, the separator between the sameness of and the difference between being and nothing, does not simply presuppose a difference between thinking and not-thinking. Even the inceptive decision to think implies the contradiction which marks all beginnings. The decision to think is not a clear-cut operation like the recognition of the fact that we do, in fact, think; it includes a remainder of that from which it separates itself, it includes not-thinking as its undecided. The beginning with thinking is only possible because—from the perspective of the result—it includes not-thinking as its not-beginning. It would therefore indeed be possible to translate the logic of pure being into the "logic of pure thinking," and to claim that pure thinking and pure not-thinking are the same, and that they are both immediate and without determinations.

Let us try to imagine Hegel's *Science of Logic* beginning not with pure being, but rather with pure thinking. This task may seem odd, at first. Within the framework of the Hegelian system the science of logic is what follows the phenomenology of spirit which demonstrated that "consciousness has the *concept* of science, that is, pure knowledge, for its result."[14] Science presupposes the phenomenology of spirit. Pure knowledge as the presupposition of science is therefore not without its history; it is already mediated. One could even object to Hegel that his supposedly presuppositionless logic apparently takes very much for granted: namely, pure knowledge itself. However, as Hegel states clearly, the science of logic is indeed pure knowledge, but only "in the full compass of its development."[15] And even though pure knowledge is something inherited from the work of consciousness, Hegel does not demand that the readers of the *Science of Logic* should first work their way through the *Phenomenology of Spirit*. In fact—as Stephen Houlgate argues—what is demanded from us in order to start in logic is rather to forget all our assumptions and thoughts, to let go of all our knowledge:

> Presuppositionless philosophy does, therefore, have certain presuppositions. Its hermeneutic presuppositions include the readiness to suspend

> or let go of what we have assumed to be true of thought and being and the readiness to focus one's attention and understanding on, and to be moved by, the minimal thought of pure being that results from letting go of all our assumptions.[16]

Hegel's *Logic* does indeed have its presuppositions, but they are not a set of principles, axioms, or ideas silently assumed in advance, but rather a form of letting go, a "spirit of radical openness."[17] This already means that what is at stake in the beginning of *Logic* and in the beginning of *Phenomenology* is, in a certain sense, one and the same thing.[18]

Let us look take a closer look at this procedure of "letting go" in Hegel's own words:

> Now starting with this determination of pure knowledge, all that we have to do to ensure that the beginning will remain immanent to the science of this knowledge is to consider, or rather, setting aside every reflection, simply to take up, *what is there before us.*[19]

Pure knowledge is a kind of void or amorphous immediacy which thus "ceases to be knowledge; what we have before us is only *simple immediacy.*"[20] I would like to put the emphasis of these words not on taking up what is "before us," words which clearly describe the object of thinking, but rather on the idea that first, we have to "set aside every reflection," and pure knowledge thus "ceases to be knowledge." Even though it may seem that there can be no logic without the assumption of the fact of thinking, Hegel's introduction to logic, perhaps surprisingly, does indeed consider the possibility of not-thinking, which, in the ultimate analysis, should be understood as the possibility of the very impossibility of logic. However, this is not done in the Cartesian manner, where such impossibility is rejected simply on account of being an impossibility *within* the realm of thought itself—claiming that even the utmost, hyperbolic doubt is still a doubt and therefore a form of thinking. Quite to the contrary, Hegel's project of the beginning not only allows for the impossibility of thinking as a legitimate possibility, it actually demands it: every reflection must be set aside, knowledge must cease to be knowledge, thought must cease to be thought. Is it really that hard to accept that for Hegel, pure thinking—as long as it remains pure—is indistinguishable from pure not-thinking?

In order to get to the truth of becoming, to the sameness of being and nothing, we had to accept the distinction between thinking and not-thinking; in order to express their sameness, we had to assume that being and nothing are actually being thought. And it seems we must conclude that in order to claim that pure thinking is the same as pure not-thinking, we must first assume the difference between being and nothing. To be more precise, we must simply accept "what is there before us." In short, it is the difference between thinking and not-thinking that enables us to claim that being and nothing are the same, and it is the difference between being and nothing that enables us to claim that thinking is the same as not-thinking. Our little thought experiment thus resulted in the idea of being as that self-referential difference that separates between the sameness and the absolute difference of thinking and not-thinking. The logic of pure being was translated into the ontology of pure thinking.

Hegelian Coordinate System

The objection that one should not read Hegel's logic of pure being charged in advance with the assumption of a rigid and immediate facticity of thinking, with the presupposition of the difference between thinking and not-thinking, proved justified to the extent that the same "mechanics" that governs such a reading can be employed to demonstrate the sameness of thinking and not-thinking, for in pure immediacy, knowledge ceases to be knowledge and dilutes into not-knowledge. This objection is based on the Parmenidean assumption of the immediate sameness of being and thinking; and it is not only justified, but also correct. And yet, what must be added to this Eleatic wisdom is what Hegel always added to Eleatic wisdom—namely its truth, which it failed to express, or rather, which it expressed inadvertently.

Beginning is a simple immediacy without determinations or distinctions; and yet one can't begin without speaking out about this immediacy. Whether we attribute the act of speaking out to the level of being, from the point of which all distinctions in thought are melted, or to the level of thinking, from the point of which pure being appears as pure void—it matters little, the conclusion is the same. Not without irony, we could call this predicament the coordinate system and picture it as the crossing of two perpendicular axes: the axis of thinking marks the indifference of thinking and not-thinking, while the axis of being marks the sameness of being and nothing. The axes cross each other and cut each other in two, producing a difference within each other: from the assumed perspective of the one axis, the other is seen as clearly separated into its opposites. For Eleatics, being and thinking are the same—this is the great achievement of Parmenides, the basis of all science, as Hegel suggests.[21] For Hegel, in a way, they are the same, too; however, as I tried to demonstrate, they are only the same at the beginning, at the origin of the "coordinate system." And just as every coordinate system requires more than just the origin, the vantage point—namely coordinates—the science of logic requires more than just the sameness of being and thinking.

In the context of distinguishing between the continuous and discrete ideas of movement, Aristotle, who of course did not subscribe to the Christian principle of *creatio ex nihilo,* creation out of nothing, constantly makes the argument that there is a certain contradiction in the concept of a beginning point in time, for at that point, the object in question would be moving and at rest at the same time.[22] One could argue that for Hegel, this apparent contradiction is precisely what is at stake in the concept of beginning: the sameness of being and not-being.[23] Perhaps one could phrase this point from a different perspective and claim that it is the beginning itself that is redoubled for Hegel: it is at the same time external and internal to the process which begins with it. Or, even better, we could claim that the beginning is in a fundamental sense displaced: one can place it neither in the pure rigidity of being, for this Parmenidean outset is not quite enough, it does not lead anywhere and is therefore not a beginning; nor in the claim that being and nothing are the same, for this would already be too much, it would fail to account for the Parmenidean monstrosity. The beginning is therefore somewhere inbetween, at an impossible intersection of the rigid, inert, indifferent, and the always-already-in-motion.

The Impurity of the Logic of Pure Being

We must address the remaining objection that by understanding the beginning as displaced, we have already entered into the logic of reflection and have therefore failed to let the logic of pure being speak for itself. Now, Hegel proposed a brief analysis of the beginning and claimed that it would lead to "the first, purest, that is, most abstract, definition of the absolute," and indeed grasped the beginning as "the unity of being and non-being—or, in a more reflected form, the concept of the unity of differentiated and undifferentiated being—or of the identity of identity and non-identity."[24] However, Hegel also warned that all he did was to presuppose a representation of the beginning and analyze its elements, adding the following famous remark:

> But the beginning ought not itself to be already a first *and* an other, for anything which is in itself a first *and* an other implies that an advance has already been made. Consequently, that which constitutes the begin-

ning, the beginning itself, is to be taken as something unanalyzable, taken in its simple, unfilled immediacy.[25]

It would be too easy to try to disperse this objection with the reference to Hegel's general claim that the beginning of science belongs to science itself and that therefore the beginning must nevertheless be precisely "a first *and* an other," otherwise it would be external to it, even if it is not a several-hundred-page-long preliminary critique of reason but only a punctual immediacy without determinations. That claim should not be understood as an outright denial of the thing-in-itself, as a complete dismissal of the idea of the gap that separates the subject and object of cognition, as a mysticism of knowledge (which is basically what Althusser accused Hegel of doing). In fact, we would do much better to understand Hegel's position not as a refusal, but rather as a radicalization of that gap. The gap is included in the absolute itself—precisely in the same sense as the beginning of science makes part of science itself, as its internal exteriority, as a rigidity that constitutes a part of movement itself, and just as a lump of cereal flakes remains dry in itself, even though it is perfectly immersed in the gooey mixture of the milk of our cognition and the cereal of the real. This goes against the concept of the facticity of knowledge expressed in the Spinozist principle of already having a true idea, *habemus enim ideam veram.* When we penetrate the lump—if we indeed allow ourselves this analogy—there is nothing to be found there, the lump has already dissolved in the general goo of cereal flakes and milk. This is precisely what happens when we analyze the beginning: it is immediately dissolved into something that has already begun, something fluid, something already in motion.

This is the gist of the answer to the objection. The beginning is indeed unanalyzable, but also inexistent and strictly speaking unthinkable; it is a perfectly smooth monolith where everything slips, it is the abyss of indifference. And yet it does not stand independently and self-sufficiently—not for Hegel, in any case—but only as a part of the movement it started; it is not completely indifferent to it, for it takes part in it. This is why I claim that the principle of Hegel's logic is the claim that pure being is the same as pure nothing, that the logic of pure being can only begin when we declare that pure being and pure nothing have already passed into each other. In part, this is to express Hegel's illustration of advancement in philosophy by taking steps backwards: while the beginning does not, in itself, include what follows, it is expressed in what follows, not analytically, but immanently, and is thus carried onwards. This is why the objection that by employing the logic of reflection one fails to let the logic of pure being speak for itself misses the point: the only way to let the logic of pure being speak out is in the language of the logic of reflection. In a formula: *as soon as the logic of pure being speaks, it speaks in the language of the logic of reflection.*

The notable Hegelian Dieter Henrich listed three of the most common objections to the logic of pure being, all of which reject the sameness of being and nothing. According to the first objection, being and nothing are but two different aspects of the undetermined immediacy; the second objection understands them as different, albeit standing under the same umbrella concept of undetermined immediacy; and the third objection sees being and nothing as two names for the same thing, the undetermined immediacy. The point of Henrich's counterargument was that these objections—as well as some favorable interpretations—share the same structure: first they separate between undetermined immediacy on the one hand and being and nothing on the other hand, and then demonstrate that it is impossible to link them. But this clearly means that they understand being as something mediated or determined, that is, not as *pure* being.[26]

Could one not use Henrich's argument to counter the reading we present here? If the logic of being is explained with the help of "the coordinate system" where the sameness of being and nothing is revealed only against the background of the decision for thinking, just as the sameness of thinking and not-thinking is revealed against the background of the decision for being—doesn't this mean that we forced a kind of scission onto the logic of pure being, determining it in some minimal sense? And if the logic of being is interpreted on the basis of (1) the unity of being and nothing understood as the sameness of sameness and absolute difference and (2) on the basis of thinking understood as a self-referential difference, a difference between difference and sameness—is it not clear that it is interpreted with determinations that include their opposites in themselves, with reflected and mediated determinations which clearly already presuppose a transition into the logic of reflection?

My general answer is that the immediacy of the logic of pure being can only be given as an immediacy which is already lost. I am not trying to pathetically claim that "we have somehow lost immediacy." The point is rather that immediacy as such is structured as something that already slipped away and that what is thus immediately given is nothing but the evasion itself, the loss itself. What we have truly lost with the beginning of logic is therefore nothing but the loss itself; it could be said that immediacy is structured as the loss of the loss itself. Hence it is indeed that which produces, inaugurates, moves; but it is at the same time also that which is produced; if it is a beginning, it is a produced beginning, the unity of producing and being produced; if it is only something negated, it is nevertheless a negation of negation and therefore a productive negation.

But let us take a closer look at Henrich's argument. His principal thesis is that one must understand the context of the logic of pure being within the system as a whole, which boils down to this: the logic of pure being *is not* the logic of reflection. He pointed out that after facing heavy criticism, Hegel reworked and corrected his entire *Science of Logic*, including the sections on the logic of pure being; however, Hegel changed only the remarks, leaving the core sections completely intact. Hegel's response to the criticism of his contemporaries was limited to underlining the separation between the logic of pure being and what followed it. For Henrich, everything comes down to this: that we may treat the logic of pure being, the unity of being and nothing, only in negative terms, only *via negationis.*[27]

Indeed, the description of pure being and pure nothing as undetermined immediacy is clearly a negation of mediation and it is therefore already mediated; with it, we have already entered the logic of reflection and distorted the beginning. The same goes for the phrase "equal only to itself." The word "only" emphasizes that this is a negation of the reflective equality, mediated by otherness and difference. In short, undetermined immediacy is the phrase Hegel uses to denote pure negation. Henrich concludes that the beginning, the logic of pure being, indeed leads to the logic of reflection, but that it is at the same time also a completely irreducible immediacy which cannot be fully accounted for. According to Henrich, the beginning is strictly speaking unthinkable. This makes continuation completely external to it. Both critics and some favorable interpreters of Hegel made the mistake, according to Henrich, of counting the interpretation of the beginning, the logic of reflection, as the beginning itself, thus failing to see that while interpretation indeed distorted the beginning, the beginning itself remained intact and pure.

If we understand the question of the relationship between beginning and continuation in its utmost philosophical importance, and not simply as a matter of philological accuracy, as a trivial matter of filing a text in the correct order—as indeed we should—then Henrich's explanation may seem at odds with the generally accepted perception of Hegel's legacy today. Who doesn't know that interpretation is never merely an external and necessarily distorting rendering of the original material, which is independent of it—but that it always penetrates and transforms the original itself! This anti-Platonic understanding of interpretation is precisely what is at stake in Hegel.[28]

Two prominent Hegelians, Marx and Gadamer, phrased this in their own, very divergent ways. Taking on the problematic of *economic production,* Marx attributed to it a certain advantage over the raw material and products, since raw material is never simply an immediate given; it is always already a mediated, complex raw material. In the final analysis, it is production that determines something as raw material. Gadamer said the exact same thing, albeit in another context, when he established the advantage of *hermeneutics*—as the procedure of understanding, explanation, and application—over what enters the process of explanation as its raw material and what is produced in this process as its result; it is only through the hermeneutic intervention that the original text is transformed from what Gadamer calls "the dead trace of meaning" back into living meaning, and this is why the result is never something that no longer requires hermeneutics and it cannot just discard it as a used tool.[29] And after all, if we take theoretical texts as the raw material of the operation that we call theoretical production, if we understand the scientific process as a process of the production of knowledge, we have already formulated the proper Althusserian position from his earlier period where "Generality II," the theoretical production as such, has an advantage over both "Generality I," words, and "Generality III," scientific concepts.[30]

This excursus on Hegel's disciples hopefully demonstrated that the tradition of the question of the (im)purity of the origin is not interesting only because of its historical value, but because it remains essential to contemporary philosophy. Aristotle's idea of the primordial mover which moves without itself moving and therefore remains "pure" heavily influenced Neoplatonism. Dieter Henrich's argument that the beginning is something unanalyzable, irreducible, and strictly speaking uninterpretable—which is to say that it always remains pure—brings us in proximity to Gadamer's reading of Schelling's idea of *das Unvordenkliche*, of that prior to which one cannot think. This is indeed a variation of the Neoplatonic concept of the One, that is, precisely of the conceptual framework that Hegel's critics reduced his system to. In order to defend Hegel, the primordial negativity should not be conceived as something indifferent, as something that produces differences only externally and never within itself. Rather, it should be conceived as a self-producing negativity, as something that is in itself a redoubled, productive negativity. In short, Hegel's concept of beginning should be strictly separated from the Aristotelian concept of beginning.

Beginning Is Polar

The mechanics of the *Science of Logic* is basically the same as the mechanics of the *Phenomenology of Spirit*, even though the precise aim of these projects is different. As Mladen Dolar explains vis-à-vis the *Phenomenology*, Hegel's paradox of the beginning—which can be detected even on the level of the text of that magnificent work where one of the principal roles of the foreword and introduction is to demonstrate that there is no such thing as an introduction into science, that there is no preliminary foreword before going to the thing itself—is not solved simply by immediately starting with the immediate; for some reason, it is philosophically important to insist at the paradoxical threshold, neither still outside nor already inside.[31] It is precisely this paradoxical threshold that is lost if we conceive the beginning as simply pure. The claim here is that this paradox of the beginning is not something that can be resolved with a proper introduction, but that it rather persists within the beginning itself, and therefore also within the body of the science of logic proper.

The problem with Henrich's position lies especially in his explicit reference to the tradition of *via negationis,* which allows for the misunderstanding that while the logic of pure being is completely inadmissible to affirmative reflection—which is in itself a correct reading—it is perhaps nevertheless admissible to a different genre of thinking altogether, to a genre that has historically used the way of negation as the only reliable form of discourse about God: negative theology. In his fairly short article Henrich uses the term *via negationis* many times: as the only possible form of explication of pure being, as the only way to see its nature, as the only way to demonstrate it, as the only way to constitute the foundation of logic itself.[32] As a consequence, Henrich's reading seems to imply that what is at stake for Hegel in the question of beginning in logic is the same as that which concerns authors like Plotinus and Proclus. Furthermore, as Andrew Cole points out in his inspiring monograph, Hegel's dialectics should indeed be studied alongside the medieval dialectics of Plotinus. Cole even goes as far as to claim that "it is not entirely clear that Hegel is willing or able in his lectures on the history of philosophy to recognize his deep methodological affinity with Plotinus."[33] However, Cole's remark is related to the dialectics of identity and difference, and does not imply that Hegel's concept of the beginning should be interpreted as a case of negative theology. As a matter of fact, Cole argues that quite the opposite is the case, namely that we should understand Plotinus's dialectics as a precursor to Hegelian dialectics precisely insofar as Plotinus arguably offers "the first example of a specific dialectical process, whereby difference emerges from the repetition of the same."[34] Cole thus effectively demonstrates that while there is certainly a relation and proximity between Hegel and medieval authors like Plotinus, Proclus, and Nicholas of Cusa, this proximity lies precisely in the fact that those medieval authors should be understood as already dialectical in the (proto-)Hegelian meaning of the term, and not in treating the One as ineffable and undialectical *tout court.*[35]

What should instead be underlined in Hegel's notion of the sameness of being and nothing is that which was indigestible for Aristotle: precisely the idea of the beginning (of a movement, a process, a transition) as a paradoxical point of neither-nor, that point of "already is, but just as much is not yet (moving, changing)." The point where Hegel's logic challenges the entire Aristotelian tradition of logic based on the principle of noncontradiction can be represented precisely as the beginning point of movement: what is demanded from us is simply to consider such a point as a *boundary*, as something that separates just as much as it binds together. The sameness of being and nothing is, as Hegel puts it, the sameness *and* absolute distinction.[36]

According to Henrich, one must immediately start with the immediate, with the nothingness, as if the beginning is not a boundary but rather that which lies *beyond* the boundary, as if the boundary between indeterminate immediacy and determinate being is a border between two regions. The reading I argue for depends on understanding this boundary as a boundary without the assumption of a region which it bounds us from. A boundary always implies its beyond (for otherwise it would not be a boundary); however, it is the hallmark of traditional metaphysics to understand this beyond as a region of its own; and since this supposed region can't be fully grasped in affirmative determinations, it is considered as an absolutely perfect monolith, as the brightest day and the darkest night. Hegel's beginning as a boundary, however, is something double-sided. It is indeed the sameness of the brightest day and the darkest night, but it is at the same time also their absolute distinction. If Henrich's understanding of the beginning of Hegel's logic can indeed be correctly summed up by the concept of *das Unvordenkliche*, the ineffable and even unthinkable, so that the continuation in the logic of reflection can only follow as something external and posterior to the beginning, then the reading I propose insists on the beginning as a double-sided boundary where the undetermined immediacy is but one of its "aspects." If the logic of being is the beginning of science in the sense of its boundary, then we can grasp it as something within the science itself, as something that properly belongs to it and is not merely its tool, but also as something external to it, something that positively limits it. However, if we think of it as absolutely pure immediacy about which nothing can be said and which we can only approach *via negationis*, then we have already surrendered it to the traditions of Neoplatonic systems of emanation. And in consequence, if Hegel's dialectics is indeed only a variation of these systems, the French materialist critique and their insistence on the legacy of Spinoza is completely justified.

In the foreword to the second edition of his *Science of Logic*, Hegel writes enthusiastically about the principle of polarity that was adopted in the science of physics in his time. He explains it as defining "a difference in which the different terms are *inseparably* bound together," adding that "an advance has thereby been made beyond the abstractive form of identity, by which a determinateness such as for example that of force acquires independent status, and the determining form of difference, the difference that at the same time remains an inseparable moment of identity."[37] This is therefore the alternative: either the principle is something independent and abstractly identical (just as it is in identity systems throughout the history of metaphysics), or this independence of the principle is already split into the difference of its two "poles" *and* their immediate inseparability. The claim here is that Hegel favored the idea of the principle as the unity of the split and inseparability.

On the one side, the undetermined immediacy; on the other side, the movement of becoming, introducing the determinations of coming-to-be and ceasing-to-be, introducing determination in general. The turn from one side to the other, from the perfect impossibility of utterance to the articulation of that impossibility, of the sameness and absolute distinction between being and nothing, is called "their truth." What is beyond this turn is therefore not unreachable, because the truth is precisely the movement by which that unutterable, unthinkable impossibility nevertheless speaks out its words. At the same time, what is found on this side of the turn is also not some hard truth or certainty. This is why it could be argued that logic does not begin with the logic of pure being, but rather with the fact that the logic of being "speaks out" its truth. The true "place" of logic is in between radical indifference and perpetual movement. In this way the immediate identity and abstraction, the rigidity of what Hegel always kept referring to as the "pantheism of the Eleatics," the "identity system of Spinoza," or the "Orient," is disallowed as an *independent* beginning, and yet at the same time is *included* in the beginning as one of its inseparable sides.

Hegel writes: "The result is the same as the beginning, only because the *beginning* is the *purpose*."[38] But the circular nature of the dialectical movement, the conflation of beginning and end, should not be understood in the Aristotelian sense, as the ideal of movement. What is at stake is rather the idea that substance produces itself. It is therefore not a monolith from which everything slides off as its external, simple negation; rather, it is a monolith which comprehends the negativity of determination as its own, internal negativity. The circular unity of that which produces and that which is produced may carry the traditional ancient Greek title of *telos.* The term, especially in the connection to Hegel, has been almost reduced to the level of an insult. And yet, even the Aristotelian concept of *causa finalis,* where the philosophical importance of the concept of *telos* originates, implies the paradoxical unity of that which produces movement or change and that which comes out of this process as its result.

2

History Is Logic

The Peculiar Placement of the Orient in Hegel's History of Philosophy

Hegel's logic of being echoes historical and philosophical questions about the Orient, the Eleatics, and Spinoza.[1] But at the same time the logical principle of the sameness of being and nothing, which is grounded on the rejection of the Oriental principle *ex nihilo nihil fit*, is also the principle of the history of philosophy according to which the beginning of the history of philosophy is possible only as a rejection of the emptiness of the Orient, where there is nothing, where nothing can come out of nothing, and where such nothingness of nothing is the main political, historical, and logical principle. Just as logic begins with complete abstraction and emptiness which must speak out, so that the beginning is placed not in that emptiness itself but in its enunciation, in the emptiness which finally spoke, so too does the history of philosophy not start immediately with the Orient itself, but rather with the "separation of the East and its philosophy" (*Abscheiden des Orients und seiner Philosophie*), which is at the same time an exclusion of immediacy from philosophy. As in logic, so in history, the beginning is displaced.

> In the East, Mind indeed begins to dawn, but it is still true of it that the subject is not presented as a person, but appears in the objectively substantial . . . as negative and perishing. The highest point attainable by the individual, the everlasting bliss, is made an immersion into substance . . . hence an annihilation. A spiritually dead relation thus comes into existence, since the highest point there to be reached is insensibility. So far, however, man has not attained that bliss, but finds himself to be a single existent individual, distinguished from the universal substance. He is thus outside the unity, has no significance, and as being what is accidental and without rights, is finite only. . . . For substance alone is the affirmative.[2]

In Hegel's *Lectures on the History of Philosophy*, the Orient has a paradoxical position since it is and is not philosophy's beginning, and it stands at the same time within and outside of it. On the one hand, the Orient is stuck motionless and can therefore not be considered a beginning, but on the other hand, it still constitutes an initial stage of the spirit, even though it is nothing true. In the logic of being, the truth, that is, the principle of the sameness of being and nothing, must not be made into something already mediated. What is at stake is the *turn* from the abstract, empty, and null immediacy to the unity of the split and the inseparability so that it does include immediacy as its inner impossibility, as the motor producing the truth, from which it is itself withdrawn. Similarly, the role of the Orient in Hegel's history of philosophy is not simply one of pure emptiness, of a nothingness that does not have a place in philosophy; rather, it is the role of emptiness about which one definitely needs to explicitly say that nothing can come of it. It occupies the place of the displaced. In the text of the *Lectures*, compiled by Michelet from Hegel's early drafts, later annotations, and students' notes, two chapters are devoted to the Orient, that is to say, to ancient China and India. The first thing that strikes us, simply looking at the table of contents, is their peculiar placement *after* the introduction to the history of philosophy and yet *before* the history of philosophy itself. This peculiar non-placement of the Orient in the formal order of the system already indicates the non-place of the concept of the Orient itself. It is quite revealing that Hegel first claims, by way of an explanation, that he is indeed going to talk about Oriental philosophy, but only to tell us that not much can be said about it.

> The first Philosophy in order is the so-called Oriental, which, however, does not enter into the substance or range of our subject as represented here. Its position is preliminary, and we only deal with it at all in order to account for not treating of it at greater length, and to show in what relation it stands to Thought and to true Philosophy.[3]

But perhaps the exclusion of the Orient can be explained by Hegel's purely doctrinary reasons, external to the historical matter itself? Generally speaking, Hegel's account of the history of philosophy is divided roughly into two epochs, the Greek and the German-Christian philosophy.[4] The Orient is then merely a superfluous member destroying the symmetry of the Greek-German axis, and it seems it was excluded more for aesthetic and hygienic reasons, due to a whim and Eurocentric bias. However, if the critique of the Orient is supported by such external reasons, it is entirely unjustified. But for Hegel, of course, as for most philosophers, the subject matter of any science is concepts, not facts. For Hegel, the conceptual reasons for making a decision, especially a decision about the very beginning of philosophy, are the only reasons worth taking into account. As Hegel wrote himself, it is quite a mistake to think that the task of a historian of philosophy is to present the historical content absolutely impartially and without the historian's own judgments. For Hegel, the most impartial are the historians who understand nothing of the matter they are discussing and have no system according to which they communicate it to others, but possess merely what he calls historical knowledge, which is to say, knowledge of accidental facts.[5] In thought in general, but particularly in speculative thought, one needs to distinguish between the understanding of grammatical sense and the real comprehension of the sense of the expressed thought. It may very well happen that someone knows the opinions of philosophers without understanding their theses.[6] We must assume that if Hegel decided to exclude the Orient from his account, it was for philosophical reasons; and these philosophical reasons, quintessential to Hegel, are what allowed the Orient to nevertheless appear on the stage of the history of philosophy, even if only to perform its vanishing act.

Hegel's partiality in reading the history of philosophy is therefore a conscious and methodical partiality: it is a way of unfolding the truth, as Gadamer would put it. The basis of such a hermeneutics, the distinction between grammar and comprehension, between meaning and sense, enables the teleological structure of the developmental system. Since its essential determination is incompleteness, sense in hermeneutics is similar to dynamism in motion. Sense cannot be captured in a final and complete comprehension because this is what makes it an opinion. "Truth is not a minted coin," Hegel warns us.[7] It is impossible to comprehend the sense of a philosophical thought once and for all because any sort of complete and final comprehension already implies the loss of sense. Sense is therefore something binding, something that leads to and directs comprehension, sense is the telos of comprehension—but it is not something external to the matter since, as Hegel emphasized, the matter itself, that is, the content of the history of philosophy, is already teleological.[8]

For Hegel, the telos of the history of philosophy is *reason*. This is why the advance in history is identical with the advance of reason. Hegel even went so far as to claim that the advance, the deepening and specification of the idea's logical content in the history of philosophy, is entirely in line with the historical sequence of philosophical views and systems so that we must relinquish any contingency upon entering philosophy.[9] *Logical* advance is thus identical to the *temporal* advance in the history of philosophy; this is why the Orient did, after all, fulfill its prescribed role, namely the role of never appearing on the stage itself, or better, of vanishing from the stage in the same instance as entering it. As the most abstract and general emptiness with ascetically allotted determinations, as immediacy, as what has not yet advanced, the Orient fulfills all the demands that Hegel expects from the beginning of the history of philosophy: "That which first commences is implicit, immediate, abstract, general—it is what has not yet advanced; the more concrete and richer comes later, and the first is poorer in determinations."[10]

If we are in a quandary whether to include the Orient in the history of philosophy or not, just as it appears the editor of Hegel's lectures was, and presumably Hegel himself, it is because we are in such a quandary in relation to *any* beginning. Just as the logic of pure being is the beginning of the science of logic, although not as something independent, but as that about which truth is enunciated, as the rigid, motionless, or dead monolith which the truth contains in itself, so too the Orient is and just as much is not the beginning of the history of philosophy. On the one hand, it belongs more to the introductory considerations, while on the other hand it helps determine that which doubtless belongs to the matter itself, even if merely "*via negationis*," merely by way of negation.

I claim there is a philosophical reason for the exclusion of the Orient from the history of philosophy, a reason internal to Hegel's philosophy. But, as one may object, did Hegel not exclude the philosophy of the Orient for a different reason altogether, on account of it actually belonging to another field, to religion? Now, Hegel did in fact connect ancient Chinese and Indian philosophies with religious thought. And he also characterized those religious ideas as purely universal, which is why they could seem philosophical to us in the first place. However, one should remember that for Hegel, the only religion in the proper sense of the word was Christian religion, just as philosophy could only be European (which means: Greek and German) philosophy. Hegel therefore did not claim that the thought of the Orient belonged to the domain of religion, but that Oriental thought was so universal and abstract that all distinctions became diluted, and *therefore* also the distinction between religion and philosophy. It is telling that Hegel discussed the separation of philosophy from other allied departments of knowledge, that is, science, religion, and popular philosophy (*Abscheidung der Philosophie von den mit ihr verwandten Gebieten*) in one chapter, and the separation from the Orient (*Abscheiden des Orients*) in another chapter altogether, namely within the chapter on the beginning of philosophy and its history. Although something similar is at stake—*Abscheidung, Abscheiden*—the fields of religion, popular philosophy, and science are quite understandably placed *outside* philosophy, while the decision on the exclusion of the Orient is essentially an *intra*philosophical decision; even more, it is a decision that initiates philosophy.

> In religion [of the Orient] we even find self-immersion in the deepest sensuality represented as the service of God, and then there follows in

> the East a flight to the emptiest abstraction as to what is infinite, as also the exaltation attained through the renunciation of everything, and this is specially so amongst the Indians, who torture themselves and enter into the most profound abstraction. The Indians look straight before them for ten years at a time, are fed by those around, and are destitute of other spiritual content than that of knowing what is abstract, which content therefore is entirely finite.[11]

Oriental religious rites are characterized on the one hand by a deep immersion into sensuality, meaning a great number of ceremonies and religious services, and on the other hand by a flight to pure abstraction. The highest point, an individual's immersion into substance and oneness with it, has the form of the most radical asceticism, such as the spiritless, motionless staring into the tip of one's nose. That which is the fullest and most variegated and colorful and has thousands of faces, rituals, and dances is at the same time also wholly empty and contingent, without value, a sort of motionless staring. For Hegel, the Oriental absolute is thus not only the sameness of being and nothing, of substance and the void, but also the indifference of the essential and the contingent, the universal and the concrete: the tip of one's nose, an entirely contingent concreteness, is a direct entry into the highest universality and abstraction. What, contrary to this, Hegel demanded from his absolute was not a distinction between universality and concreteness whereby the absolute becomes a sort of pure universality—this is basically what Plato demanded of his ideas. What Hegel demanded was that their relation be not only directly practiced or thought, but that, *simultaneously with the immediate sameness, their absolute difference be co-enunciated.* The wholly banal contingency, the tip of one's nose, must *become* the most abstract universality and vice versa. It is with becoming that we first come to the truth, which is a turn of immediacy into the movement of mediation so that both immediacy and mediation are contained in it and expressed with it.

Delimitation with Nothing

The term *Abscheiden* which Hegel uses to separate philosophy from the Orient means "exclusion," "elimination," but at the same time has the metaphysical and metaphorical weight of a farewell. In the history of philosophy, the Orient never came to life; it is some kind of an unborn being. Its mode is pure and immediate being-departed. Just as in the logic of pure being immediacy is lost in the sense of a loss of loss itself, since it is given only as already lost, the farewell from the immediacy of the Orient is a farewell from the departed, a double farewell. The word *Abscheiden* also implies the term *Scheide*, a dividing line. The question of the separation, of the farewell from the Orient is therefore a question of drawing a dividing line, establishing a boundary, a limit (*Grenze*). But how does one separate oneself from something that does not, properly speaking, exist? How can we establish a dividing line within a whole when there is no part that could be excluded from it? The problem is that the Orient was not excluded arbitrarily in the sense that Hegel simply had to come to a decision and make the cut *somewhere*, and his choice fell where it fell. For Hegel, the Orient implies pure nothing, nothing of which nothing will come of, and which has such nothingness for its supreme principle. In this specific sense the Orient does have its place in the logical and chronological sequence of Hegel's history of philosophy. Although in the *Lectures* it is strangely placed between the introduction and the beginning, we can say that it is initial in the sense of being unborn. The Orient is *precisely* the pure nothing that one needs to separate oneself from. In fact, it is the Orient itself that separates us from it: because nothing comes of it. *Scheide* as a dividing line *limits us from nothing*; it is a farewell to farewell itself. In this sense, the *Abscheidung* from the Orient is in truth the fundamental philosophical *Entscheidung*, fundamental decision.[12]

On some level it may seem that Oriental philosophy—like Spinoza's—is actually Hegel's own standpoint from which he argued against Kant. Contrary to the Kantian self-imposed limitation to the understanding and self-imposed differentiation from the absolute, one could perhaps claim that the Hegelian project is to reach the absolute precisely by radicalizing the finality and contingency of particular action so that the absolute universality is demonstrated through the banality of the contingent itself. Is not the standpoint of the Orient the truth of Hegel's standpoint?

As appealing (or inflammatory) as this proposition may seem, the problem with staring into the tip of one's nose, for Hegel, is that it understands the particular only as the negative, and the absolute substance is affirmed only through this simple negation; particular dissolves into substance without producing anything within it. Hegel's solution to the Kantian split between the understanding and the absolute is not an outright claim that the understanding is always already contained in the absolute, with the addition that the absolute itself does not have the status of something that is once and for all. The identity system abides in the immediate or, as Hegel put it, it is immersed in the absolute substance where all distinctions vanish. As such, it is itself something whose truth must yet be expressed. In the system of knowledge, the return of the particular into substance is not merely a dissolution, a simple negation of the particular and the persistence of the motionless substance in itself; rather, it is only this return that retroactively establishes the substance as a true substance. If absolute substance is identical and if the particular is something differentiated, then we can say that differences do dissolve in an identity, but it is only thus that they first positively affirm it since they make absolute substance a *concrete* universality. The standpoint of indifference, of the immediate sameness of the pure positivism of substance and the pure negativism of the particular, can by no means be equated with the heroic risk, such as the risk that the Christian God took with Jesus, although it seems that *if we compare only the results*, one death to another, non-action is quite similar to action, that is, the disappearance of the particular in the universal.

In Hegel's history of philosophy and also in his political history of the spirit, the Orient plays the role of the most abstract and the most ascetically determined universality: the role of pure being or, put differently, the role of the absolute substance where subjectivity is merely something decaying, vanishing, and negated, for it either falls away from the substance and decays as something wholly null or is identified with it, but again at the price of being annihilated as something individual. With the Orient, absolute substance is, strictly speaking, never in an *identity* with the subject or the individual since supreme exaltation has to do with immediate monolithic dilution, but it is also not in a *difference* since that which falls away from the substance is nothing substantial; it is nothing at all. The relation is rather a sort of *indifference*, abiding in immediacy. This is why Hegel claimed that there is no freedom in the Orient, merely autarchy.

The Orient is the beginning, but at the same time also a non-beginning; it is the "dawn of the spirit," but is at the same time "spiritually dead." In the account of the logic of being presented in the previous chapter, I argued that the beginning has to be grasped not as the indifference of pure being, but as its truth, as the turn of indifference into determinacy. Similarly, in the history of philosophy, the decisive step of the spirit is the exclusion of the Orient, which does not imply excluding the concrete content of the variegated Orient from knowledge or thought since it has to be grasped precisely as null, but it also does not imply making its nothingness into an indelible nonexisting non-thought, Gadamer's *Unvordenkliche*. The act of excluding the Orient is the turn of the spirit to itself as the turn to truth, that is, the sameness and at the same time absolute difference of emerging and vanishing.

Eleatic Dialectic and the Principle *Omnis Determinatio Est Negatio*

One possible way to deal with Hegel's *Lectures on the History of Philosophy* is to read them as a tireless search for dialectic proper. Even though Hegel's extravagant praise of Spinoza's philosophy, matched only by the subsequent sharp criticism of it, is extraordinary in the whole length of the *Lectures*, this same procedure is observable throughout the work. After the exclusion of the Orient, the history of philosophy was able to start with Thales—but still not as true philosophy, because it was not yet dialectic. The Ionians and Pythagoreans did not comprehend the absolute as thought. It was only in the Eleatic school that thought first freed itself and gained independence, which is why we find there "the beginning of dialectic, *i.e.* simply the pure movement of thought in Notions."[13] But already in the next chapter, we find out that Parmenides's dialectic was not real dialectic either. It appears that the actual beginning of philosophy keeps eluding us. Wherever one cuts and points one's finger and says, behold, *here* is the beginning, it is explained in retrospect that it was merely a potential beginning, it was philosophy in the making, philosophy that was still nothing *until we made the cut there and pointed at it.* The unstoppable displacing of the title of the *princeps* of philosophy in Hegel's lectures is reminiscent of the bloody change of English rulers which the well-known Hegelian Jan Kott pointed out in Shakespeare's historical plays. As soon as the pretender climbs to the highest step at the top of the tower and claims the title, he is already pushed over the edge by his successor.[14] Perhaps such a procedure is most obvious in the following passage on Parmenides:

> Since in this an advance into the region of the ideal is observable, Parmenides began Philosophy proper. *A man* now constitutes himself free from all ideas and opinions, denies their truth, and says necessity alone, Being, is the truth. This beginning is certainly still dim and indefinite, and we cannot explain in detail what it involves; but to explain it is precisely to develop Philosophy proper, which is not yet present here.[15]

The passage starts off most decisively and pompously, Parmenides is named the beginner of philosophy proper, we have before us the great emperor of the notion, free from all opinions and ideas, holding truth in his left hand and being in his right hand. But the poor man did not keep the magnificent title even for a sentence. It turns out that all the inaugurating power was contained in our gaze ("an advance . . . is observable"). It was the retrospective gaze with which we grasped and explained Parmenides as the beginner, as the *princeps*, as the prince of philosophy, that created philosophy "which is not yet present here." Parmenides's principle of identity itself is not yet philosophy proper; philosophy proper is the explanation (*Erklärung*) of Parmenides's principle of identity. We can immediately formulate several theses. Firstly, for Hegel, philosophy is essentially in the mode of potentiality—in no way can we capture it as a pool of solid, already actualized certainties since its existence is only in the making (it never appears as an already minted coin). Secondly, the history of philosophy is an increasingly more extensive, more detailed, and more specified account of its beginning. Thirdly, the beginning of philosophy has to be grasped as its telos. It is literally caused retroactively; its only tangible body is its account of the beginning as a principle.

What holds for the beginning of philosophy (for its *principium*) holds also for its beginner and emperor (for its *princeps*, or prince). And when, in the chapter on Heraclitus, Hegel provided the scheme of the internal structural moments of dialectic and at the same time of its historical development, he was concerned with the question of the principle (*principium*):

> The dialectic is thus three-fold: (α) the external dialectic, a reasoning which goes over and over again without ever reaching the soul of the thing; (β) immanent dialectic of the object, but falling within the contemplation of the subject; (γ) the objectivity of Heraclitus which takes the dialectic itself as principle.[16]

The structural elements of dialectic are arranged in a historical sequence. The term "external dialectic" probably applies to Xenophanes and Parmenides, the subjective dialectic to Zeno and his paradoxes of movement and multitude, and the objective dialectic to Heraclitus's philosophy. In the first step, dialectic is external, that is to say, dialectic is external to the *principle* of that thought: Xenophanes and Parmenides established the identity principle of absolute substance—being is, nonbeing is not—but merely as a direct assertion; all of *their* dialectics is in *our* retrospective gaze. Dialectic is external to this principle, which means: it is only when we *declare* the identity principle that we can talk about dialectic. This is why, in the first step, dialectic is contained merely in the minimal difference between the principle and its enunciation, in the difference between the identity principle and the difference itself.

In the second step, in Zeno, nonbeing obtains a validity of its own; for Zeno not only asserted the unity and unchangeability of the universe, but also turned the perspective: he used dialectics and said: let us suppose that motion and change are something true and we will show that such a supposition is absurd.[17] While in Parmenides dialectic was wholly external to the identity principle, in Zeno it became a tool for the explanation of the principle itself: *subjective* dialectic that leaves the principle untouched. It is only in Heraclitus that dialectic becomes *objective*; its point is that it is the negation of nonbeing that first produces being, and the annihilation of nothing is what is productive in the first place. The principle is then nothing but its dialectic, *the principle is dialectic itself.* That allows Hegel to claim that the philosophies of Parmenides and Zeno had remained at the level of understanding, while Heraclitus had risen to the level of speculative reason.[18]

Despite this, I do not think that we should understand Hegel's inference as the claim that dialectic is the eternal and unchangeable principle of truth. Considered as a principle, dialectic must itself be subjected to exactly the same demand it imposes on the principle of being. It is therefore more appropriate to say that the principle of Hegel's dialectic is an intermediacy between Parmenidean indifference and Heraclitean becoming, an intermediacy characterized by a turn from indifference to becoming. While the insufficiency of the principle of being is that it grasps its enunciation as its pure externalization to which it is indifferent and which, strictly speaking, does not exist or is an apparition, the insufficiency of dialectic as a principle is, on the contrary, that it presupposes only pure externalization and must so consider any kind of internality a mere apparition. Hegel's standpoint should thus—despite what Hegel himself sometimes claims—be understood not as the principle of becoming as such, but rather a turn of the principle of being into the principle of becoming; for Hegel, internality and being are not indifferently given, but are only to be considered as the product of their externalization.

In Hegel's lectures on the Eleatics, we find one of the best formulations of the principle of determination as negation which was so important for Macherey's critique. Parmenides's goddess posits two theses. Firstly, being is, and nonbeing is not. Secondly, to think that nothing is something necessary is erroneous since one cannot know or express "nothing." Hegel explained the second thesis with words that are vividly reminiscent of the formulation of pure nothing in the *Science of Logic*: as soon as you want to express or think nothing, you already express or think it *as* something. Hegel writes:

> The nothing, in fact turns into something, since it is thought or is said: we say something, we think something, if we wish to say or think the nothing.[19]

As soon as we speak, enunciate, articulate, we already say *something.* Any expression or comprehension or idea or cognition or description of nothing is already a comprehension of something affirmative and therefore of something existing. It seems that the logical consequence of this is that any determination is something non-null, something positive. But let us look at Hegel's surprising conclusion:

> "It is necessary that saying and thinking should be Being; for Being is, but nothing is not at all." There the matter is stated in brief; and in this nothing, falls negation generally, or in more concrete form, limitation, the finite, restriction: *determinatio est negatio* is Spinoza's great saying.[20]

At first sight, Hegel's explanation seems shocking. He just explained Parmenides's principle as the thesis that to define nothing already means that we have accepted it as this or that concrete being, or to paraphrase the slogan, *omnis determinatio est affirmatio.* But now he claims that Parmenides's principle implies that determination is always negative and null, *determinatio est negatio.* This apparent paradox is resolved if we understand determinateness in "tragic" or "pessimistic" terms; it is null in the sense that it doesn't have independent being, it immediately dissolves. It is negation with respect to (pure) being; it is negation of the (pure) being.

Yitzhak Y. Melamed distinguishes three distinct understandings of Spinoza's formula in German Idealism, according to which determination is negation. First, he lists the usual understanding in Jacobi and Hegel, the tragic/pessimistic understanding which asserts the unreality of the finite. Melamed here recalls Hegel's argument that Spinozism is not a form of atheism, but, if anything, acosmism, precisely in that it denies the reality of the world or cosmos and claims that the sole reality is God. Secondly, Melamed lists another meaning specific to Hegel, namely understanding the formula as a general slogan of universal dialectic; the difference from the acosmic formula being that not only is the finite a negation of the infinite, but the infinite is also a negation of the finite. This second understanding is of course the one that truly separates Hegel from Spinoza and the one-sided negation. Thirdly, Melamed lists a Kantian understanding where the formula expresses the relation between finite things and the "maximally determined Being," which is a formula referring to God as a being which possesses all realities. And finally, Melamed makes sure not to forget to point out that while the acosmic understanding of the formula is closest to Spinoza's meaning, it nevertheless does not coincide with it.[21] Melamed never claimed that his list is exhaustive, and we could add at least the understanding that Macherey detects in Hegel, namely the idea that negation is a force of determination in dialectics. Here, our interest only lies in the relation between what Melamed calls the acosmic and dialectical understanding, and what Hegel would properly call the relation between the "Parmenidean" idea that all that is is by definition (de)limited and thus null and the "Christian" idea that the ultimate negation, negation of negation itself, is productive. Our claim is that for Hegel, everything depends on uniting both of these understandings in one formula; or claiming that acosmism itself leads to dialectic, that Parmenidean Oneness is itself dialectical, that identity is already in itself the identity of identity and difference.

Hegel's thesis regarding Parmenides is not only that pure being and pure nothing are the same, but that we arrive at this by simply consistently following the path that Parmenides's goddess defined as the path of truth. The turn from determination as affirmation into determination as negation is produced immanently, with the help of the concept of the limit. The limit itself, and not only that which it limits or determines, belongs to negation. The point is not only that finite or limited things are changeable, inconstant, and therefore merely negative and null; this is already the standpoint of "Oriental" philosophy. For Hegel, that which the Orient held merely in the form of the immediate vanishing of the individual or the subjective in the abyss of absolute substance becomes a dialectical principle in Parmenides. *The delineation of the limit itself is already a negation.* The establishment of a dividing line or distinction is already the work of the negative and therefore every determination is negation. When one distinguishes between the level of that which is limited or determined in thought or enunciation and the level of the establishment of the limit, one has already entered Hegelian dialectic where negation is grasped as something productive.

Aristotle and the Motionless First Mover

One of the main questions of Aristotle's *Physics* was the question of motion, the question whether moving and changing things have the dignity of true being. The profusion of references to the Eleatics, who had a radical stand regarding this issue, is by no means surprising. Aristotle's fundamental position was that movement "is a kind of operation . . . which is difficult to spot, but of which the existence is possible."[22] In order to explain his concept of movement, Aristotle distinguished between that which moves and that which is moved. He characterized a mover as the *cause* of movement, as that which *gives* movement and is *capable* of moving something. According to Aristotle, the causing of movement happens through contact, which is why every mover that gives movement and change at the same time receives movement and change.[23]

In the phenomenal, everyday world, every mover is at the same time something that is moved, and every cause is at the same time an effect of some other cause in an endless chain. But the decisive question for Aristotle was the question of the first mover. He thereby completely transformed the premises of the problem of causality. With the first cause, he never meant the first link in the phenomenal causal chain. He repeatedly and explicitly stated that neither time nor motion can have a beginning in the sense of a point where motion simultaneously already is and is not yet. The first mover is thus not a fantastic supposition about the first link of an infinite chain, but rather a metaphysical concept whose task is to defend what is in principle the Eleatic perfection, wholeness, and necessity of pure being. The question of the first mover is the question of *ontological* causality and not the causality of the phenomenal order. This is evident from several of his views. Firstly, for Aristotle, change proper is only the change of one substance into another. Motion or change is nothing substantial, but merely something that happens to substance. Secondly, time as the measure of motion is more the reason for decay than creation. Change in itself is already degradation—on this point, Aristotle is just as much an acosmist as Parmenides was. Temporal things emerge only by chance. And thirdly, generally speaking, something completed and undecomposable is primordial to something uncompleted and decomposable.[24] It is therefore clear that, despite his expressed leniency toward the changeable, permitting its existence, Aristotle was still committed to the Parmenidean distrust of moving entities.

The question of the first mover is an ontological question: how to explain the passage from a perfect, necessary, eternal, and self-sufficient being to the world of decaying things which cause each other's motion only by chance. Aristotle's fundamental presupposition was that a thing can be in motion only due to the action of a mover or a cause external to it. This is why the first mover cannot be moved by something else, by something external to it, or else it would not be the *first* mover. But perhaps the first mover can move itself? Or, to put it in specific terms that interest us here: can a substance be the cause of itself? Aristotle considered this, and suggested that we think of the self-moving whole as composed of three parts, A, B, and C: A is the mover, B is in motion directly due to the action of A and in turn moves C, while C moves without giving motion (or gives it only by chance).[25] If we assume that the whole ABC moves itself, then the motion does not depend on C at all; rather, the mover A carries the entire causal power. For A cannot be something moved since it would then have to be moved by something else. But if we wanted to explain that part of A as something self-moving, the task would only have to be repeated, ad infinitum. In short, according to Aristotle, in all that supposedly moves itself, we should distinguish between the part that gives and the part that receives motion—but it is not possible for something to move itself in its entirety. Hence, there is *no* self-motion or self-causality proper. If we may be permitted to point out that ancient Greek, especially pre-Socratic, philosophical principles were usually also sexualized—just as Greek gods themselves—so that there is almost a binary correspondence between Sky (Uranus) and Man, Earth (Gaia) and Woman, and so on, then it is perhaps not completely outlandish to assume that Aristotle's own concept of God, the motionless mover, the generator that is itself not generated, the cause that is itself not caused, can have sexual implications as well. Aristotle's god is certainly not a hermaphrodite: his motion or causation is pure action of the mover or the cause, and the mover is never passive or receptive. To paraphrase the term which was used in the Thomistic explanation of intellectual emanation, the first mover does not include the receptive part, but merely the giving one; the action of the motionless mover is explained in the same way as the action of the intellect, that is, as pure action. Just like Zeus himself, according to Hesiod, gave birth to Athena the goddess of wisdom through his own head, so too Aristotle presents us with the idea of the motionless mover as the concept of generation or production without the receptive part, as a purely masculine affair, as a pure flowing-out.

The technical term for the metaphysical concept of generation as effluence is emanation. And Aristotle's discussion of the first cause shares many characteristics with the Neoplatonic concept of causation as emanation, and can certainly be viewed as its precursor. The first mover acts without effort. In production, it keeps out of time and out of the world of change—being motionless, timeless, and without any parts. The first cause withdraws itself from its effect since the moving thing does not affect the mover as is the case in the everyday, sublunary world. And, after all, Aristotle's conception of nature has a hierarchical ontological-causal scale. The first mover does not move mundane and accidental movers through direct contact, but through a *mediator*. In Aristotle's example of the ABC whole, the mediating part B plays a special role. The motionless mover can move only in a regular and perfect way, which is why Aristotle believed that the motion of the first recipient of motion—part B—can only be a regular and perfect motion, that is, a rotation. It is only in the last step that we reach accidental and arbitrary motions. In this way, the ontological-causal power and perfection wane when one advances from the uncaused first cause through the mediator, or a series of mediators, to the finite and accidental being. Again, the stages of such mediation are not part of a metonymic causal chain, but are thought of as concentric spheres of ontological-causal fullness—precisely in the sense of Plotinus's emanation.

Neoplatonism

The thesis that the phenomenal world is not true being—what Melamed calls with Hegel the principle of acosmism or the unreality of the finite world—is in general one of the most representative theses of Platonism. But in Plato, the phenomenal world *partakes* of true being. This is an important shift from the strict Eleatic standpoint. In the historical chapter of his notable study on expressionism, Gilles Deleuze distinguished between three elements of Plato's conception of participation: the participated, the participating, and the operation of participation itself. What is essential is that participation is external to the participated, to the true being of ideas, and takes place almost as violence against it.[26] The Neoplatonists transformed the concept of participation so that it becomes the *internal* motion in the participated. Plotinus's formula of emanation is the internal action of the participated. If we use Melamed's terminology, this already marks a dialectical moment in the otherwise still decisively acosmic principle of the unreality of the finite. The participated is the producer in the fuller meaning of the word. What participates is an effect, a product, a gift, an effusion, and not violence from the outside. But still, emanative production is something *one-sided.* The emanative One remains in itself and is hierarchically above its gifts. When it gives itself, it at the same time withholds itself from its gift, for it does not include itself in its gift.

The emanative One is closely related to the traditional Christian conception of incarnation according to which incarnation by no means degrades or transforms the superior divine order insofar as it is divine. Degradation does concern the divine Person, Christ, but merely in his non-divine nature.[27] This is why the Thomistic *emanatio intellectualis,* the reference to the relation between the intellectual process in Aristotle and the Christian process of the generation of Divine Persons, can be counted among the one-sided concepts of production, together with the Neoplatonic emanation. The primary—One, being, intellect—produces and generates from itself without emptying itself; but at the same time, *and we must add that Hegel would insist: precisely because of this,* negation does strike the order of produced being.

In Plotinus, the one-sidedness of the relation between the giver and the gifts is quite explicit: "The Principle before all these principles is no doubt the first principle of the universe, but not as immanent: immanence is not for primal sources but for engendering secondaries; that which stands as primal source of everything is not a thing but is distinct from all things: it is not, then, a member of the total but earlier than all, earlier, thus, than the Intellectual-Principle—which in fact envelops the entire train of things."[28] The One is excluded from the totality of the universe, which is why we cannot appropriately name it; we can only say what it is not, we can express it only *via negationis.* It is something unutterable and unthinkable, just as Henrich understood Hegel's pure being. "Thus The One is in truth beyond all statement: any affirmation is of a thing; but 'all-transcending, resting above even the most august divine Mind'—this is the only true description, since it does not make it a thing among things, nor name it where no name could identify it . . . we have been considering it only in its opposites."[29]

The first emanation from the One, on the other hand, which is the eternal and divine Intellect (Hegel, interestingly, translates the Greek *nous* on this occasion as *Verstand,* as if trying to hide the proximity of Plotinus to his own work), is *immanent* to the offshoots or effusions originating in it: "In two ways, then, the Intellectual-Principle enhances the divine quality of the soul, as father and as immanent presence."[30] The Intellect thus plays the role of a sort of a *mediator,* like the part B in Aristotle and like Christ in the Christian concept of incarnation. The Intellect mediates between the unitary principle excluded from the totality, on the one hand, and things as they figure within the totality, on the other hand. It has a double nature; on the one hand, it is a direct emanation from the One, but on the other hand, it becomes something intellectual only as a reflection, as a turn back to the One: "Thus in its outgoing to its object it is not [fully realized] Intellectual-Principle; it is an eye that has not yet seen; in its return it is an eye possessed of the multiplicity which it has itself conferred."[31] All subsequent emanations are subordinated to the first and are analogous to it: the primary One is in the same relation to the secondary Intellect as the Intellect is to the tertiary Soul.

Hegel explained Plotinus's One in the same way as he explained being in Parmenides and Zeno, that is, as absolute "pure being," and at the same time also in reference to Spinozism as absolute self-identical substance which "alone is true."[32] But primarily he was interested in the question of production:

> Now what is first begotten by this Unity, the Son, is finite *understanding* (*nous*), the second Divine Being, the other principle. Here the main difficulty confronts us—the task known and recognized long years ago—the comprehension of how the One came to the decision to determine itself; and the endeavour to elucidate this fact still constitutes the essential point of interest. The ancients did not frame this question in the definite form in which we have it; but they nevertheless occupied themselves with it.[33]

In a few meager lines, a lot is said. Firstly, Plotinus is topical because of the question of "how the One came to the decision to determine itself."

This is, of course, Hegel's question par excellence: how does the absolute negativity of pure being come to determination? Secondly, in the account of Plotinus, the entry point to production is the question of the Intellect. The entire production must, therefore, be explained from the viewpoint of the first emanation, the viewpoint of the direct "son."

Hegel's answer to the question of determination in the absolute was that pure being as absolute negativity is indeed merely immediacy without determinations, but once we state this about it, this statement is already an affirmation. In Plotinus's explanation, a positive determination of the One or any affirmation whatsoever distorts the original unitary principle. *Via negationis* is therefore the paradigmatic procedure of Neoplatonism. But, in Hegel's account, the immediacy of absolute substance is nothing but the lost immediacy due to which the loss of affirmation is always already the loss of loss. Absolute substance is therefore not only absolute negativity, but is at the same time also productive negativity. This is why, despite obvious similarities in the conception of the topic, Hegel rejected Plotinus's conception of the One. For Plotinus, production is merely something secondary. Hegel rejected the dry order of having first a primary unity, then a sort of a passage or production and, lastly, a secondary duality; *the primary negativity is in itself a production or passage.*

Such a distinction is essential: if we understand Hegelian pure being, as Henrich suggested, as wholly unutterable and unthinkable, something which is radically excluded from dialectic, then we should admit that Althusser's school was quite right when it reproached Hegel with inverse Plotinism. The difference between Hegel and Plotinus is precisely in the primary negativity itself being a productive and therefore differentiating negativity. This can be discerned from a somewhat concentrated passage in which Hegel distinguished his own task from that of Plotinus:

> For because the Becoming of the simple unity, as the abrogation of all predicates, is that same absolute negativity which is implicitly the production of itself, we must not begin with unity and only then pass over into duality, but we must grasp them both as one.[34]

Hegel explained Plotinus's principles from the standpoint of understanding in three stages. At the beginning, the objects of understanding are unchangeability and unity. In the next step, understanding differentiates itself from the essence, its object becomes difference itself and, in this regard, understanding is the creator of the world, multiplicity, and difference. Lastly, understanding dissolves all difference and is its own object.[35] If we try to uncompress these extremely dense formulations, we get the following picture: the first principle is the principle of inseparability, the second principle is that of difference, and lastly, the differentiating understanding grasps itself as its own object; it is the identity that in the differentiation remains in itself.

In the third step, the understanding becomes (Hegelian) reason, the thought of thought. In this way, by a minimal turn of the problematic on the basis of Plotinus's production, we can obtain Hegel's own account of production. This minimal turn already perverts the ontological construction altogether: instead of the explanation constantly moving in the mode of immediacy as if the *enunciation* of pure being were taking place directly as being itself by way of an immediate sameness of thought and being, Hegel's philosophical claim was that, with the beginning of the explanation and enunciation of being, the immediacy of being that the explanation wanted to enunciate already got lost.

Excursus: Epistrophe and Rhetorical Repetition

The turn of the gaze as demanded by Hegel is not external violence against Plotinus's conception of production. The turn or twist of the gaze, *epistrophe*, was already characteristic of Plotinus's Intellect. In Plotinus's metaphor, the Intellect flows out of the One as its emanation, but in this flowing out, it is "an eye that has not yet seen." It is only with the turn of the gaze back to the One—in which it sees difference and multiplicity—that the Intellect is constituted as Intellect, as pure difference. We can come close to Hegel's emphasis in relation to the above through the meaning that epistrophe has in rhetoric, that is: rhetorical repetition. We can thus venture the thesis that the Intellect is, in a manner of speaking, a rhetorical repetition of the One. Thought is the rhetorical repetition of being. The Intellect is the first enunciation of being, but even as the *first* enunciation, it is already a *repetition*. This does not mean that for Hegel being is a sort of a rhetorical embellishment, something that has nothing to do with the real world. The point is rather that there is no being outside language. It is with its enunciation that being is produced in the first place.

Let me borrow Barbara Cassin's terminology and define the turn of the problematic in Hegel with the relation between *ontology* and *logology*. Cassin used Novalis's term "logology" for the thesis that ontology can only take place in the field of language. In an extensive work on Sophistry, she proposed a quite unconventional view of the relation between Parmenides and Gorgias. Contrary to the traditional philosophical stance according to which being, enunciation, and thought belong together, she proposed a reading of Gorgias's essay on nonbeing as a thesis that being is an *effect* of language.[36] Parmenides's poem then does not even need Sophistry as something external to itself, because it is in itself already sophistic.[37] One of the best examples that Cassin provides of the impossibility of thinking being beyond enunciation or thought was Quintilian's sentence *philosophia enim simulari potest, eloquentia non potest,* "Philosophy can be counterfeited; eloquence cannot."[38] She explained it as the specificity of rhetoric being *index sui,* of its truth or quality being measured intrinsically.[39] This remark is brilliant, for being a good orator is nothing but giving the impression or creating the appearance of a good orator. In rhetoric, truth or quality is given as appearance and exists merely as the work of appearance, as the effect or product of appearance.

After all, it is perhaps precisely *therein* that the essential conception of Parmenides's thesis on the identity of thought and being lies. Perhaps we should not simplify it into a metaphysical or mystical fusion where there is neither existence nor thinking, but merely pure thought eternally identical with pure being. Perhaps we should rather comprehend it as a thesis that the engendering of thought is nothing but the engendering of being. Once again, this does not mean that being is merely a word and not something real. Quite the opposite: enunciation and thinking are, strictly speaking, modes of producing being; this is why language is a field where the real takes place. In this regard, with the concept of ontology as logology, Cassin quite justifiably pointed out the performative nature of truth.[40]

This is what is also at stake in Hegel's praise of Parmenides. Hegel explicated the sameness of being and thought—where determinate or explicit thought is identical with enunciation—as the thesis that it is not possible to think nothing, but at the same time he understood this in an affirmative sense, as its positive definition. If we put it with Derrida: that which escaped us leaves a trace, but because *nothing* is nothing determinate, the trace of the lost is everything that ever existed of nothing. The trace or loss is grasped as something which is not exactly affirmative, but it is nevertheless something that has its own persistence. We can list another version of Hegel's take on the formula *omnis determinatio est negatio*: with determinacy, pure nothing is lost, but this loss is a productive one, the loss of the loss itself.

Spinoza against Trickle-Down Metaphysics

This brief and very selective overview of the history of the One finally brings us to Spinoza. As was already pointed out, Hegel classified

Spinoza's system basically as an emanative system of the gradual degradation of being: from absolute substance to parts with increasingly less perfection, increasingly less being, from the hierarchical and logical primary to the secondary, from the absolutely infinite substance to the only relatively infinite attributes and from there to the finite modes. The tripartite division into substance, attributes, and modes is indeed reminiscent of Aristotle's tripartite scheme of metaphorical causality that connects the motionless mover, the mediating moved-mover, and the merely moved. The special role of attributes—for they are the ones that enunciate or form the substance in a determinate way, they modify it—corresponds to the role of the mediating Intellect or Christ in Hegel's explanations of Plotinus's emanation and the Father's engendering of the Son in the Christian conception of incarnation. But the explanation of Spinoza's triad as a hierarchical and logically ordered ontological-causal scale makes the Spinozist concept of causality just a variant of emanative causality. French materialist readers, and among them Gilles Deleuze, vigorously emphasized distinctions between the emanative causality and the concept of causality proper to Spinoza: immanent causality.

Among the characteristics of emanative production, Deleuze emphasized the postulate that the One is not affected by what expresses it.[41] Emanation is a one-way operation, it has no consequences for the One. Deleuze makes it quite clear that emanative and immanent causality do have something in common. In both, the cause, after having produced its effect, remains in itself. Deleuze writes: "Their common characteristic is that neither leaves itself: they produce *while remaining in themselves.*"[42] Spinoza's system is an heir to the emanative tradition; the substance is expressed in infinitely many attributes and affected in infinitely many ways without lessening or exhausting itself by this operation. In this regard, Spinoza's conception was truly not Christian in Hegel's meaning of the term: the concepts of the negation of negation and the contradictory being-in-and-for-itself are foreign to Spinozist substance, because in Spinozism negativity does not produce its own effects; negation is merely a weakening, and substance cannot decrease or be decreased.

But does the fact that the Spinozist substance is "in itself" suffice to infer its incapability to be thought of as the actual cause of itself, as the mover of itself? Neither in Plotinus nor in Spinoza does the absolute act under the constraint of imperfection; it does not produce the universe from a need or a desire, for it lacks nothing, but merely acts according to the necessity of its nature. Spinoza writes: "God acts solely from the laws of his own nature, constrained by none."[43] But one needs to distinguish between the declarative and the reflective level of philosophical systems.

Hegel's objection is aimed at the insufficiency which is visible in the absolute in itself only from the reflective level, only from the standpoint of its enunciation, since it cannot entirely or completely enunciate itself in it; for Hegel, the Christian idea of Incarnation involves precisely what systems of emanation lack, namely the concept of God literally becoming human. If we measure the emanative absolute by its enunciations and in this sense take it at its word, only then does it prove to be inadequate for its own task.

Can we also say the same of Spinoza's immanent absolute? An emanative cause is superior to its effect; it marks it with inner imperfection, a distance that separates it from the giver, from what is most characteristic of it, a distance which in the moralistically theological interpretation becomes debt and guilt, a deficiency that needs to be eliminated, a task and a telos that need to be fulfilled. In principle, the emanative cause is the mechanism employed by contemporary metaphysics to explain the concept of "trickling down" (of wealth, for instance: as if guided by some invisible hand, the Neoplatonic concept of effluence of being migrated through centuries and was adopted by contemporary economics as the concept of effluence of wealth). But in immanent causality, it is not only the cause that "remains in itself," its effect also "remains in it."[44] Following Deleuze, we can assert that an effect is therefore not a falling away from the cause, it is not its discard, it is not emanation. In the immanent system, the effect is not indebted to the giver for its gift, for what it is; it does not have an inner gap that would have to be filled with a teleological ecstatic return to the origin; it is not deficient, but has its own kind of perfection.

But this means that an emanative cause is said to be "in itself" in a *different meaning of the term* than an immanent cause is "in itself." An emanative cause is "in itself" in the sense aimed at by Hegel's objection. It is *merely* "in itself" because its adventure of giving is an adventure merely for the gifts; with this adventure, it squeezes out *its own* imperfection, and this imperfection is therefore merely that which the absolute, in order to remain in itself, leaves behind itself. Contrary to this, the modes of immanent substance are not imperfect compared to the absolute. The power (*potentia*) of existing and acting is the *same* in God, who has it absolutely, and in the mode that has it as part of absolute divine power. As Deleuze has emphasized, the second important difference between an emanative system and (Spinoza's) immanent system is the univocity of being.[45] Being is one, and all beings are equally close to the absolute and the absolute does not have more or less distant gifts and does not act as a more or less distant cause—even more: the absolute is no closer to *itself* than it is to its manifestations and, in comparison to the unnecessary existence of its modes, its necessary existence is not—as existence—in any way a superior kind of existence.

Spinoza writes that although nothing can exist or be conceived without the substance, substance does not pertain to the essence of human; and the same holds for the essences of other things.[46] But even though substance does not pertain to the *essence* of humans, it necessarily pertains to their *existence.* Humans exist as part of the existence of substance, they exist in the same sense that substance exists; the point is not that they exist only *if* substance exists, but first and foremost that they exist precisely *as* the existence of substance itself.[47] The difference between substance and mode thus concerns their essence, while existence is univocal or even one single existence.[48] That is why, in Spinoza's immanent system, it is possible to formulate a real difference between the One and its gifts, without the gifts being merely refuse, merely leavings, "gifted" with a binding deficiency. The one is included in the existence of the multiplicity; when it is expressed in multiplicity, the multiplicity "remains within it."

Deleuze's point about the univocity of being is related to the univocity of the action of the causal force. Spinoza writes that God is named the cause of all things "in the same sense that God is said to be self-caused."[49] This is his grand philosophical achievement. Not only is substance the cause of itself—which already implies a break with Aristotelian doctrine, because substance is on some level also its own effect, which Aristotle did not allow—but its causal power is not hierarchical. Individual things are merely determined ways in which the affection of substance, its mode, is expressed. This is why in the Spinozist system there is one single causality just as there is one single being. Spinoza rejected the metaphysical distinction between metaphoric and metonymic causality, that is, the relation between the ontological-causal hierarchical scale and the accidental causation in infinite chains of moving things. There is no ontological-causal hierarchy since the metaphorical level of causation is something real only when it is at work in a metonymic chain.

3

Telos, Teleology, *Teleiosis*

Ontological Slime

Pierre Macherey claims that the philosophy of Spinoza is something that the Hegelian system cannot digest, something that cannot be integrated in its "totalizing dialectics." It is for this reason that Hegel "obsessively" returns to it: "Spinoza haunts the Hegelian system throughout its unfolding. The obsession, of which he is a symptom, is not immediately undone; it reappears continuously in the discourse that itself never completely finishes with its beginning."[1]

Of course, Macherey is criticizing Hegel, but in the critique he nevertheless gives us a useful description of the constitutive decision of Hegel's philosophy; all we need to do is to replace the term "Spinoza" with the term "logic of pure being." What if the complicated relationship between the logic of pure being and the logic of reflection—where the logic of pure being is precisely that which can never be articulated in the logic of reflection—is the fundamental characteristic of Hegel's philosophy as a whole? Shouldn't we—just as Hegel insists—understand the logic of being not only as the beginning of logic proper, but also as the underlying logic of any beginning in philosophy? It is what persists in the development of the dialectical thought as its undialectyzable and unanalyzable "real kernel."

One of the key distinctions between Kant and Hegel was described by Slavoj Žižek as a shift in the understanding of the thing-in-itself.[2] The formula that Žižek uses to distinguish between the phenomenal and the noumenal is a one-sided limitation. In his reading, the experience of the sublime basically describes the dissolution of the idea that beyond the phenomenal there lies the unreachable, yet substantial thing-in-itself.

> In other words, this experience demonstrates that phenomena and noumena are not to be conceived as two positive domains separated by a frontier: the field of phenomena as such is limited, yet this limitation is its inherent determination, so that there is nothing "beyond" this limit. The limit ontologically *precedes* its Beyond: the object which we experience as "sublime," its elevated glitter, *Schein*, is a mere secondary positivization of the "nothing," the void, beyond the limit.[3]

Beyond the limit there is "nothing," there is only the void. We can add, specifically referring to the *Science of Logic*: the void of pure being. The positive object that we experience in the experience of the sublime—namely the full, substantial Beyond—is always just the "shining of the appearance." Nevertheless, this object underscores the irreducibility of the limit itself. The limit thus functions as both the limit *and its beyond.* What we are dealing with here, contrary to the idea of the distant origin, is rather some repeatability of the original determination, of the constitutive, purely formal determination.

In traditional metaphysics, the Beyond is what causes all beings within the confines of this world, but also determines and binds them as their purpose. Žižek does not suggest a Beyond in an affirmative meaning of the word, and yet his understanding of the limit retains the formal characteristics of a positive Beyond. His limit is an attempt to formulate how something radically un-integrable persists inside the given positive domain (within the order of being, within such and such discourse, etc.). The "void beyond the limit" is, of course, the Hegelian void of the absolute substance, the ontologically primordial or original nothingness of being, which is at the same time that from which a limitation delimits and the limitation itself.

The most widely used examples of this void throughout Žižek's work are the examples of an unknown yet indestructible horror from television culture, such as the undead creatures from countless zombie movies and TV shows, or the alien from Ridley Scott's 1979 film *Alien.* What these examples suggest is the idea that the established, positive order is on the one hand constituted by, but on the other hand also threatened by an "ontological slime," that is, by a substance where all distinction is dissolved.[4] In this regard, Žižek's explanation of the limitation as a purely formal distinction is analogous to Gadamer's concept of that abyss, prior to which no thought is possible (*die Unvordenkliche*).

To be sure, Žižek's idea of the ontological slime as the ontological primordiality of the limitation over what it delimits corresponds to the gesture of inauguration in the Hegelian discourse; whether it is the separation of the Orient from the history of philosophy, the void of the absolute substance, or the nothingness of the immediate, pure being: for Hegel, the proper beginning in philosophy, logic, or thought is always a question of delimitation from a limitless, distinctionless, indeterminate substance. This, in fact, is what makes it a primordial gesture. However, the point is that the "slime" survives the inaugural scission and haunts the positive order as an irreducible foreign object, as the undead persistence within the positive order itself. For Macherey—notwithstanding his general rejection of Hegel—Spinozism functions precisely as the "slime" that fuels the Hegelian system and gives it its purpose just as it at the same time threatens to dissolve it at any given time.

Origin as Produced and Repeated

Both Gadamer and Žižek address the questions of the unfinished beginning of the Hegelian discourse, of the persistence of the slime, of the repetition of the original act of decision. Their paths diverge, but they nevertheless share the rejection of the traditional metaphysical formula of the distant, yet binding Origin persisting in the process as its transcendent Beyond. They point out that the origin is a produced origin insofar as the gesture of original scission precedes the origin as such (Žižek); or that it is an ever-renewable origin insofar as it requires repetition in order to function as origin at all (Gadamer). Production versus re-production.

The in-itself is the original object, for which it is demonstrated, in retrospect, that it has always already involved the subject, or that it could only have been an object for that particular subject. Žižek and Gadamer share the idea according to which that which is original already involves its repeatability and according to which the purely formal act of drawing a demarcation line irreducibly persists in positive, determinate things it constitutes. For Žižek, the phantasmatic Beyond is only constituted as something secondary to the real and actual experience of the separation of the phenomenal world from its determining boundary, from its limit. For Gadamer, the authentic understanding of the text we are reading can only establish itself through a positive application, since the "resurrection of the meaning" always demands a positive Word, even though the meaning itself remains *Unvordenkliche.* For Žižek, the task of the philosopher is to suspend the mechanism of the spontaneous formation of the ontological slime into a concrete, ready-made being, and to insist on the limitation as such. For Gadamer, the task of the understanding is to immediately look for an authentic affirmation, to give to the original limit some shape and substance, to bring its relationship with the truth of the text it is reading into a positive application.

The difference between the two positions is best explained by analyzing their understanding of Christianity. For Žižek, what is at stake in the advent of Christianity is its purely formal intervention in the conjuncture of the world, its destructive and alienating form, which is why he insists on understanding it as Evil—that is, not only unbound to the practical morality of everyday life, but in fact disturbing, even threatening the stillness of the practical morality of everyday life. In other words, Žižek is interested in Jesus's entrance on the stage of world history to the extent that it is a formal act, an intervention, a radical gesture that reshaped and reformed the existing order and brought about a new type of discursivity. This approach falls into the tradition of the Christianity of Saint Paul and Martin Luther and its orientation is close to that of Alain Badiou; Žižek's concept of production is a concept of reformation.[5]

For Gadamer, quite to the contrary, the essence of Christianity is the revelation, its capacity to produce positive application again and again, its unstoppable faculty to reproduce itself. Gadamer's example from *Truth and Method* is the Scholastic explanation of the Christian sermon as proclamation of the Word, where "the Christ of the resurrection and the Christ of kerygma are one and the same."[6] The everyday ritual of proclaiming the word is therefore a repetition of the original event itself; in fact, it is nothing short of the new happening of the event of resurrection itself. Gadamer's concept of repetition is reading in the sense of re-reading, and production in the sense of re-production.

Both Žižek and Gadamer subscribe to the idea of the priority of the limitation to its beyond. However, for Žižek, the limit is purely formal; it is a gesture which is repeated throughout history and can take the form of conflicting positive manifestations. The task of philosophy or science is to insist on its original negativity. In this regard, Žižek follows Althusser, for whom science does not construct a positive ideal model of reality, but rather engages in a symptomal reading of the reality, that is to say, it understands reality literally, as if reading from a page in a book but stumbling upon paradoxical points, where reality simply does not say what it is saying. For Gadamer, on the contrary, the focus is on the positive expressions, on the positive understandings, even though none of these enjoys the status of the ultimate expression, for they are all ontologically posterior to primordial negativity.

Subject as Lack or as Torsion

But there is a third possibility to be considered alongside the paths that Žižek and Gadamer have taken. They both claim that the affirmative construction of reality is ontologically unfinished; the totality is marked by an inner lack or limitation. Gadamer exploits the more or less familiar religious category of the finality as the irreducible framework of human understanding. Žižek evokes either the category of the real kernel which cannot be integrated in or successfully explained by the symbolic order, or the category of the subject as an empty place in the structure of reality, as a crack in the substance.

But there is yet another way to understand the one-sided limitation. One could claim that the limitation does not only precede what it is delimiting from, its beyond, but that strictly speaking the boundary is all there ever was and that existence is a function of that delimitation line, that it is its curvature or torsion. The line of limitation itself remains seamless; it includes no gaps or lacks (such as supposed by Žižek's understanding), it is in itself not limited or imperfect (Gadamer): providing, of course, that it is nothing but the limit-line, without any content to be a limit to, only a transition, a pathway, only a substance that is never anything else but a subject. Instead of understanding substance as an unfinished, non-total substance, where the subject is the name for the crack in the substance (Žižek) or its finite and therefore deficient counterpart (Gadamer), one can understand it as pure transition, as both vanishing and becoming. This prompts the alternative: either the subject is the lack in the substance, or it is simply the name for the curvature or torsion of the substance.

Admittedly, the examples where Žižek evokes the image of torsion in reference to his concept of negativity are scarce. But he does make an interesting use of it in the context of his discussion of Keynesian economics. The idea is that when a capitalist government prints money for which it has no cover in whatever it is that the "science of economics" considers real value—there is no pot of gold, not anymore at least, at the bottom of the long chain of financial maneuvers—in order to stimulate the growth of the economy by borrowing from the future, it is living at the expense of the future by constantly deferring the time of the final reckoning. Under the Keynesian premise, the art of economic politics is precisely to make sure that the time of reckoning never comes. Žižek transformed this idea into an ontological thesis and claimed that such an economy is virtual insofar as it is supported and fueled by debt that will never be repaid. The debt which constitutes the economy, explains Žižek, corresponds to the Lacanian concept of debt which is characteristic of the symbolic order as such; the meaning of words or other signs in the chain is always "borrowed from the future" and therefore only exists as the future meaning, or as virtual meaning.[7] In this regard, Žižek's thesis of the virtuality in economy and language subscribes to the famous Althusserian claim—proposed in the context of the critique of the relationship between the infrastructure and superstructure in classical Marxism—that "the lonely hour of the 'last instance' never comes."[8]

If we accept that the hour of reckoning between the real and the borrowed value never comes, then their difference vanishes and the debt becomes a characteristic of the reality itself. The reality itself becomes something deferred, something virtual. Reality is understood as dynamic, as pushed from the "real" value towards the "printed" value, as *torsion* that can never be put back straight again, since it is primordial or ontological.

The German philosophical tradition was always very fond of the etymological relationship between debt and guilt, since the German word *Schuld* expresses both. Nietzsche famously analyzed a specific economic logic of debt behind any moral concept of guilt.[9] In *Being and Time,* Heidegger went so far as to propose the thesis of the original debt/guilt of the human existence.[10] But perhaps we could add a certain geometric aspect of this etymological link, one that is founded upon a simple distinction between a straight line and a curve.

When we want to "set the record straight," we want to rectify a mistake in the account of something. Does this not imply that the blame that was wrongly put on us, as well as the guilt that followed, is imagined as something which is not straight, as something crooked or contorted? Similarly, to pay one's "debt to society" requires incarceration in a correctional facility, a term that implies that the felony is imagined as some bending of the rules of law (and perpetrators are imagined as crooks). To take the cue from the imagery of the common language, we can understand debt as either a lack, as an unevenness or a gap that needs to be filled, or else as a torsion or bending that needs to be rectified, that needs to be set straight. The images of the language confront us again with the alternative: whether to understand the substance as a curtailed substance, that is to say, as a substance with a constitutive lack, or to understand it as a substance which is bent. To put it in two words: lacuna or torsion?

We usually understand debt as a matter between a person and a bank; alternatively, and more dramatically, between a person and a usurer. One only has to think of Shakespeare's *Merchant of Venice* to remember that it is not only in German philosophy but in English literature as well that debt functions eminently as something void and non-existing, but nevertheless pertaining to human flesh itself. The image of financial debt is the lack that the bank agreed to fill on the promise that the person will, over time, fill the lack that opened on the side of the bank. Debt opens up a question of filling the gap or correcting an unevenness on the premise of a temporal delay.

This is a similar structure to that of exchange. One could say that the difference between debt and exchange is that a debt always implies a temporal delay of reckoning, while an exchange can easily be carried out instantaneously, with both the merchandise and the payment exchanging hands at the same time. But in truth, the contract between the buyer and the seller is only possible on the assumption of a gap or lack that the exchange fills on both sides: the buyer owes payment, the seller owes the merchandise. We must think of exchange in terms of Derrida's thesis of the primacy of writing over the spoken word: even when the exchange is taking place "live," "in real time," and the merchandise and the payment are given simultaneously, we should still not think of exchange as something immediate; it still requires the structure of debt as something essentially atemporal—and hence as something mediated.

Debt is therefore, before it is anything else, an atemporal exchange of something for something else: *it is a sign.* If we transpose the thesis of the existential debt from the relationships of an exchange onto the field of ontology, then the question is how exactly to think that atemporal relationship, that signification. Is it a gap in the structure of being, a gap of the deference of the reckoning? Or is debt the torsion of being itself, an ontological spring? Žižek's reading of the relationship between the actual and the potential is Deleuzean to the extent that his focus is on the actuality of the potentiality itself:

> The status of possibility, while different from that of actuality, is thus not simply deficient with regard to it. Possibility as such exerts actual effects which disappear as soon as it "actualizes" itself.[11]

The possibility Žižek is writing about possesses an actuality of its own, an actuality of the potential that does not need to actualize itself in order to produce actual effects. We can speak about the ontological debt of the economy, its virtuality, because it functions and is something actual precisely because there is never the final moment of Judgment Day, Parousia, when the time itself is at an end and all debts are paid for good. We should even claim—as does indeed Žižek—that economy does not consist of the real and the speculative sector (industry and financial institutions), much in the way that philosophy in early Hegel breaks down into logic and metaphysics, but that the real sector is already speculative, just as logic in the later Hegel is already metaphysical. Again, we can attribute this to Žižek's Althusserian philosophical foundation: the concept of the actuality of potentiality is of the same order as the Althusserian concept of the theoretical practice which was coined to reject the naive materialist distinction between the economic practice, supposedly working hard, with sleeves rolled up, and the speculative theoretical reflection of that practice. There are passages in Žižek's work that are not only much more elegantly explained with the concept of a curve rather than that of a gap, but perhaps these are also precisely those passages that effectively demonstrate that Hegelian philosophy is not a philosophy of Parousia.[12]

The distinction between the two conceptions of the subject, either as the gap in the substance or as its torsion, may seem of little importance. In the final analysis, they are merely images and not precise conceptualizations. In both cases, it is the category of the subject that suspends the idea of the substance as a well-rounded totality, as an all-encompassing unity, and enables us to think it as not-whole and as in transition. But the importance of this distinction becomes more visible in the context of Spinoza's philosophy, where there is no concept of lack or imperfection, either on the level of the substance or on the level of the modes. To be more precise, Spinozism does not recognize the idea of a *productive* lack or negativity. This was the fundamental reason for Hegel's rejection of Spinozism as a project that never really moved from the beginning. And it is true, if we accept Deleuze's and Negri's readings and understand Spinozism as a vitalistic philosophy of pure affirmation, that we have reduced it to a somewhat naive position that will inevitably prove to be unsatisfactory in contemporary debates, where the actual effects of negativity and the generally accepted idea of the primacy of negativity have grown roots. Can Spinozism account for the structure of language and the symbolic order? Does it even have a proper concept of the sign, a concept that is not exhausted with the notion of inadequate ideas? This depends ultimately on whether we can demonstrate that Spinozism is capable of thinking something like debt: something that is neither pure actuality nor pure potentiality. It is clear: perhaps it is precisely the concept of the substance as a bent or curved substance, as a substance with torsion, that enables Spinozism to not only survive in contemporary philosophical conflict with Hegelianism, but also to find answers to the questions that Hegelian philosophy could only perpetuate. Perhaps there is a way to use Hegel's reading of Spinoza's concept of the substance to help Spinozism consequently push itself to the frontiers of its hypotheses, without ceasing to be Spinozism.

Telos and Dynamism

The question of debt as an atemporal exchange, or as a kind of a contraction of time, allows us to formulate an ontologically very interesting dimension of something that does not exist, at least not in the simple meaning of the term, and yet clearly affects reality. This is precisely what is at stake in the notorious Aristotelian and Thomistic, but also Hegelian, concept of *telos*. Perhaps it is time to rehabilitate this heavily criticized concept . . . But firstly, why is the concept of telos so problematic? In the world of habit, we always already find ourselves in a concrete situation where, to use a Heideggerian term, telos is nothing but the organization of our pursuits according to our givens and our expectations (*Ent-*

wurf). Part of the problematic aspect of telos arises when we connect this concept with the general notion of free will: by this coupling, human subjectivity becomes a kind of puppeteer organizing the body according to its design, its goals, its wishes and whims, pulling its strings from a level above the mechanistic, deterministic level of the physical body. This is—*in nuce*—what the Cartesian concept of subjectivity amounts to. And this is precisely the concept that lies at the center of Spinoza's sharp critique in the addition to the first part of the *Ethics.* For Spinoza, even God, the sole cause that may be called free, does not act "from his free will or absolute pleasure, but from his absolute nature." At the root of all misconceptions, or "prejudices" as Spinoza calls them, is precisely the idea of telos: "Now all the prejudices which I intend to mention here turn on this one point, the widespread belief among men that all things in Nature are like themselves in acting with an end in view."[13]

As Spinoza explains, people are not only wrong about their own free will, but furthermore ascribe voluntary actions to God himself—which is the second aspect that is problematic with the concept of telos. In this case, the question of telos becomes the question of the Divine Plan and thus we are already entangled in the discussion about Divine Providence that leads its course in history, driving its agents with an invisible hand for the greater good of all, until all is fulfilled in the time-ending event of Parousia. This second problematic aspect of the concept of telos comes to the fore when we ontologize or universalize the everyday experience in the world of habit so that we understand nature itself, or history itself as organized toward an end-goal. On this point, again, we can easily see that the contemporary metaphysicians, gathered under the banner of the "science of economics," have been able to convince us that we do not need to worry and that we do not even need laws and regulations of this world, because the "free market" will move in its mysterious ways and make sure that justice is delivered, much better than any human institution could. The metaphysical argument has not changed one bit over the centuries: the reason for the superiority of the "free market" over human institutions is that humans are frail and weak and finite, they are corruptible . . .

In order to dispel the grip of this "prejudice," Spinoza does not simply brush it off, but teaches us to distinguish between the concrete and the abstract generality. The generality is abstract if it is merely a consequence of the fact that we can never imagine very many singularities in detail. Spinoza's example is the abstract image of man, which involves only those details in which all people we have made contact with overlap; such images are quite accidental.[14] Spinoza does not regard the abstract generality as an elevation of the concrete accidental material to an ideal form, but quite to the contrary as an accidental conjunction that fails to grasp the real. The blunder about the teleological activity of individuals as the expression of their free volition is connected precisely with this kind of generality. Spinoza opposes it to his concept of common notions (*notiones communes*), the concept of generality which is rooted in the concrete, in the affection of our body.

But perhaps we can use the concept of telos not as an abstract generality, not as a naive image where God's intellect is basically nothing but a powerful version of our own, but by understanding the fact of concrete existence as an ontological category. In this context, Spinoza's insistence on concrete generality is revealed as a gesture which is in its nature very similar to that of Heidegger and his thesis of Dasein as the being that exists ontologically, a thesis of the existence that already involves the ontological dimension and is therefore not merely some debris, emanating from the level of being; it is not imperfect in comparison to the perfect being, it is not unfinished in comparison to the original totality, *since perhaps being itself is something unfinished.* Could telos be a working concept of the ontological finality?

We can lay a foundation for the concept of the telos of the universal substance by exposing the relationship between the Aristotelian pair of telos and dynamism. Let us take Althusser's example for his thesis that the interpellation of a material individual into an ideological subject has always already happened: the rituals and expectations surrounding the birth of a child. These rituals are mostly carried out even before the "material individual" is born, but certainly long before one could claim that it is capable of voluntary submission to ideological initiation.[15] It may seem that this suggests that there is actually no such thing as a material individual, that this was just a temporary working hypothesis which turned out to be irrelevant in the course of the analysis. But in truth, this hypothesis should be seen as a *necessary hypothesis.* While it is true that the material individual never sees the light of day, that it is something negative, it is at the same time something without which it is impossible to think the symbolic or ideological "birth." We could then claim the following: what is born is an ideological subject, but the material individual remains within this subject as something radically unborn.[16] The Althusserian material individual as the unborn within the born itself is precisely the crossing of telos and dynamism we were looking for. On the one hand, it is the name for the unfinished, uncompleted, unperfected nature of the subject, for its actuality of the potentiality; on the other hand, it lies in the core of the web of the teleological structure of planning and preparation. Althusser's material individual is what the Lacanian theory of the subject understands as the subject's real kernel.

The problem of the Aristotelian concept of the final cause is that it seems to simply transpose the result of the process to its beginning and call it its purpose, its reason, its cause. The teleological structure was at the core of Spinoza's critique, and this is why he wrote that nature knows no purpose and that "all final causes are but figments of the human imagination."[17] However, even in Aristotle himself, at the very root of the problem, the notion of *causa finalis* should be explained in the light of the concept of potentiality. One should not forget that the idea of the fourfold of causes as Aristotle developed it in his *Physics* was invoked as part of the discussion of the broader question of movement and change, the question that was resolved, in the end, by distinguishing between the actual and the potential. This is the reading I argue for: the causal power of the final cause (telos) should be explained in exactly the same way as we have explained the actuality of the potentiality. When we observe a house under construction, the final cause is the name of the inner dynamism of this movement, something that cannot be exhausted with the explanations of the material (the planks) or the form (that shape that is the reason why we say that a house is being built and not a ship). And even the effectuating force (work) is not enough, because it only explains the actuality of things in motion but says nothing about the direction, the goal of that motion.

However, the final cause is also not merely the end of construction, its external purpose or goal, retroactively transposed to the beginning as its prime mover. In fact, the entire fourfold of causes should be understood as a totality of causality. Telos is not the end point, but rather the work of perfecting or completing itself. This is why for Aristotle telos as the final cause is present throughout the process of construction and not just at the end. Just as the dogmatically interpreted relationship between actuality and potentiality required its transformation into the concept of the actuality of potentiality itself, we should also reconstruct the opposition between the process and its result into the concept of a processual telos, telos which exists only in the process of its fulfillment, internal to the process.

From Fourfold to Fourfold

The question of telos was one of the central questions in Heidegger's reconceptualization of the Aristotelian fourfold of causes. In his lecture "Building Dwelling Thinking" given in the context of a gathering of architects, he took the example of bridge-building to consider construction. Of course, one can always say that the *purpose* of the construction is human dwelling; this makes the construction a mere tool or means to achieve the end. But Heidegger's point was that building is not only a means for dwelling, but dwelling in itself: "For building is not merely a means and a way toward dwelling—to build is in itself already to dwell."[18] To use Hegelian terms, purpose or end are simply not enough to explain the concept of telos, since the point is rather that the thing is in itself teleological.

But even more explicit is Heidegger's explanation of the essence of technology in the lecture "The Question Concerning Technology." Again, his argument is that we usually consider technology as a means to an end. This is why Heidegger briefly debates the historical background of the concept of instrument before he comes to the core of the problem, the Aristotelian concept of the fourfold of causes, one that dominated centuries of philosophy.[19] He pointed out, firstly, that the four causes should be considered as a totality. Secondly, the concept of cause should therefore not be understood from efficiency (and reduced to it), but rather from what binds the four causes in a unity. For Heidegger, this concept was that of *verschulden*, "indebting"—or, as noted above, being guilty of, being responsible for: a chalice is indebted to its material, to the form of the chalice, to the silversmith.[20] Thirdly, the entire fourfold should be reformulated and reconceptualized, which was the task of his own fourfold: sky and earth, mortals and divinities.

After the logically precise and conceptually honest *Being and Time*, a reader may wonder what happened to Heidegger in later years to produce the pathetic phrases about sky and earth, and so on. The curious fourfold may seem completely out of touch with any reasonable philosophical tradition. I believe that many commentators have taken those words too literally and reduced their response to parroting the phrases and humbly praising the mysterious concept of the fourfold. On the other hand, critics were also too fast in giving up and ascribing the whole story to the blunders of an aged philosopher. In my opinion, Heidegger's concept of the fourfold becomes much clearer and much more reasonable if we simply ground our reading of it in the introductory notes to "The Question Concerning Technology," that is, to the discussion of Aristotle's four causes. If we bear that in mind, then it becomes clear that the earth and the sky are, in principle, critical reformulations of the material and the formal cause; while divinities and mortals are perhaps—at least to some extent—reformulations of the final cause and the efficient cause. For Heidegger, the challenge is to salvage the concept of causality from the instrumental understanding, where it is reduced to a question of means and end, and settle it in the domain of production (*Hervorbringen*, or *poiesis*). Here is what he writes about the chalice and its telos:

> But there remains yet a third that is above all responsible [*verschuldet*] for the sacrificial vessel. It is that which in advance confines the chalice within the realm of consecration and bestowal. Through this the chalice is circumscribed as sacrificial vessel. Circumscribing gives bounds to the thing. With the bounds the thing does not stop; rather from out of them it begins to be what, after production, it will be. That which gives bounds, that which completes, in this sense is called in Greek telos, which is all too often translated as "aim" or "purpose," and so misinterpreted. The telos is responsible for what as matter and for what as aspect are together co-responsible for the sacrificial vessel.[21]

Telos is certainly an end and a completion, though not in the meaning of goal or purpose, but rather in the sense of determination. We should understand the end as something productive, as something determining; not in the sense of confining, but in the sense of inaugurating. Heidegger's understanding of telos as determination, and not as a simple negation, is perhaps yet another formulation of the principle of *omnis determinatio est negatio.* Telos is therefore not something that only comes in the game at the end, it does not simply mark the end or the limit of its existence, but properly completes it and is in this sense something that is in play from the very beginning, something without which that process cannot even start. Telos is interior to the process of which it is telos. And if we remember that in Aristotle, telos—along with the entire concept of causality—should be understood on the basis of debt and guilt, the link between telos and dynamism becomes transparent: to involve dynamism is but to carry debt.

This telos that operates only from within the process of its fulfillment can be given the name *teleiosis,* in honor of Franz Brentano, who invented this concept in the context of his discussion on the continuum.

Franz Brentano's Geometry

One of the most interesting paradoxes we inherited from antiquity, specifically from Aristotle's discussions, is Zeno's famous paradox of the arrow. The challenge is to explain what, if anything, is movement, by discussing a flying arrow. If we observe it in any given moment of its flight, it fills its space and rests in it. But this goes for every singular moment of the flight—the only sensible conclusion seems to be that the arrow never moves! This is one of the paradoxes of movement that Zeno offers us in defense of the Eleatic concept of being. The commonsense intuition that movement is simply not the same thing as rest will not help us resolve this paradox any more than would the mathematical calculation of the arrow's speed at a given point in time. We would still need to give an ontological explanation of what we are talking about when we talk about movement. And this was the task for Aristotle in his *Physics*.[22]

Aristotle refutes Zeno's paradox by distinguishing between continuity and discontinuity; a continuous process or object can be divided in parts that are themselves continuous, which makes a continuum infinitely divisible. Aristotle thus famously claimed that a spatial line does not consist of points (since they are indivisible and therefore not continuous), and time does not consist of singular moments or "nows" (since they are indivisible). For Aristotle, in a "now," we strictly speaking cannot see movement, and even about rest we can only speak in a special meaning of the term. This was the reason for Zeno's mistake.

However, Aristotle's solution of the arrow paradox has a flaw: it fails to account for the success of geometrical representation, where the spatial movement and the duration of time are observed precisely in singular points, in indivisible moments, producing correct results every time. How is that possible, if time and space, as Aristotle assures us, do not consist of indivisible parts, but are strictly to be discussed as continua? We could say that Franz Brentano took it upon himself to address the philosophical urgency for an ontological explanation of movement in a way that was also applicable to the geometrical representation of movement in its singular, noncontinuous part. The task is actually a brave attempt to propose an impossible mediation on the question of continuum, where the result would be something like a point in motion.

A plastic artist creating an image of a person or an animal in movement faces the same paradoxical task; they must literally capture movement in a material that is as immovable as stone or bronze. The famous sculptor Auguste Rodin believed that this task was handled best by making sure that the complete sculpture composes several phases of movement in one piece. As the gaze drifts along the sculpture, those parts each in turn reveal another phase of the movement so that the synthetic totality produces a surprisingly powerful effect of life or movement. Rodin went as far as to prefer the traditional way of depicting a galloping horse, that is, with all four legs lifted in the air at once and extended, even though it was proven by photography that such a pose never occurs in nature. (As Eadweard Muybridge famously proved, the horse *does* lift all four legs during gallop, but *not,* as was usually depicted, with front legs extended forward and hind legs back.) The photograph of a gallop was considered too static from the point of view of artistic truth, its effect basically corresponding to that of petrifaction. For Rodin, this makes such photography less plausible than a sculpture which is capable of synthetically capturing several phases of a gallop in one stroke. We could say that Zeno's understanding of movement is precisely a kind of "photographic image" of a gallop, to be strictly separated from Rodin's synthetic paradigm. Brentano's task was perhaps precisely to argue for the paradoxical photograph-in-motion.[23]

Brentano's concept of the continuous was heavily concentrated on the question of boundary. His little known but extremely productive concepts of *plerosis* and *teleiosis* are an attempt to explain the finite and noncontinuous part of the continuous whole only by referring to the whole it is a part of.

Firstly, let's take a look at the definition of *plerosis.* Imagine there are two disks; one is a disk of completely blue color and the other is a disk parceled into four quadrants: one quadrant is white, one is blue, one is red, and one is yellow. The center of the sectored disk, if observed as the outer boundary of the blue sector, has only a quarter of the *plerosis,* compared to the full *plerosis* of the center of the completely blue disk.[24] The essence of Brentano's move is that one and the same point has different properties when observed as a boundary of different entities. We may add to Brentano's example that in the case of the parceled disk, the geometer must decide whether the center point is white or blue or red or yellow (if indeed they allow for a point to have the quality of color). This is because a point, for a geometer, is completely independent of the whole it belongs to, and so one can easily either count it in or subtract it from the continuum. A Brentanian, on the contrary, can claim that the center point is shared by all four sectors of the disk, with the stipulation that for each sector, the center has only a quarter of *plerosis,* which is also differently oriented for each of the sectors. This is why, in Brentanian geometry, we can draw not only one, but infinitely many straight lines between two points—but their *pleroses* are only partial and are oriented differently.[25] By introducing *plerosis,* we can resolve the question of the beginning of movement that puzzled Aristotle: we can determine a clear boundary for each interval of movement or rest of an observed body; it is just that the *plerosis* (or fullness) of the boundary is shared with the next interval.

The concept of *teleiosis* is even more interesting, insofar as it generalizes the idea of the variability of *plerosis* from the outer boundaries of a continuum to all, that is to say, also to the inner boundaries of a continuum. This makes the boundary the crucial determination of the continuum. Brentano explained the concept of *teleiosis* by positing a rectangle of continuous color transition from blue on the one side to red on the other side.[26] Let us compare the color of any of the horizontal lines (that is, lines that pass from blue color to red) with the color of the diagonal in the point of their intersection. From the abstract mathematical point of view, the color of the diagonal and the color of the horizontal line in their intersection is the same, since this intersection is exactly one point which is independent from the lines that intersect in it and is certainly of the color, identical to itself (again, if indeed it could even be said that it can have the property of the color). But if we observe the intersection as the inner boundary of the diagonal and compare it to the intersection as the inner boundary of the horizontal line, then, in Brentanian geometry, its *teleiosis* is different. The diagonal is longer than the horizontal line, and therefore the grade of the color transition is different: this is why the *teleiosis* of the intersection depends on the line it belongs to. And if we compare the blue vertical line of the beginning of the rectangle of color transition to any vertical line of a completely blue rectangle, their *teleiosis* is also different. The outer boundary on the blue side is not completely blue, just as the outer boundary on the red side is not completely red, as one may conclude on the basis of an abstract representation. For every vertical line of the rectangle of continuous color transition we must assert that it is *in itself on the way* from blue to red. The beauty of Brentano's solution is that it does not flatly reject Zeno's geometrical representation of movement—a "photographical" representation that is commonly used even today—but rather comprehends it as part of a more complex understanding of movement in space.

The defining characteristic of Brentanian geometry is that boundaries as parts of the continuum cannot be considered as independent from the whole they belong to as parts. This is why Brentano allows us to speak about the seemingly paradoxical dimension of a dimensionless part of the continuum. The examples listed above all attest to the spatial dimensions of a singular point: orientation, fullness, grade of variation.[27] In contrast to the Aristotelian notion of the continuous, the concepts of *plerosis* and *teleiosis* do allow us to observe movement in a singular point. It is therefore clear that the mathematical procedure will always produce the correct result; but when we are interested in the ontological status of movement or rest, we must take into account that the object in movement, observed in the given moment, has a *teleiosis* which is different from that of an object that is at rest at that same moment. This resolves Zeno's paradox: the flying arrow, observed at any given singular moment in time, has a different *teleiosis* from that of an arrow which is at that moment at rest. A moving arrow cannot be said to occupy its place in the exact same way that a resting arrow is said to occupy it.[28] Even though movement can be observed in a singular point or "now," this point inherits, so to speak, all the characteristics of the continuous whole it belongs to as a part.

In the light of the Brentanian conception of the continuous, we can claim that movement is at work in the singular moment, or that the singular moment as a part of the movement is itself moving. Brentano's interpretation of movement is radically different from the mathematical. Mathematics finds infinity, characteristic for the continuum, always somewhere in between or outside of the indivisible parts of continuum—for instance, the mathematical definition that in between two given points we can always find another point is infinitely reiterative, but does not speak of the infinity belonging to the points themselves; the infinite recourse is strictly external to points, it lies in between them. Brentano's geometry, however, allows us to understand a singular point, if observed as an inner or outer boundary of a continuum, as a point with such and such a *teleiosis*, that is to say, as a point that is always already on its way from one end to the other end, as a point that is in a way in itself continuous (though, paradoxically, dimensionless). Brentano's infinity of movement is neither Eleatic indeterminacy nor abstract external reiteration, but an infinity already at work, an infinity internal to its finite parts. Unlike in Aristotle's explanation, the continuous is not in opposition to the discontinuous, since the discontinuity, the singular moment, the point of "now," is recognized as a *part* of the continuous; in other words, the continuous is not some glue that intervenes from the outside and binds discontinuities together, since it only exists as working at the level of the discontinuities themselves. If we understand the concept of *teleiosis* in this way, as a concept that enables us to comprehend the unity of the process and its end, then we have already grasped one of the aspects of the processual telos that was advocated by Hegel.

Telos, Teleology, *Teleiosis*

For Hegel, the history of philosophy is teleological, because the matter itself, philosophy as dialectics, is teleological. But does this telos as an inner telos ever get perfected—can it ever be fulfilled? Can there ever, to be quite explicit, come an End of History? Hegel's answer to this question is emphatically yes. However, the fulfillment of telos does not come as new philosophical knowledge in the sense of a positive content; it comes as a formal structure of fulfillment, as the system of the history of philosophy itself, as the system that was constructed by following the trace of the intellect in historical development. The telos of the history of philosophy is fulfilled as that philosophical system that explains the development of the history of philosophy as the internal development of its own logical categories: that is, in Hegel's philosophy. It is clear that this can mean a fulfilled telos only in a special sense of the word. The perfection of the telos is identical to grasping telos not as the result that is revealed only at the end, but as the entire path, drawn up by the succession of actualizations of telos. Hence, we get a wonderful Hegelian paradox: the fulfillment of telos is in understanding telos as the path of its fulfillment.

The telos of the history of philosophy has a double function. On the one hand, it is a *principle* in the sense of the *motor* of history, invisible and withdrawn from its current. On the other hand, it is the proper *beginning* of the history of philosophy and therefore a paradoxical point where its movement starts, whether this is the troublesome Orient as the vanishing emergence of spirit, whether it is Parmenides as the prince of dialectics, or whether it is Spinozism and its principle of the negativity of the determinate. The starting point is the principle that nothingness cannot be thought or expressed in words since in determinate thinking or speaking we immediately grasp it as something. But it is precisely the nothingness of nothingness that keeps trying to get expressed in the history of philosophy, with the initial contradiction acquiring more and more complex form.

The famous criticism (by Althusser) states that the Hegelian system is the ultimate incarnation of historical metaphysics in its teleological and theological aspirations. On the one hand, this seems justified. The logic, phenomenology, and history of Hegel start with the poorest and most abstract beginnings and gradually climb towards more and more complex forms and knowledge, until they finally reach the point of the absolute system, the absolute knowledge itself, which is the breaking point that gives meaning to the entire process. If we look at Hegel's hierarchical and progressing structure as a totality, as a clearly defined succession of elements, then his dedication to teleology—in the sense of the concept of telos as an external purpose or end—is evident. But on the other hand, absolute knowledge as the conclusion, as the telos of the process, does not bring about the mythical ultimate understanding. At the end of the process, knowledge and truth are no more united than they were at any other stage of its development.

And even if we turn to the beginning of the process where such a union may be given in its pure and immediate state, one should bear in mind that the immediacy of the beginning is only a lost immediacy, since it is given only as something insufficient or lost in advance. If we look away from the totality to its parts as they are thought, however, the picture we see is quite different: every stage carries true tension and contradiction. At the level of the part of totality, the outcome is far from certain, even though in retrospect it turns out time and again that it could not have been otherwise. Contemporary Hegelians underline precisely this perspective; let me just point out the special attention that Catherine Malabou dedicated to the questions of the "becoming essential of the accident" and the "becoming accidental of the essence" and her conception of the Hegelian interplay of necessity and surprise with the French phrase *voir venir* (meaning both to anticipate what is coming and to let oneself be surprised by it).[29] Hegel himself appears to have been far more impressed by the glorious, straightforward, and neatly arranged structure of the system than could be said for contemporary Hegelians. They prefer the importance of accidents, immanent to the process of truth, and the central role of the difference and differentiation as the motors of that process. From this perspective, Hegel's telos is probably the best example of what is dead in Hegel, to use a famous expression by Benedetto Croce. But the wager I propose is that this notorious and arch-metaphysical concept should be defended: it should not be read as the foundation and crown of a teleological edifice, but rather as a processual telos, as telos which is at work in the particular part of the whole; as telos that is expressed by the Brentanian concept of *teleiosis.*

In order to properly defend Hegel on this point, one would have to painstakingly work through the vastness of references throughout the body of his work to the conceptual nest of purpose (*Zweck*) and purposivness (*Zweckmäßigkeit*), and weigh the correlation to his account of natural teleology, as well as to other pertinent concepts and terms like goal, result, end, and so on. Here, let me only sketch the argument in brief stages. First of all, Hegel completely adopted the Kantian distinction between the external and internal teleology. External teleology denotes the idea that we can ascribe some external purpose to natural processes, like for instance explaining the stroke of lightning as God's punishment. Not only Spinoza, but Kant and Hegel as well abhorred this ridiculous notion. The internal teleology, on the other hand, denotes the inner purposivness of natural beings and allows us to claim, for instance, that the purpose of the germ is to grow into a tree. Secondly, Hegel in fact used the example of the inner teleology of plants as a metaphor to describe the dialectical process of the spirit, or the self-development of the concept. Therein lays the greatest problem: Althusser criticized Hegel's concept of totality precisely as an "expressive totality," containing its entire history in its germ, so that the process of development is but a gradual manifestation of what was already laid in the beginning. Thirdly, it is therefore important to note that Hegel himself limited the usefulness of the organic metaphor. Hegel argues, for instance, that in nature the germ indeed comes back to itself, just as spirit does; but that in nature, the return of the germ is not for the original germ, but for another, while in spirit, the returning spirit is for that same spirit. Hegel writes: "As with the germ in nature, Spirit indeed resolves itself back into unity after constituting itself another. But what is in itself becomes for Spirit and thus arrives at being for itself. The fruit and seed newly contained within it, on the other hand, do not become for the original germ, but for us alone."[30] And fourthly, when Hegel, in the *Encyclopedia*, comes to the point where he must specifically address the difference between nature and spirit, namely at the point of transition from the philosophy of nature to the philosophy of spirit, he is forced to use a completely different metaphor. He writes, perhaps a bit shockingly: "The purpose [*Ziel*] of nature is to kill itself [*sich selbst zu töten*], and to break through its rind of immediate and sensuous being, to burn itself like a Phoenix [*sich als Phönix zu verbrennen*] in order to emerge from this externality rejuvenated as spirit."[31] The only proper metaphor for the dialectical process of the spirit is the metaphor of rejuvenation through death, a metaphor which resonates with the Christian concept of Resurrection.

When Hegel declared himself the great emperor of history, logic, reason, and spirit, the fulfillment of the historical philosophical telos, et cetera, et cetera, et cetera, this gesture was performed with the full knowledge that he will share the fate of Parmenides, who was cast into the abyss immediately after his inauguration, indeed in the same sentence. It is important to understand this gesture as precisely that: as a gesture; it is important to underline its formal status. This gesture is principally the same as that of a full stop at the end of the sentence, the stop that makes the story or the thought reach its logical or meaningful conclusion. To put the full stop at the end of the sentence always involves taking a risk. We are always in danger of not having said the essential, or at least not in a satisfactory way. We are always in danger that the readership will understand our meaning not only as our *complete* position, but also as our *dogmatic* position: this is exactly what we mean, even if you shoot us this instant! We are always in danger of not being regarded as human beings with a soul, as hermeneutical creatures in an infinite relationship with ourselves, a relationship of constant interpretation and reinterpretation, but as a one-dimensional, rigid force.

And yet we would face an even greater danger, should we avoid this one by trying to preserve the unforeseeable nature and the real surprise of the explicit formulation of thought and deny our sentence its full stop at the end. The most obvious proof for this is the disappointment and sheer disgust we are filled with when watching, listening to, or reading stories with the so-called open ending. By these, I do not mean stories whose ending is quick or abrupt, where the story ends immediately after its peak—in fact, that is usually a sign of a good story. Open ending, here, does not necessarily imply stories that end in a suspense or with a cliffhanger, like for instance in thrillers; nor does it imply stories where the ending scenes somehow repeat or reenact the disposition of the beginning. What I mean are the stories that simply do not end and are even impudent enough to parade this obvious flaw as their point, as if saying, with a benevolent didactic tone: we wanted the recipient to write their own ending. These lousy stories without ending, without plot, and without courage clearly show that to put down the full stop is far from being a means to evade the risk, the labor, and the true surprise; rather, it is precisely the gesture of taking the chance and throwing the dice. Putting the full stop means accepting all the consequences. Putting the full stop means saying something.

The Napoleonic gesture by which Hegel declared himself the emperor of thought and grasped absolute knowledge is the gesture of putting the full stop in described paradoxical, aleatory meaning. On the one hand, this is how the dialectical movement reached its ultimate ending, how the potentiality was actualized; this is how, as Malabou put it, the "forms already actualized discharge their potential energy and consequently liberate future possibilities of actualization."[32] On the other hand, the dialectical movement started to work only by reaching this point, since it was only in this full stop that it has finally said what it said. The final ending is therefore its new but also its true beginning, just as Heidegger spoke about the telos of the sacrificial vessel.

This is also revealed by the well-known thought from the preface to the *Phenomenology of Spirit*, where Hegel declares that the speculative or philosophical sentence requires a double reading. The first reading, where we are trying to move from the subject to the predicate, fails, because we find ourselves wandering from the subject to the predicate and back. But it is in the very failure of this first reading that the speculative reading is born.[33] This principle of double reading actually goes for the sentence as such: when it reaches its full stop, *it dies*; but precisely the moment of the sentence's death is also the moment of its speculative resurrection, the beginning of its second life, that is to say, its second reading.

The critique of the Hegelian teleological totality is quite futile in the contemporary conjuncture since there does not seem to be anyone among Hegelians willing to hold the banner on this issue. Contemporary philosophy is so thoroughly marked by the idea of the primacy of negativity, of the primacy of limitation over its beyond, of the originality of nothingness (thought as the void, rupture, lack, etc.), that the story about the organic growth and development in the wholesome totality is simply dead and uninteresting. To paraphrase Hegel: it seems that contemporary philosophy can only begin from this point onwards, only when we have already bathed ourselves in the ether of the organic totality which hides in its ultimate fruit only the path back to its renewed growth and development. The true impasse and the true battleground that determine why Hegel is inspirational for contemporary debates lies in the concept of absolute knowledge itself, in the telos of thought itself, understood beyond the framework of naive external teleology, but also beyond the framework of the organic metaphor of purposivness. The questions are how to conceptualize movement within the absolute and how to understand the working of telos at the level of the part of the process. The true impasse lies in the fact that the concept of telos faces us with two conflicting demands. On the one hand, the process needs to come to a definitive conclusion, the abstract indeterminacy must be transformed into the mode of concreteness; the absolute knowledge must bring the dialectical movement to the end, and this means that it needs to possess the power to give meaning to it. But on the other hand, how do we conjugate this demand for a definitive ending with the concept of the ontological indeterminacy, that is, indeterminacy which is not simply a privation of the actual existence, since being is considered as something radically incomplete?

Nothingness eludes us as soon as we try to think it, but Hegel's point was to consider that it is precisely in this elusive nature of nothingness—as the monolith form upon which everything slides, as the Žižekian ontological slime, as the Lacanian lamella, as the Hegelian Orient—that it nevertheless produces actual effects. We cannot simply discard it or think it away; quite to the contrary, it rather functions as the motor of thinking. This is what Lacanians call the real remainder, by which they imply that the symbolic order of language, which could also be understood as the order of existence, is not constructed in its totality; in a manner of speaking it is simply incomplete. In his lecture on materialism and infinity,[34] Žižek explained this thought with an example from the field of video gaming: the game creators defined a world with "superb graphics" and "realistic effects," but there is inevitably a limitation, for instance a house whose interior is undefined; it was never a part of the game and it therefore never existed. The point is that the world of the symbolic order should be understood precisely as that "unfinished house" (Žižek's own phrasing). Contrary to Aristotle's example of a house in construction, one must claim that the incompleteness of the house is not some ontological deficiency with respect to the purely actual primal mover, *but is in fact the only way that something actual can even exist.*

How do we think the incompleteness of the world without assuming an openness which could be easily substituted by arbitrariness? How do we insist on the concept of the end and nevertheless think the original incompleteness? In a way, the answer is quite simple: absolute knowledge is precisely the conceptualization of this paradox. It is the gesture of putting the full stop, the gesture of making a decision, the gesture which is at the same time the ultimate and the inaugural gesture, the end of the sentence (as an irreversible sequence of words in time) and its new beginning (as a symbolic, atemporal piece of signification). We understand telos as the punctuation mark which is constitutive for being itself. In other words, being is incomplete precisely because it is nothing but an end, being is only if it is at an end. But this simple answer tells us nothing about the relationship that we underscored as essential: should this incompleteness be understood as *lack* or as *torsion*?

4

Death and Finality

Death of Spinoza

With almost every historical philosopher he discussed, Hegel pointed to at least some sort of an interesting relation, if not full accord, between his life and his philosophy. In his account of Spinoza's philosophy, he put a special emphasis on Spinoza's ethnic descent. In fact, Spinoza was born in a Sephardic Jewish family, which emigrated from the Iberian Peninsula to France at the time of expulsions and forced conversions, was later exiled from France, and finally settled in the Netherlands.[1] In the seventeenth century, it was not easy for a thinker like Spinoza to openly discuss his views on nature, God, and the true meaning of human freedom; for a Jew, it meant putting oneself in mortal danger. The Jewish community in Amsterdam was in a precarious position, and it did not want to risk being blamed for actions performed or views expressed by one of its members. Spinoza was excommunicated at the age of twenty-three. Even though the ban, or *cherem*, pronounced by the Amsterdam Jewish community was usually only a means of putting pressure on an individual, an attempt to bring him back to the flock, and was not meant as a permanent ban, in Spinoza's case, the language of the expulsion was extraordinarily violent and the *cherem* was never lifted.[2]

Hegel, however, was not particularly interested in Spinoza's relationship with Judaism. For him, the key to Spinoza's philosophy was not in understanding him as a European Jew, but rather as a *European Oriental.* It is with Spinoza, according to Hegel, that the Oriental understanding of absolute identity first came close to the European mode of thought, through a radicalization and consistent development of Cartesian philosophy.[3] This also explains why Hegel was interested in the fact that Spinoza's practical profession was that of a lens grinder. Indeed, it was impossible for Spinoza, given that he had no intention to teach anything else but what he considered to be the truth, to make money by teaching, and so he had to rely on the financial support of his friends and the modest earnings he received for building delicate optical equipment: by lens grinding. Spinoza's interest in optics was not a mere biographical contingency for Hegel; he saw in this a reference to what he understood to be one of the fundamental categories of the Orient, the category of light, an image of the principle of the absolute identity. In the *Science of Logic*, one of Hegel's explanations of the unity or sameness of being and nothing is the kinship between light and darkness. Both pure light and pure darkness make it impossible to distinguish anything determinate; determinateness already requires a shadow, an outline.[4]

But the agreement between Spinoza's biographical details and his philosophical teachings that is most often and most pointedly mentioned in Hegel's work is the circumstance of the death of Spinoza.

> Spinoza died on the 21st of February, 1677, in the forty-fourth year of his age. The cause of his death was consumption [*Schwindsucht*], from which he had long been a sufferer; this was in harmony with his system of philosophy, according to which all particularity and individuality pass away [*verschwindet*] in the *one* substance.[5]

What Hegel found interesting about this was the wordplay on "consumption," *Schwindsucht*, and the passing away itself, the *verschwinden* of a particular individual; *schwinden* means to wane, to disappear, to shrink into nonexistence. It is as if the cause of death, in Spinoza's case, was not so much the particular sickness of the body, the consumption, but rather passing away as such, the death itself. Spinoza as something particular and individual disappeared (*verschwindet*) in the abyss of the absolute substance where there is no distinction and where all particularities are dissolved into nothing (*in dem alles nur dahinschwindet*). It is as if it were the accidental and banal biographical detail, the cause of death, that put the finishing touch on Spinoza's philosophy of the one substance. It is as if Spinoza's death establishes a standpoint from which we can say: "Look, he was absolutely right, all individual is consumed in the universal." All individuality disappears in the abyss of absolute substance, and Spinoza's consumptive death is the highest affirmation of this principle: the system of the absolute substance itself disappears in the abyss. Hegel did not quite say it, but it is clear enough: Spinoza's death is the disappearance of the system of disappearance, or the "death of death."

Consumptive death includes an element of self-reference. Spinoza the individual disappeared into the abyss of the substance by way of disappearance, he died of dying. This is not a death for such and such a reason, but a death out of principle, a conceptual death, a dialectical death of the concept. It is the self-referential element that is for Hegel the basis on which Spinoza's absolute substance can be brought from its status of the "true" to the status of the "wholly true:" the principle of disappearance must take itself seriously and disappear itself, the principle of absolute negation must negate itself. Spinoza himself would never accept death as a concept; for him it was simply a question of succumbing to external powers. It seems, however, that his own death both confirms and subverts the system, and what is more, it subverts it by confirming it. Spinoza's death proved to be perfectly in accord with his system, which, however, means that it apparently *did* operate on the level of the concept.

According to Hegel, all Oriental conceptions about "emptiness" and "nothing" and the "transience of everything" should be taken at face value, we should hold them to their word, so that Oriental philosophy in its entirety is comprehended as null and excluded from the actual history of philosophy not as something substantive, but as pure nothing which we need to separate from, which we say farewell to. The thesis related to Spinozism is the same: the nothingness of individual existence, the disappearance into absolute substance, is a burden that absolute substance has to "take on," an effort it itself has to undertake. The principle of identity, if it is consistent, is transformed into the principle of becoming.

Let Die: Kenosis

Spinoza's conceptual death—if we follow the meaning of Hegel's somber joke—enables the speculative death of the concept. Absolute substance turns the work of negativity, the incessant vanishing, on itself, negates itself, whereby the universality of absolute substance becomes concrete universality; it becomes something "literal," it is held to its word and embodied. We could express this with the slogan: *let die.* This retrospective move is the hallmark of Hegelian dialectics; sometimes it is formulated as the question of substance identical with its own disappearance, or as the question of substance as subject, and sometimes as the question of infinite judgment in which the spirit's being is identical with the dead bone, but often also as the question of Christian mysticism in which Jesus is the incarnation of God.

In the Christian theological tradition, the degradation of absolute substance is known as the question of Christ's humility, or *kenosis.* This term comes from a somewhat mysterious passage in Saint Paul's letters: "Christ Jesus . . . emptied himself [*eauton ekenosen*] by taking on the form of a slave, by looking like other men, and by sharing in human nature. He humbled himself, by becoming obedient to the point of death—even death on a cross!"[6] This is closely related to the paradoxical humanness of God the Son. The Christian concept of incarnation is essentially different from other concepts of incarnation, for instance in Pythagoreanism, for it does not entail God only *showing* himself in human form, but rather

God *becoming* a human being. Christ feels the pain, fear, and sadness (of his human body); he is subject to the external and internal causes of the suffering of body and soul. Kenosis is therefore the degradation (humiliation) of God into human nature.

From the very beginning, the Christian *theological* tradition provided widely divergent explanations of divine incarnation. These partly revolved around the extent to which Christ is subject to "humanness," and partly around the question of how exactly to ground the unity of the divine and the human in him. But the *philosophically* essential idea contained in the Christian notion of incarnation is the paradoxical unity of the finite and the infinite. This is where Hegel's interests in kenosis lie, and so do our own.

In dogmatic theology, the relation between the divine and the human remains fundamentally one-sided. God created the world, and yet suffered no change thereby; it was the world alone that underwent change, for God's existence is considered to be pure actuality. The incarnation of God in Jesus also effected no change in God per se, but merely the change of the world, which was "saved." We could say that at the same moment when Christian theology discovered the fascinating point of the unity of the divine and the human, it also covered it up: for, in Christ's death, it was not his divine nature that died since it was not and could not in any way be affected, and as divine it also did not suffer. Such an idea of incarnation remained, at least from the Hegelian point of view, insufficient. In dogmatic Christian metaphysics, the one-sided relation between the pure actuality of the absolute and the potentiality of the world remains, in its core, Aristotelian or Neoplatonic. At all costs, the prime mover must remain unmoved.

In explaining the relation between the divine and the human, Hegel leaned on the tradition of Christianity that was established by Saint Paul, and especially the Protestant conception of kenosis, Luther's in particular, which proved decisive for his argument. Speculatively, the most interesting for him was the "infinite grief" of Easter Friday, the feeling that "God Himself is dead."[7] This religious feeling implies, if expressed in philosophical terms, the mortality of the divine itself, which Hegel took very seriously as a thesis about the finitude, paradoxically pertaining to the absolute itself. Based on Luther's translation of "kenosis" as *Entäusserung* (emptying), Hegel explained incarnation as God's passing into being.[8] Hegel's thesis was that God's death on the cross concerns God's being itself. Incarnation and the related death on the cross are something that God *had to* take on in order to disengage from the abstract universality of the pure concept. This was and remains unacceptable for the dogmatic view; Hegel was reproached for introducing into

God, which could supposedly be thought of only as pure actuality, a sort of potentiality and therefore an imperfection or a deficiency, or even a hunger for being.[9]

The objection that Hegel introduced into God a kind of a lack—as if the perfect being does not act from its overfull presence, from pure actuality characteristic of a transcendent being, but according to a sort of necessity, under compulsion, out of need or even a hunger for being—is grounded in the traditional explanation of Aristotle's distinction between the actual and the potential, and in his concept of the "unmoved mover." But the negativity within absolute substance that Hegel had in mind is not a potentiality in the sense of a deficiency or the absence of the actual but rather an actual potentiality (virtuality). Potentiality within God has its own actuality and is not only privation or an action postponed to the future.

Catherine Malabou pointed out that a similar discussion developed about Hegel's account of Aristotle's conception of nous.[10] For Hegel, nous includes negativity. But again, he thereby did not force nous into potentiality, insufficiency, or passivity since nous includes the paradoxical dimension of actual potentiality, virtuality.[11] The point is that nous has the capability of self-determination. For Hegel, God, or absolute substance, is not an unfinished project. But it is also not a self-sufficient and purely universal abstraction that produces its products or gives its gifts or emanates the waves of its being without being affected in any way by such action. It is not a despot arbitrarily issuing decrees (on this, Hegel and Spinoza agree entirely).

The virtuality of God is a concept that enables one to understand his activity as free, but at the same time not as arbitrary, even though it is open to real surprises and daring risks. Contrary to the notion of the divine as an abstract universality which, abiding in its safe haven, establishes itself over the dead bodies of concrete, material individuals, Hegel construed the Christian God as the absolute which is willing to put everything at stake, including his own absoluteness, omnipotence, and omniscience, and perhaps, if we follow Žižek's reading, even his own faith in God.[12] Incarnation is precisely the concept of absolute substance as substance that takes on the entire burden of risk and establishes itself *over its own dead body*. We can see in this the influence of the Protestant account of kenosis as the Word that became a finite human soul: it staked its word and became something literal. The Word limited, and in this sense, humbled itself, but its finitude, its punctuation mark, its full stop has to be taken seriously: it was not only Christ's human nature that died on the cross, and not only his Person, but also God the Father himself, the initial pure abstraction.[13]

The traditional explanation of the relationship between the Divine Persons is a process of emanation. Hegel found it insufficient, since in the relation between the divine and the created only the latter is negated. The production, characteristic of emanation, is a one-sided or simple negation. The viewpoint according to which God produces out of his grace, overabundance, and inexhaustible and unsolicited generosity without thereby suffering any damage is production as giving without losing. This is very concisely encapsulated by Gadamer in a passage summing up Thomas Aquinas's account of the concept of *emanatio intellectualis*:

> Thus we can see how the creation [*Erzeugung*] of the word came to be viewed as a true image [*Abbild*] of the Trinity. It is a true *generatio*, a true birth, even though, of course, there is no receptive part [*empfangenden Teil*] to go with a generating one [*zeugenden Teil*]. It is precisely the intellectual nature of the generation of the word, however, that is of decisive importance for its function as a theological model. The process of the divine persons and the process of thought really have something in common.[14]

Thomas's theology provides an account of the relation between intellectual generation and the generation of Persons. While it may still seem to some that the question of *gender* or sexuality does not or should not arise in the context of the metaphysical or theological concept of the process of *generation*, it should be clear that discussing the similarities and differences between the organic process and the conceptual process is a productive way to explain them. In a Thomistic theology (or, to make things even clearer in the pursued line of thought: in an Aristotelian theology), production is perceived as a kind of monosexual, purely masculine generation, more specifically, as generation that does not require conception. Conception presupposes, firstly, *passivity* and *receptivity*, perhaps a void that can take something in or into which something can penetrate, a dimension that God definitely does not possess. Secondly, if God could conceive, he would have to subject himself, or a part of himself, to change, which would already imply a sort of *potentiality* within his being. This is why generation is explained as the action of the "generating part" without any cooperation of the "receptive part." To spell it out, this is a purely masculine generation, but not in the sense of penetration—for there is nowhere to penetrate—but in the sense of pure auto-affection, the *noeseos noesis* (thought of thought), which results in emission or emanation, or in the infamous trickling down of being.[15]

For Hegel—and this is the most important difference from dogmatic Aristotelianism—these processes should not be understood as *giving without loss*, but as the *loss of the loss itself*, the emptying of emptiness. For Hegel, the death of God is "an event of his self-negation."[16] With the death of the Son, the heavenly Father also dies; but this does not imply an imperfection of God; rather, it is to be understood as a productive death, as *the death of death itself*. The latter formulation, coined by Luther to express that in the death of Christ human mortality also died away, was explained by Hegel as a negation of negation.[17] With death on the cross, God is by no means revealed as something imperfect; rather, he is shown to be something productive.

Comedy: The Mortality of the Divine and the Immortality of the Corporeal

The starting point of Hegel's explanation is the perception of God in the Enlightenment and pietism, in which God became a dry universality and emptied abstraction, and in this sense something void, lost, and dead. In his early publication *Faith and Knowledge* we can already find the relation between "infinite grief" captured by the event in Christian religion, namely the death of God on the cross, and the conception of God as an abyss of infinity unreachable and unknowable for the finite subject. Hegel writes:

> But the pure concept . . . must signify the infinite grief [of the finite] purely as a moment of the supreme Idea, and no more than a moment. Formerly, the infinite grief only existed historically in the formative process of culture. It existed as the feeling that "God Himself is dead," upon which the religion of more recent times rests. By marking this feeling as a moment of the supreme Idea, the pure concept must give philosophical existence to what used to be either the moral precept that we must sacrifice the empirical being [*Wesen*], or the concept of formal abstraction [e.g., the categorical imperative]. Thereby it must re-establish for philosophy the Idea of absolute freedom and along with it the absolute Passion, the speculative Good Friday in place of the historic Good Friday. Good Friday must be speculatively re-established in the whole truth and harshness of its Godforsakenness.[18]

The emptiness on the side of the subject agrees with the emptiness on the side of God. In a certain respect, the viewpoint of *Phenomenology of Spirit* and *Lectures on the Philosophy of Religion* only sharpened the thesis from *Faith and Knowledge*. While in the earlier text God as such was something dead, in the later texts death is conceived as an event in God's being itself. Death, for Hegel, also means the death of the (dead) abstract universality, its negation. This is precisely why it is so important for Hegel that it was not only the Son that died on the cross, but also the Father: it is only thus that death on the cross can be grasped as a productive death, as a death that saves God himself, as the negation of his pure negativity, as the dying away of his deadness. Death on the cross is thus a matter of God's capability to follow through.

Hegel allows us to talk about the immortality of the non-transcendent, even corporeal order. Whether it is the tireless persistence of unanalyzable and undialectyzable pure being in dialectics, or the unwaning persistence of ontological slime which eludes every attempt at determinate comprehension, there is always a dimension of something inexhaustible in the very process of determination. At the same time, at the level of the absolute substance, negativity can be thought of as a paradoxical mortality of the divine, as a productive mortality. Just as the immortal dimension within the corporeal order is in fact its motor, its causal power, so the mortality of the divine is by no means merely a limitation or a deficiency of the absolute, but precisely its capability of production as self-production. The (Christian) God can produce himself only because he involves negativity, the paradoxical dimension of divine mortality.

Malabou noted that if we separate kenosis with which God disappears into its otherness from the corresponding self-differentiating movement within reason, we really should admit that we have introduced a sort of lack into God. This is why she rejected the theological criticisms of Hegel precisely with the argument that they explained the negativity of absolute substance in isolation from the negativity within the subject as modern subjectivity. She stressed the relation between the suffering of God and the suffering of human subjectivity deprived of God, concluding that the negativity in God is not a lack or passivity, but actual potentiality or, as she terms it, *plasticity*.[19]

A special relation between the dimensions of the mortality of the divine on the one hand and corporeal immortality on the other hand was also pointed out by Alenka Zupančič in her book *On Comedy*. In her initial thesis, she distinguished between conservative comedy (or also just bad comedy) and subversive comedy (good comedy) on the basis of the relation between the concrete and the universal. Conservative comedy makes fun of the universal or the exemplary—embodied in a king, a bishop, an officer of the law—by means of staining it with concrete, everyday human flaws; we laugh at the awkward connections of the universal with the concrete whereby the concrete is graciously allowed its place in the sun. She offers the example of a "toffee-nosed baron" who "slips on a banana peel" but keeps getting back up on his feet as if nothing had happened. This is not comical because we see that the baron, too, is subjected to the law of gravity, just like everyone else, but rather because he never stopped doubting his immense importance. The thing that makes him human is therefore precisely the belief that he, as the baron, is raised high above the merely human.[20]

We can explain the difference between good and bad comedy with a reference to the Aristotelian "poetic license" granted to the concrete. Just as moving or changing things, for Aristotle, are far from the perfection characteristic of pure actuality, but are nevertheless accorded a certain dignity of being, so does conservative comedy preserve the primacy and purity of the ideal (its truth and seriousness), but at the same time grants the mud of the concrete a certain right to be, an ontological license to match the poetic one. Perhaps the most obvious event where this kind of comedy (the conservative) is played out is an annual festival in Washington, D.C., where they hold a White House Correspondents' Dinner to praise and glorify the president by throwing mildly amusing insults at him and hear his mildly amused laughter at his own expense. The problem with conservative comedy is that it simply doesn't take itself seriously enough.

Zupančič's thesis was that subversive or true comedy can by no means be sufficiently explained by the resistance of the concrete or a benevolent gesture allowing the concrete to be. She employed Hegel's triad of the "spiritual work of art" from *Phenomenology of Spirit*, in which the Greek genres—epic, tragedy, comedy—follow in a logical and historical sequence as a gradual abolition and elevation of *representation* as the means of the phenomenology of the spirit. She then went on to define the comic as the "concrete labor or work of the universal" or as "the universal at work."[21] Her point was that it was only in comedy that the universal obtains its concreteness so that it is not only a dead and empty abstraction, existing merely in itself, but precisely the dying away of such deadness.

Of course, such "concreteness of the universal" is directly related to the mortality in the order of the divine. Zupančič pointed out a possibly surprising move that Hegel made in *Phenomenology of Spirit* when he jumped straight from discussing comedy (as a spiritual work of art) to the question of the mortality of the Christian God—how on earth could the death of God be something comical or happy? She pointed out Hegel's line of argument in which Christ's death is seen as a turning of the unhappy consciousness into a comic or happy consciousness, and explained the concreteness of the universal along the lines of Luther's *Entäusserung*: as incarnation.

For Hegel, the comic and comedy are in a special way related to mortality (and negativity) within the divine order. But they are also related to the immortality within the corporeal order. This was the dimension that Zupančič also, or better yet *especially*, pointed to in arguing that human existence includes something that transcends it—but not an additional being, a divine soul, for example—as this is a dimension that Lacanian psychoanalysis usually conceives as a void or a lack at the level of the human being itself.[22]

In the genres of comedy, we can find hundreds of illustrations for the immortality of the body. Animations and cartoons feature a sort of indestructibility: a hero falls a thousand meters deep, is blown to bits in powerful explosions or run over by a train or a tanker, and yet, in the next scene, he is already at work again, hunting the rabbit or chasing the mouse or following the Road Runner or plotting to take over the world just as before and without a single scratch. The indestructibility is pushed so far that it also applies to the hero's clothes, which always miraculously return to their initial condition. Robert Pfaller suggested that one of the essential modes of producing comic effects be named the "paradigm of success." This refers to how, in a comedy, "everything succeeds—often too much so."[23]

One of the most famous examples is probably the role of Jerry/Daphne played by Jack Lemmon in the superb classic *Some Like It Hot* (directed by Billy Wilder in 1959). In order to hide from the Mafia, Jerry disguises himself as a woman and pretends to be Daphne, a musician in an all-female band. He manages to play the role so convincingly that he catches a rich suitor. Things get out of hand and he cannot drive the suitor away, not even after finally, at the very end of the film, revealing that he is actually a man: the suitor doesn't even blink and delivers the ultimate punch line, "Nobody's perfect." The silly, improbable cross-dressing was so successful that it took over the reins completely. But does the paradigm of success rely simply on the fact that the world is happy and not sad—after all, they do say that tragedies end with a funeral, and comedies with a wedding. The answer is a straightforward no. Pfaller's point with regard to the paradigm of success is that the comic lies precisely in the *too much* of the success. The true place of the (Hegelian) comic is the excess of success, when the success of the disguise produces quite unexpected effects. The excessiveness and inexorability that this absolutely silly game acquires—one can hardly imagine a sillier way of trying to escape the Mafia than by dressing up as a beautiful woman—is precisely the dimension of the immortality within the order of the body, for it is not driven by an otherworldly force, but by that body itself.

Let us recall the scene in which Jerry dressed as Daphne tangos with his suitor. At first he seems annoyed, but soon the movement of his hips reveals that he is not *playing a role,* but at that moment *is* the role, that the role of Daphne becomes alienated from him and begins acting independently, starting a life bigger than Jerry (or Lemmon, for that matter), and that in a sense it got ahead of him so that perhaps "the role is playing him" and not the other way around. The essence of the paradigm of success, if it is to apply to comedy, truly lies in there being *too much* success. It is not that everything always goes smoothly for the hero, that the world is just and happy, but that the appearance acquires the fullness of being, that the appearance *produces* being.

Pfaller emphasized the produced nature of being in his discussion of success by formulating another principle of comedy as "play becomes reality" (*aus Spiel wird Ernst*); he provided several examples of comedies where a true love emerges from a faked one.[24] Zupančič expressed a similar viewpoint when she argued that in comedies a baron (or other vehicle of the order of the universal) is not comical simply because he is haughty although he, too, urinates, just as a peasant is not comic in the proper sense simply because he is impersonating a baron with a loaf of bread to serve as a hat. Merely mixing the high and the low, the universal and the concrete, does not suffice—what is actually comic is, as Zupančič tells us by using Lacan's famous remark, "a king who believes that he really is a king"; what is comic is a king who has been taken in by himself.[25] What is characteristic of comedy is a literalness which is close to the Hegelian understanding of incarnation. If incarnation implies that the Word is held to its word, that it stops floating in the other world and is incarnated in concrete letters, in a concrete being, in such and such an individual from a random place in the desert, then comedy truly is incarnation.[26] Monty Python's *Life of Brian* captures much of the Hegelian understanding of the concept of kenosis, of the humbling of God as the unity of the most abstract universality of God and the most contingent particularity of a human being.

These examples corroborate that in comic genres, there is at work a dimension of infinity, inexhaustibility, or indestructibility of the corporeal order, of the order of the letter. Hegel's thesis about ancient comedy as part of the representational triad can thus also be applied to contemporary comic genres. At the same time, the examples also indicate the "ontological thesis of comedy" which claims, in short, that being is something produced or caused, or that it is the effect of pretense or appearance. This has led us to the proper sense of the agreement between the negativity of the corporeal order and the negativity of the divine order: being is something produced.

But again, this does not mean that the sequence in which the relation between being and appearance is traditionally explained is simply overturned. The point here is not to substitute the primacy of the truth of being over the acted appearance by the primacy of appearance over being, to posit naive materialism instead of naive idealism, a kind of post-metaphysical thought in place of metaphysics. Being is produced because it produces itself; it is performed. Because being produces itself, it is necessarily ahead of itself, or it lags behind. Such a delay of being enables us to think of it as the cause and the effect at the same time, as its own cause. Being causes itself, it produces itself, it is indebted to itself. There is no primacy either of being as the cause or being as the effect, for we have to think of being from causing, production, becoming.

Spinoza and Death

Given the extent of the speculative implications of death in Hegel's philosophy, one is forced to ask oneself: does Spinozism allow for the concept of death not as something merely negative, not as a mere weakening or degradation, as something that is not a mark of imperfection, but rather as something productive? The first, most direct answer can only be a decisive no. In Spinoza's philosophy there is no such thing as a productive death. Generally speaking, Spinoza does not even deal with death. "A free man thinks of death least of all things, and his wisdom is a meditation of life, not of death."[27] Suffering, pain, losing strength, and death are all merely the weakening of the body effected by external causes. "No thing can be destroyed except by an external cause."[28] Death is not an inner necessity of human existence,[29] but merely the disintegration of the characteristic "relation of motion-and-rest" of the parts of a mode. The endeavor to persist in the existence of a certain mode (*conatus*) is even its actual essence.[30] All feelings of pain are merely the ideas of unwanted, weakening affections of the body. This is why it can by no means be said that the existence of individual things, modes, includes contradiction or imperfection—opposition can only come from the outside. In this respect, Hegel's explanation of modes as something merely negative and dissolving is wholly incorrect. The disappearance of modes is by no means their task or their inner telos. Even suicide was explained by Spinoza with the operation of external causes and with an explicit reference to the principle *ex nihilo nihil fit*:

> Nobody refuses food or kills himself from the necessity of his own nature, but from the constraint of external causes. This can take place

> in many ways. A man kills himself when he is compelled by another who twists the hand in which he happens to hold a sword and makes him turn the blade against his heart; or when, in obedience to a tyrant's command, he, like Seneca, is compelled to open his veins, that is, he chooses a lesser evil to avoid a greater. Or it may come about when unobservable external causes condition a man's imagination and affect his body in such a way that the latter assumes a different nature contrary to the previously existing one, a nature whereof there can be no idea in mind (Pr. 10, III). But that a man from the necessity of his own nature should endeavor to cease to exist or to be changed into another form, is as impossible as that something should come from nothing, as anyone can see with a little thought.[31]

And of course, it doesn't make any more sense to talk about death or nonbeing at the level of the substance. Even if we take into account the justified objections and critiques regarding Hegel's account of Spinozism, he nevertheless seems to have captured something essential about it. It is obviously impossible within Spinozism to think negativity at the level of being. If we really see Spinozism as a philosophy of "pure affirmation," then it becomes questionable to what extent Spinozistic philosophy can even be relevant for those contemporary philosophical discussions that rest on the initial assumption about, in Heideggerian terms, the primacy of the negative phenomenon, on the thesis that being can be glimpsed only against the backdrop of negativity, the thesis of being as produced being.

And was not Hegel's account of Spinozist production as a variation of "the intellectual effluence without penetration," to paraphrase Gadamer's account of the Thomistic concept of emanation, also adequate in a sense? If substance produces without any consequences for the substance itself, if in production it does not produce itself anew, then Hegel's account of the system of substance, attributes, and modes as an essentially emanationist conception of production was fundamentally correct after all—even though we are talking about emanation without ontological hierarchy. While for Hegel, production is the action of a self-referential negativity, a self-differentiating difference, in Spinozist philosophy, if we construe it in view of the principle that there is no nonbeing, production is a variation of the Aristotelian (or neo-Aristotelian) concept of pure activity.

We run into similar difficulties if we want to capture with Spinozism the dimension that came to the fore in Hegel's conception of the comic and the account of Christian incarnation. In Spinoza's theory of affects, which he developed in the third and fourth chapter of *Ethics*, there are two fundamental emotions, pleasure (*laetitia*) and pain (*tristitia*). All other, more complex emotions are in various ways, with the addition of this or that image or the absence of an image, composed out of pleasure and pain. The emotion of pleasure is determined as the process in mind that results from an affection of our body by an external body that *increases* our powers to act and comprehend, while pain results from an affection of the body that *decreases* the power to act and comprehend.[32] Here, we also have to take into account the difference between active and passive affects. Active are those where the cause of affection is internal, and passive those where the cause of affection is external. It follows that pains can only be passive. The existing mode cannot include anything that could weaken its existence, which is why the decrease of power, that is, pain, can be caused only by external causes. As consequences of external causes, pleasures are also passive, but if they are caused by internal causes, they are active and are called blessedness.[33]

But the limitation of Spinoza's theory is very clear if we try to employ the concepts of pleasure (or joy) and pain (or sorrow) to say something about the comic and the tragic. Since pain can only be passive, it cannot be productive. Aristotle's conception of tragedy, according to which the feelings of pain (specifically, empathy and horror) must provoke a catharsis of pain, already demands something that cannot be reduced to the Spinozist concept of pain. Furthermore, Hegel's account of Christ's suffering on the cross, firstly, does not focus on mere pain, but rather on excessive pain, as it is the God Himself that is dying, but secondly, and even more importantly, the excess of pain generates immense happiness, so that the pain itself, the ultimate pain, appears as the path to salvation not only of all creation, but of God Himself as well.

Comedy, too, lies beyond the boundaries of the Spinozist theory, even though pleasures or joys can be active and therefore, in some sense, productive. Comic effects, as described by Pfaller and Zupančič, are produced as the *excess* of success so that in comedy an ontological delay or anteriority is always at work. Being follows the acted appearance; it is something produced by appearances. Such a dimension of being cannot be captured with organic strengthening or weakening. While Spinoza's theory can explain why our mind experiences pleasure or pain by watching a theater performance or a film, it is quite useless to discuss the dynamics or the structure of the artwork in question.

Why is the pleasure-pain pair incongruous with the comic-tragic pair? Comic and tragic are aesthetic effects characteristic of theater and film, of the order of the performed, played, imaginary. Comedy produces truth from something which is a mere deception, a mere appearance; the assumption is that appearance is inscribed in being itself.

Performances or enactments are not later or a posteriori actualizations or re-actualizations of being; they are inscribed into being itself so that repetition is possible only as production. This means that, as paradoxical as it may sound, repetition is a production of something new—at least in the domain of the aesthetic. In the realm of the comic, appearances are not mere reflections of being but are anchored in being; they are what constitutes being in the first place.

In Spinozism, on the other hand, the faculty of imagination (*imaginatio*) is related to a lower kind of knowledge and comprehension. This is precisely why Spinozism finds itself in an awkward position when defining the comic and the tragic; they cannot be adequately grasped without the assumption of presentation, demonstration, enunciation, performance, and repetition as gestures that are inscribed in the order of being and even produce being. When it comes to the question of illusion, falseness, and mistake, it seems that the quandary of being is redoubled.

Spinoza's Concept of the False: On Constitutive Distortion

In Spinoza's epistemology, in which according to the *Ethics* we have to distinguish between three kinds of knowledge,[34] and according to the *Treatise on the Emendation of the Intellect* between four modes of perceiving,[35] a mistake seems to be defined in the framework of rationalism as a consequence of besmearing our intellectual faculties with the filth of the imagination. In our senses, individual things appear to us fragmentarily and without order. Knowledge that leans on "unreliable experience" with the help of imagining is called knowledge from symbols (*cognitio ex signis*) and is of the lowest kind.

> Falsity consists in the privation of knowledge which inadequate ideas, that is, fragmentary and confused ideas, involve.[36]

It seems that Spinoza's view of the false is a sort of epistemological Eleaticism. Inadequate ideas contain absence, imperfection, deficiency—just like for the Eleatics moving bodies necessarily include a sort of indistinctness and indeterminacy—which is why, strictly speaking, they cannot belong to true being. A similar deliberation also applies to the question of evil or the bad: "Knowledge of evil is inadequate knowledge," argued Spinoza.[37] The bad is, strictly speaking, nonbeing.[38] Spinoza resolved the question of evil much like Nietzsche: good is that which benefits us, bad is that which hinders us in our striving for good, which is why the difference is not between Good and Evil, but between good and bad, between benefit and hindrance.[39]

However, a mistake or a fallacy does not result from an internal deficiency of the imagination. Imagining, as an affirmative faculty of the mind, as a positive modification of substance, is something perfect in itself and therefore cannot include any deficiencies. Many contemporary interpreters criticize a dry rationalistic take on Spinozism, where imagination is in itself considered as the cause of the false. Genevieve Lloyd pointed out that Spinozist ethics does not claim that we should get rid of affects and live a life without them, but that we should understand them and thus transform the passive passions into active, rational feelings that are a source of freedom and virtue.[40] Deleuze pointed out that the falsity of inadequate ideas originates in the fact that, with the idea of our body being affected by an external body, we do not yet know the essence or nature of the external body since such an idea is actually an imaginative mixture of our body and the external body. Knowledge based on images or signs (symbols) is therefore merely knowledge by effects.[41]

Spinozism is not epistemological Eleaticism because inadequate ideas are not something void and null, but have their immanent necessity and positivity. But the quandary is thereby not eliminated. Error still has the characteristic of absence, a kind of privation of knowledge involved in inadequate ideas. If you grant error the dignity of being, then there is no reason to still call it error, for it is indistinguishable from the truth of being. Error thus, in the final instance, cannot belong to the positive modifications of substance. But if you push it out of absolute substance, you have pushed it into pure nonbeing. Are there no mistakes, then? Spinoza does indeed write: "In Nature nothing happens which can be attributed to its defectiveness."[42] But if there is no defectiveness, how should we formulate the difference between adequacy and inadequacy?

Deleuze's answer was that we need to distinguish between ideas as modifications of absolute substance under the attribute of thought and ideas as they appear in our mind. Ideas in the first sense cannot contain any imperfection or error—and, in this respect, there is no error or imperfection or inadequacy at the level of fundamental ontology. It is only in the case of ideas in the second sense that we can talk about inadequacy, for the ideas in our mind are almost exclusively inadequate ideas, that is, ideas as images of the affections of our body and external bodies. However, even in Deleuze's account, it seems that one must assume a certain kind of negativity, characteristic specifically of the level of the modes. It is, after all, merely finite (human) beings who have inadequate ideas. If one wants to talk about the false, one might still have to assume a sort of deficiency of the finite spirit, which leads to the erroneous assumption that the ideas of the affection of an external body are already adequate ideas of that body. This is why Hegel's account is precious in a way, as it points out an important question for Spinozism: how can we comprehend difference as such without leaning on the hierarchical ontology of metaphysical systems of emanation or on traditional identity metaphysics?

If we construe Spinozism by insisting merely on the ontological principle according to which nothing comes out of nothing, it seems that it cannot be read as a theory of the signifier. It was especially Deleuze and Vinciguerra who have shown that such an account is insufficient and that in Spinoza's philosophy difference can by all means be thought of as something productive. Contrary to traditional accounts, according to which the faculty of imagination (*imaginatio*) was often simplified into the immediate source of falseness, contemporary Spinozists have stressed its productivity; even more, they often even moved it to the fore. Spinoza's definition of imagination as knowledge by signs (*cognitio ex signis*) was even the starting point of Vinciguerra's account of Spinozism as a theory of the sign.[43] Lloyd believes that Spinoza did subordinate imagination to reason, but that this cannot be understood in the framework of an unequivocal rationalism, for the faculty of imagination can also be an ally of reason. This is why she rejected Hegel's account of singular things in Spinozism as illusions caused by inferior knowledge associated with imagination, and emphasized the specific actuality of images that reason cannot simply transcend.[44] For Spinoza, a true idea cannot dispel the action of inadequate ideas merely as something true, but only insofar as it acts as a stronger affect.[45]

Negri went even further than Lloyd. He rejected the assumption that imagining (*imaginatio*) is a *distortion* of reality and wrote that it is a *constitution* of reality. Imaginative images constitute the world of everyday experience so that truth exists in the world of imagination.[46] Thereby, Negri's explanation of the faculty of imagination came close to what Louis Althusser writes about the necessary imaginary relationship between people and their relations to the immediate circumstances in which they live. For Althusser, the question of the theory of ideology is by no means answered with the explanation that people live their imaginary, fictional representations of the actual relations, their imaginations that supposedly give a distorted image of actual conditions. Ideology is not simply a distortion of reality. Ideology is a relation to reality.[47] The essential question is thus the following: why is an individual's relation to their everyday reality necessarily imaginary?[48] Paraphrasing Negri, Althusser's thesis can also be summed up by saying that the imaginary character of ideology does not *distort* reality because it *constitutes* it. Althusser's theory of ideology shares Spinoza's view that the faculty of imagination should be considered a positive faculty and not simply as an illusion or mist.

One of the essential Hegelian objections to Spinozism is that negativity is seen merely as something external to being and not as its internal capability of self-transformation, as the capability of being to produce itself. But the inspiration found in the question of the imaginary in Spinozism indicates that the negativity of being can perhaps also be considered as something that we can call "constitutive distortion." The question of the capability of the imaginary is not only extremely interesting for Spinozist studies, but can perhaps even be placed in the foreground. The following thesis can be formulated especially on the basis of Negri's and Althusser's account of the imaginary: the Spinozistic conception of the imaginary does not talk about an erroneous, mistaken, or distorted image of reality, *but enables us to think about the distortion at the level of reality itself.*

Determination of the Substance: Spinoza and Negativity

If being does not include any negativity and if negativity is something external even for created beings, then Negri's and Deleuze's assessment that Spinozism is a system of pure affirmation is perfectly justified. Can we employ Spinozism to point out that which in Hegel's logic of being emerges as a crossing of thought and being? Does Spinozism enable us to think the self-productivity of absolute substance? Herein lies the essential stake of Hegel's account of Spinozism. The problem of Spinozist substance is supposed to be in its not being in a relation with itself. It is not only that in Spinozism the individual (the mode) is merely something null and is directly dissolved in absolute substance, but above all that substance does not comprehend such negativism as its own negativism, that is, it does not enter in a relation with itself, it is not substance *and* subject, and is therefore only pure being or pure nothingness that does not yet comprehend itself as the unity of the producing and the produced.

Nevertheless, it can be shown that Spinoza's substance actually *is* in relation with itself, although not in a relation of negation and the negation of negation. This is the essential difference; for Hegel, self-relation is possible only as self-negation. Contrary to this, I believe that modes need to be consistently understood as modifications of substance, as its modalities, inclinations, or inflections. Thus, one can argue that substance is never in an immediate or pure state, but is always given in such and such a "mode"—just like we must not think of Heidegger's Dasein as a self isolated in immediacy, but always as such and such being, as being-in-inclination, and even as an original inclination (*Hineingehaltenheit*).[49] Just like Dasein is a sort of being-towards-being, the relationality of being with itself, its determinateness, so the Spinozist substance is posited only with its modifications. Hegel's thesis that Spinoza did not consistently develop the conception of *causa sui* (cause of itself) is therefore quite tendentious. In Spinoza, *causa sui* does not mean, as Hegel suggests, "the establishing of itself as an other" and it is not "loss or degeneration, and at the same time the negation of this loss."[50] As opposed to Hegel, Spinoza also never wanted or needed to establish the initial simple principle from which it would be possible to derive more complex concepts; he was never interested in the question of beginning with the simplest and most indeterminate abstraction. This is why many commentators and Spinozistic philosophers have emphasized that we should not be blinded by Spinoza's geometric method of proof.

Spinoza defines *causa sui* in accordance with the classical ontotheology as that whose essence includes existence, which Hegel quite accurately related to the unity of thought and being. But Spinoza's *causa sui* does not establish itself as an other and is therefore not lost to itself; rather, as I have suggested, substance is constantly "modified," it is always already "modified," it is always substance-in-a-mode. In this respect, Spinoza's idea of *causa sui* as that whose existence is included in its essence is related to a sort of original curvature of substance, an original modification. Because being is unequivocal (or univocal), the existence of substance is not more perfect compared to the existence of modes; we should even go so far as to claim that the existence of modes *is* the existence of substance. And because the modifications of substance are included in its essence, the original inclination of substance can be explained with its essence that includes existence. In short, the Spinozist substance is in relation with itself without at the same time being a loss of itself or a negation of itself or the establishing of itself firstly as itself and then as an other. Self-relationality of substance does not mean, for Spinoza, that substance is posited against itself or that it is itself and at the same time the loss of itself, but that it is always already in motion without having any isolated initial and final point from or to which it is inclined. If it is even possible to talk about a telos in relation to it, then it is certainly an internal telos.

Since Spinoza quite clearly and emphatically declared himself against any concept of the final cause, the infamous Aristotelian *causa finalis*, or telos, it is of course highly controversial to speak about purposive causality in Spinoza; Gueroult, Macherey, Žižek, and many others have explicitly rejected any such attempts. Despite this, a number of scholars, coming from both the analytic and the dialectic continents of philosophy, felt the need to demonstrate that there is perhaps a way to speak about teleology in Spinoza, especially with regard to the concept of perseverance in being (*conatus*). In his monumental study, Knox Peden puts the finger on the reason why this task is so important for contemporary materialism. He criticizes Althusser's staunch defamation of teleology in Hegel and argues that "a Marxist politics hostile to the concept of telos hardly seems to be a Marxist politics at all."[51] Here we shall simply follow the Kantian distinction, to which Hegel subscribed as well, between external and internal teleology. Most, if not all, of Spinoza's explicit arguments against final causes refer to the notorious external teleology, counting something like "God's punishment for allowing gays to serve in the military" as a sufficient explanation for a contingent event of the death of a soldier. About the notion of internal teleology, such as we can describe in plants and animals, or in reading a text with that text itself and developing its own internal purposes, Spinoza does not speak—at least not as a final cause. However, as was argued above, his concept of *causa sui*, even if we do not accept it to mean what it means for Hegel, nevertheless already involves a concept of self-referentiality that especially and explicitly comes to the fore in the concept of perseverance (*conatus*). Put simply, for Spinoza, things do not only exist, but also tend to exist in the future; which means that existence as such, finite or not, substantial or modal, reaches over itself, transcends itself, and is not, as Hegel insisted, fixed in its own inertial being. This interpretation is the cornerstone of any concept of teleology in Spinoza.

Negri, too, was of the opinion that, in relation to Spinozism, it is by all means possible to talk about negativity that is not merely something external. In his terms, the question of production is formulated as the question of the organization and the expansion of being. Negativity is included in the expansive being at its margin and is subordinated to the level of being. It is an emptied, evacuated space, something that first needs to be constructed in order to be later included in the infinite. Negativity is a singular, contingent being considered as the future that human praxis integrates into positive infinity.[52] In his characteristic style, Negri's conception shoots into several directions at once, but a common feature of his determinations of negativity can nevertheless be discerned. It is the question of the margin as the dividing line with which emptied space is included into a positive whole, with the integration of emptiness being thought of as the integration of a temporal lag into positive being. Negativity is related to the Aristotelian notion of potentiality since negative or subordinate being is understood as something not yet constructed, while the integration of that emptiness is a question of the power of action.

Negri's comprehension of negativity as potentiality and temporal contraction should certainly be commended. His idea that being organizes itself and expands is also useful because it grounds its self-referentiality and the orientation towards itself. But what is questionable, and too Aristotelian, is his insistence on the conception of being as an absolutely affirmative area where negativity is only a marginal phenomenon. I believe that it would be more appropriate to say that being takes place *precisely at the margin*, precisely as a dividing line; and that it is not something in itself first and only later decides to expand and organize, but that it is something real only insofar as it is expansive and only insofar as it organizes itself. Or, put differently, there is no being beyond the level of the production of being: in this respect, substance is always already in such and such a mode, it is always already determined, it is always already oriented.

A somewhat different argument in favor of the self-referentiality of substance was formulated by Pierre Macherey. He expressed certain doubts regarding the adequacy of Deleuze's account of Spinozism as a philosophy of pure affirmation, and in a surprisingly Hegelian manner wrote that such a definition had already passed into Hegelian "negativism."[53] Let us leave aside the fact that he mistakenly ascribed pure negativism to Hegel and overlooked his fundamental demand to grasp productive negativity. Contrary to Hegel's formula according to which determination is always negation, Macherey pointed out that Spinoza's concept of determination has several meanings. On the one hand, substance truly is something indeterminate since it is not limited or finite. In this sense, determination truly does include negation for Spinoza.[54] But determination also has a purely positive meaning which is at work in the definition of the free cause. Spinoza writes:

> That thing is said to be free which exists solely from the necessity of its own nature, and is determined to action by itself alone. A thing is said to be necessary or rather, constrained, if it is determined by another thing to exist and to act in a definite and determinate way.[55]

Substance itself is also determined; it is something caused and produced in a special sense (by itself alone). Furthermore, if we take into account the principle of the uniqueness of cause, then it is clear that the determinateness of the free substance differs from the determinateness of things-not-free only in that it is a self-determination, the turn towards itself. In this respect, Macherey believed that Spinoza's notion of *causa sui* entails the conception of a live substance, a substance in motion. And as it is a kind of a movement towards self, it turns out that Spinoza's substance not only is not motionless, but is characterized by the very self-referential movement demanded by Hegel.[56]

The listed examples hopefully demonstrate that it is possible in Spinozism to think negativity and determination at the level of substance itself; that it has to be thought of as a turn to itself or self-referentiality; and that it is grounded in the immanent conception of the cause, according to which determination at the level of substance has the same meaning as the determination at the level of modes. Spinoza's substance is in motion without the reference to Aristotle's motionless mover which is the foundation of all Neoplatonism. In a system of production in which substance is expressed in the modes of its attributes, substance is not a cause excluded from the causal chain. I would wager that the uniqueness of cause has to be explained in the strong sense so that the self-determination of substance is not merely *homonymous* with the determination at the level of modes, but is *nothing else but* the working of determination at the level of modes. That is to say: the determination of the substance is precisely the modification of the substance. Substance is a live or an active or a movable substance, but its activity is not elevated beyond modal existence, because it has to be comprehended precisely as, to paraphrase Alenka Zupančič, the substance-at-work. The thesis is that not only do the modes exist merely as a determinate existence of substance, but that in a sense the opposite also holds, that substance, too, exists *precisely as* the existence of its modes. Modes are not the expansion of an already existing being, they are not its organic accretion, for being is nothing but its own expansion.

5

Ideology and the Originality of the Swerve

The productive philosophical opposition between Spinoza and Hegel may be seen as a rearticulation of the ancient principles of Parmenides and Heraclitus, principles of being and becoming. At the same time, the philosophical reverberations of the event of "Hegel and Spinoza" reach well into contemporary discussions. This is perhaps nowhere more evident than in the opposition between Deleuzean and Lacanian theories. For Deleuze, everything seems to be alive; even inorganic entities like cities are to be understood as living organisms, as springs of indestructible vital energy. Everywhere you look, life is in overabundance. For Lacan, quite the opposite is true: death is everywhere, even within living organisms; it is as if death has already occurred. The catastrophe already occurred and we are already dead.[1] In postwar French thought, however, there was another influential thinker who was heavily inspired by both Spinoza and Hegel, and whose peculiar philosophical endeavors must be thought as a productive confrontation between Hegel and Spinoza, as the embodiment of the problematic of "Hegel and Spinoza." It is no coincidence that the theses of the Marxist philosopher Luis Althusser have come up so often in the analysis so far. This chapter explores in some detail the core problematic of the Althusserian theory of ideology, which is not inspired only by Spinoza and Pascal and their radical theory of the materiality of religious belief, but also by Lacan and his theory of the subject and its imaginary relationship to himself or herself. As I will try to demonstrate, the only way to successfully explain the nature of ideology is for Spinoza's concepts working hand in hand with those of Hegel.

The Spinozist Basis of Althusser's Theory of Ideology: Belief

Two of Althusser's most fascinating and apparently paradoxical concepts are those of *theoretical practice* and *the material existence of ideology*. What exactly is expressed in them? If they suggest that, on the one hand, theory is determined by practice, and on the other hand that all practice already includes something theoretical, then these concepts are nothing but corrections of an inflexible, naive distinction between the pure, innocent gaze of theory and the unreflected, immediate work of practice. It could be argued, however, that the concept of theoretical practice completely negates the distinction between theory and practice as principles, since it allows for no theory as purely theoretical; there are only various forms of practice, among those, theoretical practice. Something similar can be said of the idea of the material existence of ideology. In contrast to naive materialism which sees ideology as a kind of mist rising above the chimneys of economic production (by Althusser's account, this includes Marx's own theory of ideology in *German Ideology*),[2] Althusser stated that ideology exists as practice, that it possesses a material existence.

In his later work, Althusser would repeatedly point out that his decisive theses had been largely Spinozist. He even regarded the appendix to the first part of *Ethics* as the first theory of ideology.[3] Therefore, it seems convenient to approach the concepts of theoretical practice and the materiality of ideology from the standpoint of radical Spinozism, in keeping with Hegel's (or Jacobi's) thesis that a philosopher must necessarily begin as a Spinozist. Both concepts share a Spinozist trait: they inscribe the spiritual dimension (theory, ideology) on the surface of the material practice in which this dimension is manifested. The spirit is immanent to the letter. The order of ideas is never contrasted to the order of actual existence as something external to it; we could say that the order and connection of ideas are explained as the order and connection of an actually existing practice.[4]

Althusser's example of the material existence of ideology was from the realm of religious belief and faith. In the traditional understanding of faith, believing is usually portrayed as a profound psychic experience of the believing subject, an activity of the soul. Contrary to this, Althusser suggested that faith exists entirely on the surface of its religious rituals. He recalled Blaise Pascal's somewhat scandalous advice to the unbeliever, who is seeking to believe, which is basically this: fake it until you make it.

> They are people who know the road you want to follow and have been cured of the affliction of which you want to be cured. Follow the way by which they began: by behaving just as if they believed, taking holy water, having masses said, etc. That will make you believe quite naturally, and according to your animal reactions.[5]

Althusser summarized Pascal's point in a short formula and suggested that the existence of belief is woven into the surface of its material rituals. Generally speaking, ideology is not something hovering beyond rituals, which are always to be observed as inscribed into material, practical state apparatuses, but only exists in the very existence of those rituals, and hence possesses a material existence.[6]

One could make the reproach that this concept of ideology is an a priori acceptance of faits accomplis, and that it avoids the risks and the drama of human actions. It might even seem that Althusser completely mangled what Pascal had been saying. Pascal's point was not—or so this reproach may claim—that ideas and consciousness have no independent existence, as Althusser argued, but rather that rituals are not merely a useless appendix to religion, since belief in the true sense of the word can only arise through the formal, ritual humility of the believer. The humbling of the subject in rituals has a productive role in a purely Hegelian sense of the word: the abstract, proud mode of belief has to be humbled, it has to be made concrete in material rituals, and it is only as its own product that it becomes true belief. It might seem that, in contrast with Pascal's injunction, Althusser's explanation can only take effect once the action is over. Instead of belief, it refers to religious formulae, and does so invariably after the fact. When someone prays, they are characterized as a believer, without any reference to the meaning of what they are doing, without any reference to the symbolic function of their actions. This is as if during a nerve-wracking soccer match, someone claimed that they were rooting for the winner. That is ridiculous, because it is the contest, the struggle, the effort that makes the winner, just as it is the effort of the belief, the patient work of the ritual, that makes the believer!

In fact, a similar reproach could be formulated against a number of Spinoza's conceptions. Consider the following thesis from his *Political Treatise*: an individual's right is always correlated to their power or capability.[7] The capitalist idea of the self-regulation of the free market seems to rest precisely on this Spinozist premise. The natural functioning of the free market is much better at making sure that all is well in the end than even the best thought-out interventions by the state. In the struggle for survival, one subject lives, another fails. But necessarily, by definition, it is always "the best" who wins; that is, the one to win is the one who wins; the winner is not determined by the judgment of some intrinsic qualities but by the formal fact that they have won. Isn't Spinozism just as silly as the idea of the self-regulation of the free market?

But such a reproach misses the point of Spinozism at work in Althusser's thesis on the material existence of ideology: the thesis that ideology only exists as the existence of its apparatuses has to be understood in a positive and active sense, not as merely noting a statistical result. Firstly, the point is not to arbitrarily assign an ideological affiliation to a subject inserted into the functioning of an apparatus; the point is that beyond its functioning within apparatuses, ideology does not exist at all. Secondly, the functioning of ideology in apparatuses is not merely a mechanical persistence but a productive action, since the functioning of the apparatus constitutes not only the ideological subject but the ideology itself.

In Althusser's text "On the Material Dialectic," the term "practice" is quite unceremoniously defined to mean: production.[8] We can therefore distinguish elements of production in theoretical practice: raw materials, means of production, products. I suggest that even the infamous operation of ideological interpellation should, accordingly, be understood as an operation of production whereby "human individuals" (its specific raw material) are shaped, selected, and processed (for instance through education and training) to produce ideological subjects (products which are dependent on it even when they are "bad subjects"). Furthermore, the operation of production functions, to put it in Spinozist terms, within its own order; the terms "human individual" and "ideological subject" do not refer to ontologically different orders somehow bridged by interpellation. Althusser emphasized that the pure material individual is only an abstract assumption, and hence it is not Aristotelian matter that only acquires form at a later stage, but an *always already* complex raw material.[9]

Practice and Theoretical Practice

However, in Althusser's texts, the strong, Spinozist sense of the idea of the materiality of ideology is interwoven with a weak sense. The two can be distinguished by answering the question whether ideological production is (ontologically) dependent on some other production or is independent and explainable on its own terms. Althusser's answer seems to be very clear (and orthodox): in the last instance, ideological production depends on economic production.

In order to revisit this ancient question and the all-too-familiar answer, I suggest differentiating between ontological-causal and conceptual dependence. Ontological-causal dependence presupposes that the dependent order is hierarchically lower than the determinant one, while in conceptual dependence the determinant order is simply a model which serves to explain the dependent order. The notion of the materiality of ideology is a weak notion if and when it presupposes that ideology is ontologically-causally dependent on economy, while the strong or Spinozist notion of the materiality of ideology presupposes a relation of only conceptual dependence between them. While it is possible in both cases to speak of the primacy of practice, in the second case the ideological order is simply explained or understood in economic terms: as production.

To illustrate the lack of clarity in this concept, let us consider the passage where Althusser mentions "a theory of the differences between the modalities of materiality" of ritual practices such as shaking hands, prayer, making the sign of the cross, and repentance.[10] This formulation permits an ordering of these practices on a hierarchical scale where some are more material and others are less material. But if these *practices* are to be understood as *productions*, they should be seen as specific ideological productions. For a believer, these actions are entirely automatic, and the cry of mea culpa perfectly corresponds to the example of interpellation, when at the sound of a police hailing, a person in the street automatically assumes that it is him or her who is being hailed. All such automatic, spontaneous, and perfectly mundane acts should be viewed as productions whereby ideology produces subjects. Rather than categorizing some gestures as "more reflective" and others as "more practical," I think it is important to stick to the Spinozist point and understand all acts of belief as material actions inscribed on the material surface. This does not rule out assigning them varying degrees of *intensity*. In this perspective, while the believer's actions all remain on the *same surface*, not all of them possess the same power; depending on the circumstances, it is perfectly possible for a (material) blow with a hammer to be an act less intense than the (material) act of reading a book.

A similar oscillation of Althusser's theory can be found in the distinction between theoretical and practical ideologies as defined in the lectures on *Philosophy and the Spontaneous Philosophy of the Scientists*. In this context, Althusser would seem to have given primacy to practice in the ontological-causal sense, not only in the conceptual sense: theoretical ideologies supposedly acquire their raw materials from practical ideologies and are therefore dependent on them. Pfaller interpreted Althusser's stance on this issue in similar terms to the stance of those who give primacy to ritual over myth and according to whom myth is merely a later and distorted explanation of ritual.[11] Similarly, Althusser repeatedly asserted that the law is merely a legal cloak over reality: a story that explains reality after the fact. Yet we should not overlook that he also strongly criticized the conflict around de jure and de facto guarantees, characterizing it as a conflict between accomplices obeying the same rules.[12]

Althusser's definition of *practical* ideologies is the following: they are "complex formations which shape notions-representations-images into behaviour-conduct-attitude-gestures" and therefore function "as practical norms."[13] That is, they are always already ensembles of thought and action. But does this mean that theoretical ideologies are pure concepts devoid of any action? Or are they still ensembles, but containing a larger proportion of thought? I think this is a false dilemma. When defining theoretical practices, we can not overlook material apparatuses with their branching practices and rituals whereby knowledge is produced and maintained. We have to approach them in the same way as when defining ideological practices (practical ideologies). The distinction between practice and theory, between ritual and myth, can also be drawn in the case of belief. But the Spinozist point made by Althusser was that this distinction should in fact be discarded and the believer's actions understood as material actions, that is, actions existing on the same surface and differing, at most, in their degrees of intensity. In order to be consistent, then, we have to say that the same holds for the surface of theoretical practice: we can distinguish between practice (the scientists' institutional rituals, the appearances) and theory (the content of theories, the truth behind the appearance), but what Althusser is saying here is actually close to Foucault's concept of sciences as disciplines: such a distinction only makes us overlook that the interior of a theory is entirely contained on its institutional surface.

Let us consider another example. In order to be consistent, we have to insist that it is not the case that some modes of production—their definition and number vary, but generally included are economic, political, ideological, and scientific modes—are more practical, such as economic or political practice, while others are more theoretical, such as legal or ideological practice. Yet Althusser stated:

> We think the content of these different practices by thinking their peculiar structure, which, in all these cases, is the structure of a production; by thinking what distinguishes between these different structures, i.e., the different natures of the objects to which they apply, of their means of production and of the relations within which they produce (these different elements and their combination—*Verbindung*—obviously vary as we pass from economic practice to political practice, then to scientific practice and theoretico-philosophical practice). We think the relations establishing and articulating these different practices one with another by thinking their degree of independence and their type of "relative" autonomy, which are themselves fixed by their type of dependence with respect to the practice which is "determinant in the last instance": economic practice.[14]

As we pass from economic practice to political and to theoretical practice, does the "combination of the different elements" vary, so that it gradually reaches increasingly theoretical spheres? And is this "degree of relative autonomy" not perfectly proportional to the passage from the determinant economic practice to more theoretical practices? Although the spheres are relatively autonomous, it seems that they are strictly hierarchically ordered according to the degree of their dependence on the fundamental sphere, like successive levels of a pyramid: at the lowest level, there is the economic order, followed by the political and legal-moral orders, and finally, the ideological order.

But let us attempt a thought experiment. Let us say that in the last instance, the economic order is embodied in a blacksmith, reeking of onion, his hands forging the world. Let us wash him and perfume him with angelic scent, call him the Demiurge, and place him on the top of the pyramid. What has thus changed? We would be forced to say: *absolutely nothing has changed.* We have produced a hierarchical ontological-causal model, various iterations of which are very familiar in the history of philosophy, from Platonism and Neoplatonism onwards. Questions of what came first—for instance, ritual or myth, or de jure or de facto guarantees—that is, questions on whether determination runs from the top of the pyramid towards the bottom, or from the bottom up, can be promptly dismissed as so many theological pseudo-problems.

The Real and the Material

Deviations from the Spinozist sense of the concept of theoretical practice can be found in Althusser wherever the economic order is explained as the real order, which is in turn understood as a kind of the most practical form of practice. In my opinion, we need to take on board all the consequences of the concept of theoretical practice and state, in the spirit of Spinoza, that the economic order stands in the same relation to the real world as do the political, ideological, and theoretical orders; it is no closer to the real world and other orders are not more distant from it. The real world does not function as a distant cause in the Neoplatonic sense, whose causality and ontological power decrease in the more distant spheres. In other words, the order of economic production is not identical to the real world, just as in Spinoza the attribute of extension is not identical to the real world. Hence, scientific theoretical production does not, by itself, produce insights about economic production but rather produces insights about the real world. Theories of economy are simply special cases of theories of the real world—special cases of what Althusser, following Marx, summarized as the "*mode* of appropriation of the world peculiar to knowledge."[15]

Besides the cognitive mode of appropriation, Althusser also discusses other modes of the appropriation of the real world, such as the artistic, the religious, and the political modes. But if we are to remain consistently Spinozist, we have to add one more mode to the list: namely, the economic mode. To each of the "modes of appropriation of the real world" we can assign a corresponding order of production: to the economic order we assign the economic mode of appropriation, to the theoretical order the cognitive mode, and so on. Just as Spinoza's substance is not identical to any of its attributes, Althusser's real world is not identical to any of the orders of material production. The economic order is no exception. Just as Spinoza's attributes of substance are not hierarchically organized, there are no relations of subordination or ontological-causal dependence among Althusser's orders of production. And just as substance is expressed *in all its perfection* in each of its attributes, the orders of production are their own measure, that is, they are ontologically complete or total.

Up to this point, Althusser's theory of ideology can and according to this reading should be explained with a consistently Spinozist approach. However, we have not yet truly addressed the important question of the *real*, the instance which Althusser calls the real object, the real order, the real process, and so on. This is certainly not the same as the material—material practices, apparatuses, processes, in short, the surface of production. Althusser repeatedly stated the need for a sharp distinction between cognitive and real objects and between cognitive and real processes. Nor is the real, as we have already seen, identical to the order of economic production—the order of economic production is itself one of the material orders and has to be understood as a production surface on which raw materials, means of production, and products circulate with varying degrees of intensity. The economic order, like other orders, is in relation with the real only through the economic mode of appropriation of the real world.

What, then, of the real world, the real object, the real? It is neither production nor an element of production, neither surface nor an intense part of the surface; in fact, it is the negativity of that surface itself. If the order of production is explicated as surface, then the notion of the real that is not identical to the material surface can perhaps be explained with the metaphors of the torsion of the surface itself, or of the break of the surface itself. The idea of the appropriation of the real world therefore implies that the positive material surface (the material order) is constituted as a grasping of the negativity of the real. To take cognitive order as an example: what is at play is a conceptual mode of grasping the real.[16]

But isn't such an understanding of the real as negativity in conflict with Spinozism; in fact, is it not closer to the conception vehemently and doggedly rejected by Althusser on almost every occasion: that is, the Hegelian conception? According to Althusser himself, his theory of ideology was almost entirely Spinozist—all its central elements, from imaginary reality to the illusion of subjective causality, are already present in Spinoza's texts. Almost entirely: for Althusser would appear to have added something after all, namely, *the concept of contradiction,* which Marx had inherited from Hegel and developed into the idea of class struggle in history.[17] However, adding the concept of contradiction to Spinoza's theory is no trivial matter; it is certainly not a simple addition, since contradiction is perfectly impossible in a Spinozist universe. It seems we have thus already entered a Hegelian space, where the complex Spinozist ontology of nonhierarchical material surfaces is assigned the role of a beginning, of a necessary first step, which, however, does not yet amount to a solution.

Ideology and Negativity

The relationship between the real and the material can be expressed dialectically. The real is the constitutive negativity of the material, it is a gap in the surface which the surface grasps in order to (retroactively) form itself. Since the gap is nothing but a rupture of negativity in the material surface, without any affirmative quality, the difference between the gap and the material surface is the gap itself. In other words, the real is only the difference between the real and the material; the real is pure difference; it should be understood as the difference as such. The surface is constituted as a grasping of the real, but this grasping is a failed grasping, since the real, as pure difference, cannot materialize at all and is lost at the moment it is grasped. This may sound quite abstract; but this dialectical relation is in principle the same as the relation Hegel analyzes between identity and difference in his *Science of Logic.* Hegel writes that identity is identity of identity and difference; the difference is constitutive for identity in the same sense as the real is constitutive for the material.[18]

The distinction between the real and the material can help explain many details of Althusser's theory of ideology. Consider the distinction between individual ideologies (in plural)—which, as Althusser assures us, in contrast with Marx's thesis in *German Ideology,* certainly do have their own histories—and ideology (in singular), which indeed has no history, because it is omnipresent historical reality. It would be too simple, and wrong, to say that the difference between ideologies and ideology lies only in that the latter is a general case of the former. Specific ideologies as specific forms of ideological production are not merely reflections of real history but have affirmative histories, since their existence is always an existence of material ideological apparatuses. In contrast, ideology in singular is eternal, in a similar way as the Freudian unconscious is said to be eternal, or rather, timeless.[19] While ideologies (plural) are explained as material ideologies which exist in material practices, what is at stake with ideology (singular) is not the dimension of material, but that of the real. Ideology (singular) is not eternal in the meaning of an endless timeline of history or as an abstract omni-historical structure, but should rather be understood as the very possibility of history (as the history of class struggle), because it is precisely a moment of the *real* within this or that *material* ideology, which is just what permits ideologies to become historical, that is, to embody their concrete historic forms of class struggle.

The distinction between the real and the material can also help explain the relation between science and ideology, which is crucial to Althusser's theory (at least in his earlier period). From a Hegelian point of view, while ideologies (plural) are always merely material, science is material *and* real; science trains its gaze to perceive the real or, in other words, that which is the real itself. Because science is nonmaterial, it cannot be reduced to the material surface of the subjects' practices; rather, it is the constant *negative movement of transformation of such a surface.* According to Althusser, "there is no practice except by and in an ideology,"[20] and science is composed of "shocks of scientific breaks"; the shocks of the real that destroy ideologies.[21] And if science really is a process without a subject, this is the case precisely because in Althusser's theory of ideology, subjects are always material ideological subjects.

Based on Hegel's formula of identity as identity of identity and difference, we can now also proceed to clarify the Hegelian-Lacanian criticism of the concept of interpellation by Žižek and Dolar.[22] In contrast with the suggested Spinozist explanation where interpellation is, in fact, a name for material ideological production, Žižek and Dolar stressed the issue of self-recognition in interpellation. For them, interpellation was a Lacanian question of the constitution of identity in the mirror. They drew attention to what they referred to as the remainder of the real, something which is radically impossible to be successfully integrated into the identity of an Althusserian subject of ideology. They explained this remainder as a gap, a hiatus, a void, and it is only in this gap that what Lacan would call a subject emerges, the gap-subject or so-called hysteric subject: that is, precisely what can never become a successfully functioning material ideological subject. Taking into account Dolar's warning that, on the one hand, the remainder of the real functions as that which enables ideology to successfully recruit subjects, and on the other hand, because it is a gap, it already anticipates its internal dissolution, we can see that this explanation perfectly conforms to Hegel's formula about identity constituted by difference.

Finally, the distinction between the real and the material can also help to explain the concept of symptomatic reading which Althusser developed in his contribution to *Reading "Capital."* As a first step, symptomatic reading can be defined as a kind of literal reading, because it does not attempt to reach spirit beyond the letter or meaning beyond what is literally being said, but in a way clings to the letter, takes the text by its word—just as Pascal's believer can only believe by clinging to rituals and practices. Althusser's example of symptomatic reading was Marx's reading of texts of classical political economy: Marx did not read them through the lens of his theory, but on their own terms.[23] Symptomatic reading is literal in that it assumes that the meaning of the text being read is entirely contained in its literal utterance. This first step can rightly be called Spinozist, since it corresponds to Spinoza's "literal reading" of the Bible.[24]

A suitable explanation of symptomatic reading, however, requires another step. When Marx read a text of classical political economy on its own terms, he would point to its symptoms, that is, the points where classical political economy had produced surplus answers, answers to which none of the questions it was asking corresponded. This reveals another, Freudian element of symptomatic reading, because an answer that does not answer a question that has been asked exhibits a structure typical of Freudian negation (*Verneinung*).[25] The material surface of the texts betrays itself, slipping on the smooth surface of itself. Symptomal reading demands that the reader pay special attention to the points where the gaze breaks despite looking forward, where it encounters a void contained in what the text affirms, that is, when the total surface of the text being read appears as perforated, when it turns out that the *material* existence of the text is constituted as a grasping and simultaneously as a missing of the *real*.

Clinamen

We have seen that the dimension of the real in Althusser can be explained with the help of the metaphor of the lack on the level of being or text. Further justification and confirmation for this explanation are provided by a somewhat unusual text from Althusser's later writings which bears the title "The Underground Current of the Materialism of the Encounter." This essay elevates the void to a paradigmatic object of philosophy. Althusser begins by claiming that philosophy has to empty a space for itself. It does so by emptying itself, which is to say, by removing classical philosophical questions and proceeding exclusively from nothing.[26] The problem with classical philosophical questions is that they always presuppose the originality of being, sense, cause, and order, and presuppose "the priority of Meaning over all reality."[27] Indeed it might be said, even if it is a simplification, that Platonism (and Eleaticism) were characterized by the assumption that the phenomenal world is secondary, derived, reduced, and imperfect and that it can only be assessed against the upright, unblemished, and flawless being as its source. Contrary to the classical metaphysical tradition, Althusser drew attention to the tradition of philosophical materialism that does not define itself as the antipole, as the symmetrical counterpoint of idealism but rather with the help of the concepts of encounter, surprise, and chance. Althusser ordered his reflections on the "materialism of the encounter" or "materialism of contingency" in a loose historical sequence, which he introduced by linking Epicurus and Heidegger. More precisely, he introduced it with the concept of the swerve (*clinamen*).

Althusser begins by recalling how Epicurus pictured the beginning of the world: atoms raining in the void. Suddenly—by pure coincidence, for no reason, without sense or cause in the proper meaning of the word—something happens: an atom swerves from a straight line and collides with another atom. A world is born.[28] Althusser emphasized that it is only this encounter that makes atoms real. Atoms, as far as we can imagine them before the swerve and the encounter, are purely abstract and do not possess existence in any real sense of the word: "The *atoms' very existence is due to nothing but the swerve and the encounter* prior to which they led only a phantom existence."[29] Atoms as they are before the swerve occurs have therefore exactly the same role as the material individual before his or her interpellation into a subject in Althusser's theory of ideology. The "individual" (which is of course only the Latin version of the Greek term "atom") is merely an abstract assumption, a phantom; from the point of view of interpellation, things are very different. Once the symbolic or ideological order of sense is established, it has always been in effect: it spreads out over its obscure past, appropriates the status of anteriority and antecedence, and it can certainly function as a Platonic idea.

As opposed to the metaphysical assumption of origin as something straight, where swerves of the phenomenal world with regard to it are secondary at best, the basic thesis of the materialism of the encounter is the thesis about the originality, the primordiality of the swerve itself.

> That the very beginning of the world, that is, of all reality and all sense, is due to the swerve—that the world begins with the swerve, not with reason or with a cause—this gives us the full measure of the audacity

> of Epicurus' thesis. Which thinkers in the history of philosophy have adopted the thesis that the swerve is original and not derived?[30]

According to Althusser, the authors to adopt, defend, and develop this thought were principally Machiavelli, Spinoza, Rousseau, and Marx. But the one most immediately associated with the Epicurean swerve was, perhaps surprisingly, Heidegger's philosophy of the factual, where it turns out that there is no point in asking about the origin of our being in the world, since being is possible as being only in such and such a world, only as determined being, only as Dasein. Althusser goes on to affirm that it is only with Heidegger that the question of void was given its full philosophical weight.[31] The point is not that there is first an upright being, which is only produced as determined being by the swerve, but that before the swerve (of being), there is no being at all.

While Althusser argued that Hegel's conception of void and of the functioning of negativity was more or less a case of "false words,"[32] it is important to note that in reality Hegel had suggested a specific twist in the metaphysical perspective, an about-turn in metaphysics. His task was a recapitulation of what metaphysics or ontotheology had got right, and not a wholesale repudiation. Hence we might indeed say that in Hegel, production is an event whereby determined being is produced out of pure being. Yet here, pure being is anything but straight perfection, since it is indistinguishable from the movement—if I may be allowed to use this term—of the "swerve" of negation from itself, and in this sense it is a self-referential negativity. The thesis about the originality of the swerve can certainly be understood as a Hegelian thesis; in chapter 2, we attempted to demonstrate that what separates Hegel from Plotinus is precisely the idea that the epistrophe, the return of the eye of the intellect back to the One, must be thought as the very same movement as the flowing out from the One, and not, as in Plotinus, as a separate event. While Plotinus distinguished between the principle of unity and deviation from it (the epistrophe), Hegel thought that the absolute negativity was, by itself, a deviation (a swerve) from itself, and that was precisely the reason why it was productive, "generative," or even "world-creating."[33]

The question of the *fall* of atoms is another one directly linked to the question of the swerve.[34] The assumption about the parallel falling of atoms through the void is pure abstraction, hence the fall is, in the ultimate analysis, nothing but the swerve itself. Perhaps we could explore the thesis on *clinamen* a bit further and add a demonstration from the field of grammar, specifically, the question of cases. What is called *Fall* in German and *casus* in Latin—case, *Fall,* and *casus* are all etymologically linked to "falling": *cadere*— is known as *sklon* in some European languages (for instance in Slovenian, my own language): there is an etymological link to "being bent," "inclined," "bowed." The metaphor of curvature or torsion gets another interesting layer, a grammatical one. In modern English, the declension of nouns is almost nonexistent, to the point that even the term itself may sound unfamiliar. In most European languages, however, like Latin (*declinatio*), the declension of nouns is extremely important, and it implies a metaphysics of its own. If we recall that the term *declinatio* shares the meaning of the swerve or declination, then we could say that the metaphysical claim of traditional linguistics is that words possess an original substance, which is why a noun is called a substantive, and that concrete examples of words in actually uttered sentences are merely something derived, something added to the root from the outside, bending it, taking away from its original straightness and forcing it to adopt a bowed posture, inclining the substantive this way or the other. A grammatical case, the specific way a noun falls, can also be seen as a specific way a noun is inclined. Contrary to the spontaneous (or deliberate) grammatical metaphysics, Althusser's view can be summarized as the thesis that words never appear in their purity, but are always already parts of sentences, where they appear in various declinations: they are always already curved or bent. Grammatical declension is thus not a secondary transformation of words but something they possess originally, so that words originally appear in *casus* or *declinatio*: falling, or bent.

To develop the linguistic metaphor even further, dogmatic Platonic metaphysics could be defined by the thesis that concretely uttered words are merely attempts to reach a transcendent truth which is fundamentally distant and unreachable for them. Contrary to such a view, Gadamer, drawing on the tradition of preaching God's word, noted that the original sense has to be renewed in the spoken word, it literally has to rise from the dead and be repeated, be read again. Hence, for Gadamer, the standpoint of finality has a specific advantage, since the original sense can be renewed and transmitted only through concretely uttered words.

But Althusser made an important step further: it is not only that transcendent truth is renewed in concretely uttered words, all the while retaining its transcendence and exceptionality. His thesis could be summed up as the thesis that it is the act of uttering itself that produces the truth which has been uttered. This is well documented in the practice of psychoanalysis, which has been famously called the "talking cure" by one of Freud's patients. But we know this even from everyday experience. Something is bothering us, something unpleasant that we do not want to speak about; but it is only when someone pokes us that we finally say something about it. And it is only then that we really find out, for the first time, what it was that was bothering us. And by saying and defining it we have not only found it but—often to our surprise—have already made a first step to avoiding or even solving the issue. This is exactly how Althusser's concept of surprise works: the truth is an effect of the surprise provoked by its utterance.[35]

Another thinker included by Althusser in the tradition of the materialism of the encounter that I wish to look at more closely is Karl Marx; specifically, let us consider the question of the modes of production. Althusser's thesis was that the capitalist mode of production had arisen as a result of an encounter, as a combination of elements with independent histories.

> When Marx and Engels say that the proletariat is "the product of big industry," they utter a very great piece of nonsense, positioning themselves within the *logic of the accomplished fact of the reproduction of the proletariat on an extended scale,* not the aleatory logic of the "encounter" which produces (rather than reproduces), as the proletariat, this mass of impoverished, expropriated human beings as one of the elements making up the mode of production.[36]

The point is that before the encounter that gave rise to capitalism, the proletariat did not exist at all; there was only a "mass of impoverished, expropriated human beings," a rain of abstract atoms. It is in this respect that Althusser's modes of production as modes of appropriation of the real world have to be explained in terms of the swerve or declination. For the cognitive mode, Althusser used the same pun as in the epistemological text in the collective volume *Reading "Capital"*: conceptual grasping (*prise* in French) is only possible as a surprise (*surprise*). The grasping of the real world takes place as, quite literally, a "surprise." Its product includes something that was not planned.

Another detail worth paying attention to is Althusser's critique of what he calls the logic of the accomplished fact. With it, he certainly refuted suspicions that his theory was "functionalist," just as Spinozism was supposedly merely "determinist." However, his stressing the role of coincidence should not tempt us to make the opposite mistake and adopt an anarchistic explanation. Rather, his is the paradoxical thesis that the source of the meaningful order is not Meaning with a capital M, but non-meaning—it is a thesis on Non-meaning with a capital N. It is not the thesis that the source of all being is the most perfect being, nor that the source is something dirty, but the thesis that the source is always inseparably present in what stems from it. He writes in an almost Hegelian passage:

> The world may be called *the accomplished fact* [*fait accompli*] in which, once the fact has been accomplished, is established the reign of Reason, Meaning, Necessity and End [*Fin*]. But the accomplishment of the fact is just a pure effect of contingency.[37]

Historical orders (the capitalist order, the feudal order, etc.) are simply specific ways in which atoms met and grasped each other and the ontological slime coalesced—but there is no guarantee that these coalesced forms will endure; on the contrary, it seems rather, to paraphrase what Kierkegaard said about repetition, that all that endures in history is the impossibility of enduring. "History here is nothing but the permanent revocation of the accomplished fact by another undecipherable fact to be accomplished."[38]

The key emphasis in Althusser's text is on the question of surprise, success, and coincidence. But, once again, this is not about the rebellion of coincidence against a strict and rigid symbolic order. Althusser's point is much more far-reaching: coincidence has to be understood as the very source of the symbolic order, since the symbolic order can only be instituted as a grasping of the original coincidence. Spinoza sharply distinguished between freedom and free will; by the same token, we have to say that Althusser's surprise is not about arbitrariness but about what we can, in the context of a Hegelian account of comedy, explain using the concept of the surplus of success. Just as in comedy, being either overtakes itself or lags behind (and this is constitutive of comedy), so with Althusser's Epicurean rain, being is in the constitutive declination.

Finally, Althusser's idea of the materialism of the encounter leads us to revisit the question of whether negativity on the level of being, its constitutive indebtedness, is to be understood as a gap or as curvature. The images used to illustrate the materialism of the encounter—declination, fall, swerve, as well as, more generally, inflection and modification—certainly count among images of curvature. On the other hand, in Althusser's work, the negativity of the real world is often interpreted in terms of a cut or a rupture. The cut between the real object and the object of cognition, and the epistemological rupture between ideology and science are modes where negativity included in cognition, ignorance included in knowledge, or oversight intrinsic to active observation are understood in terms of the concept of the gap. This is illustrated by voids in a text registered by symptomatic reading. On the one hand, they are what makes the discourse possible: classical political economy was organized so as to be perfectly blind to problems with its basic approach. On the other hand, it was just that void included in the approach of classical political economy that turned out to be a *productive* void. The task taken up by Marx was after all nothing else than *reading* classical political economy; a special kind of reading that did not overlook the voids but used them as a basis to create a whole new approach.

In Althusser, then, both types of conceptions of negativity are at work simultaneously at all times. Althusser is the incarnation of the problem that we have decided to call the problem of Hegel and Spinoza. It seems that the conception of lack is more present in his epistemological theses (cuts, ruptures, gaps), while in the historical and what we could call ontological theses it is the conception of curvature that takes center stage (falls and swerves as a basis of historical transformations, the ineradicable character of imaginary distortion in ideology). These notions can certainly be conceptually distinguished. But what may be more important is distinguishing them from traditional metaphysics and its contemporary incarnations. The psychoanalytic lack is never just a lack, since it is always a productive lack, a lack that is at the same time a surplus; castration, for instance, far from being a concept of the destruction of enjoyment, is precisely a concept of its production. The trouble with pleasure, to use the title of Schuster's book, is precisely that there is too much of it.

In Hegel, in (Hegelian) psychoanalysis, as well as in Althusser, we are dealing with a specific meaning of the paradoxical original divide, or cut. Therefore we could say that the concept of lack is an inadequate one precisely when it is tied to two classical themes in metaphysics: the deficiency and limitedness of human existence. On the other hand, the concept of curvature should not be taken lightly either. The thesis that being is originally curved or fallen or thrown or that it is always given only as modified can easily degenerate into an identitary thesis, that is, the thesis that being is identical to itself; except that, unlike in Platonism, this thesis is not about the identity of perfect being with perfect being, but about the identity of imperfect or deficient being with imperfect or deficient being. So it is when we wish to make curvature a quality of the content of being instead of grasping it in its negativity that we have a problem. Being is being only by being curved, or in other words, *being is curvature.* The concepts of lack and curvature are both materialist in the sense that they refuse external intervention into the order of being or into the order of cognition as well as any external model, criterion, or cause. They are ways of thinking about the transformation or the event as intrinsic to being itself.

Conclusion

Substance and Negativity: The Primacy of Negativity

One of the most fundamental theses of contemporary philosophy is that of the *primacy of negativity*. Of course, the question of negativity itself has been present in philosophical tradition since its very beginnings. In a way it is *the* philosophical question, discussed throughout history in antiquity, by the Scholastics, in philosophical mysticism, in German idealism and even in modern times, under various names such as nothingness, void, nonbeing, lack, and many, many more. But in contrast to contemporary thought, traditional, especially classic philosophy was in principle determined by a choice *against* negativity. The course of thought in antiquity is perhaps best expressed in the claim of Parmenides that only being *is*, while nonbeing *is not*. It seems that the choice for being is in itself a negation of nothingness.

The Eleatic theoretical position is brilliant in its radical simplicity. Yet this simplicity should not be underestimated, because it has some far-reaching consequences. For Parmenides, things that are said to be changing or in movement fall in the category of nonbeing. Plato and Aristotle proposed more refined ontologies, according to which negation and negativity are still considered as outside of being proper, but at the same time form a relation with it. Negation and negativity do not belong to (pure) being and can only be considered as logically secondary and as temporally posterior, as degradations of being. This concept was further developed in Neoplatonism and upgraded into a hierarchical system of emanation, where the One, which is above being itself, "emanates," radiates more and more determined and less and less perfect beings. The greatest change of perspective that Neoplatonism brought in comparison to Plato was precisely in the conception of determinate, finite beings. While Plato explained them as some sort of *external* violence, distortion, or degradation of original unity and perfection, Plotinus, Proclus, and others considered determinate beings as necessary products of an *internal* activity within that unity and perfection itself.

In an obvious disparity with antiquity, which determined centuries of (European) metaphysics, contemporary philosophy proposes the thesis of the *primacy of negativity*. This thesis possibly deserves a central place among all tectonic theses of modernity, since it does not only incarnate a break with traditional Christian-Platonic metaphysics, but also continues to break, even today, with all those theoretical formations, thought patterns, and spontaneous opinions and habits that perpetuate it in the "science of economics," as well as in our theoretical, philosophical, and academic "problems" and political and moral struggles.

The idea of the primacy of negativity can be found in the most divergent theories. Even with paradigmatic authors of affirmation such as Deleuze who was referred to by Benjamin Noys as "*the* central figure of contemporary affirmationism,"[1] one can, in certain contexts, speak of the primacy of negativity. As the title of Deleuze's famous book indicates, difference and repetition have replaced the original and the identical as privileged objects of philosophy.[2] Deleuze came to regard that which traditional metaphysics considered as something rupturing original unity or something merely imitating primary principles (an imitation that necessarily failed) as the very productive force. What tradition understood as negativity—that which is accidental or destructive, that which doesn't exist in itself, but only receives being from some distant and elevated Origin—thus takes center stage in philosophy, since it needs no Origin to be what it is.

Difference and differentiation play a central role in Derridean deconstruction and in structuralism. The best example of this is the idea that writing has a specific advantage over the spoken word. Tradition preferred the immediate presence of the latter. Writing was considered as an attempt to re-produce, or re-present, that original presence, an attempt that necessarily leads to a deformation of truth—precisely like the Platonic theory that actually existing things are nothing but deformed and inherently weak copies of their original ideas. Derrida proposed the thesis of the primacy of writing, pointing out that the negativity of writing, namely its necessary delay and deformation, is in fact inscribed in the essence of language itself. The very possibility of language is based upon an interrelated network of signs; and a sign always implies a delay, or a detachment from what it signifies. The question of whether language is formulated in writing or in the spoken word seems a secondary one.

In the initial sections of his *Being and Time*, Heidegger maintained that being can only be discussed through negation, which allowed him to propose the thesis of the ontological difference. Apophatic or negative theology similarly claimed that the supreme being (God) can only be described by negation (*via negativa*). But Heidegger's point was not that the human mind is deficient in expressing what is primary, but quite the opposite, that what is primary "expresses" itself only through negation. Heidegger did not understand being as an original fullness which human language (supposedly finite and imperfect) can only speak of by denying what it is not. Rather, according to Heidegger, negativity is internal to being itself. We can take an ordinary chair as an example of how the primacy of the negative phenomenon is revealed in *Being and Time.* We don't even notice the chair if it is in its place, stationed in its usual and average use, behind the desk. But if it is broken or lying on the floor, we not only notice it, but are also aware that there "*is* something the matter with that chair." Thus, a mundane object becomes a phenomenon of worldliness only in the background of negativity. In other words, the phenomenon as such exhibits certain negativity.[3]

Gadamer's hermeneutics drew from Hegelian and Heideggerian philosophy in demanding a turn in traditional hermeneutics. In Gadamerian perspective, the understanding and interpretation of a text are not merely methods by which one approaches the truth of that text. They are in a manner of speaking two ways of *production* of the truth of the text. What we are dealing with here is yet another idea of something that, at first glance, seems logically and temporally secondary—since we usually and naturally assume that text is primordial to its interpretation—but turns out to be an original production of meaning. The underlying proposition of such hermeneutics is the Hegelian idea that the truth can never be found outside of its protocol, outside of the "method" which expresses it. The hermeneutical delay—which is typical for explanation, understanding, and interpretation, for these are all temporally *posterior* to the text they refer to—is inscribed in truth itself. If Derrida considers writing as primordial to the immediacy of spoken language, perhaps we can claim that, for Gadamer, the interpretation of a text is in some way more original than the original text itself.[4]

In a somewhat unorthodox text on "The Underground Current of the Materialism of the Encounter,"[5] Althusser analyzed a series of thinkers of a radical materialist ontology where the entire order of being is founded upon an original act of chance. Among authors like Spinoza and Machiavelli, the series (surprisingly) also includes Hegel and Heidegger. The basic thesis of the "materialism of the encounter" is best expressed in Althusser's account of Epicurean ontology. Atoms are falling like raindrops through the void, parallel to each other. Suddenly, one of them swerves and collides with another. This accidental encounter, based upon a chance decline (*clinamen*), creates the world. A complication is inscribed in original being itself (as the being of the world). To this we must add that such a breakthrough event cannot be successfully pinpointed to a singular historical occurrence. Strictly speaking, this event is still going on, and if we accept Althusser's premise of the undercurrent of the materialism of the encounter, it has never ceased to be, nor will it ever cease. It may sound contradictory: we have, in Althusser, on the one hand a break and its transformation or change, and on the other hand the unchanging nature of transformation itself. Contrary to traditional metaphysics, where eternity was understood as an attribute of the idea of the perfect being, its unchangeability, the surprising point here is rather that what is eternal is the struggle itself, changeability itself.

Other ways to think the primary negativity within the topoi of contemporary philosophy were introduced, for instance, by Lacanian psychoanalysis in its concept of *pas-tout*; by Catherine Malabou in her concept of plasticity; but also by the Deleuzean concepts of curve and fold, by the idea of art as production of being (Zupančič, Pfaller, Gadamer), and by practically all contemporary theories drawing from Hegelian dialectical negativity.

Hegel and Spinoza

It can thus be said, firstly, that the question of the primacy of negativity is the key to understanding contemporary philosophy. It is its nexus, uniting under one banner otherwise quite divergent, even combatant thinkers. It is obvious, secondly, that negativity is considered from many different angles and in many different contexts. This fact, we argue, gives rise to fierce philosophical controversies. This is perhaps especially apparent in the polemics around the "philosophy of affirmation" versus the "philosophy of negation." It seems that the question of negativity that stirs an increasingly high level of interest in contemporary debates is in many ways a productive repetition of the question that determined the principal battleground of German Idealism in the nineteenth century. In controversies between contemporary Deleuzeans and contemporary Lacanians, for instance, we can hear the echo of tectonic struggles between two giants of philosophy, Hegel and Spinoza, who have both inspired generations of theorists and left us as their legacy two extremely influential schools of thought. Thirdly, it seems that such controversies are perpetuated mostly at the level of the external discord of concepts, without an explicit understanding of the proximity of and the distance between their fundamental theses. For the most part, this chapter attempts to tackle the question of contemporary negativity precisely by examining the polemics between Hegelianism and Spinozism. We can formulate it as a question of negativity inscribed in absolute substance, and therefore as a question of Hegel and Spinoza.

Almost all listed champions of the break with traditional metaphysics—

perhaps with the exception of, in part, Gadamer—understood Hegelian philosophy not only as a part of that ontotheological and teleological tradition that they sought to break with, but sometimes even as its most elaborated form, its radical peak. At the same time, Deleuze and Althusser, but at least to some extent also Agamben, Negri, and many others, looked to Spinoza as their philosophical ally in the struggle against the Hegelian pestilence. Nevertheless, the very least we can say in Hegel's defense is that his role was a controversial one. His philosophy invested the activity of negativity with a radically new meaning. To put it bluntly, negation holds the precise power to fluidify the ossified structure of metaphysics by inscribing something quite contingent into the very core of its elevated conceptions; and vice versa, to recognize the conceptual necessity in something completely aleatory, or in some immediate factuality. Moreover, what makes Hegel a contemporary philosopher, and not only in the negative sense, merely as someone digestible, but in the affirmative sense as someone who helped contemporary philosophy formulate its own field and start on its own path, is perhaps best shown precisely in what he relentlessly criticized in Spinozism and, more generally, in systems of identity. According to Hegel, any kind of identity can only be thought on the background of difference. An identity always implies an internal split into two; what is identical with itself is identical only insofar as it produces a difference within itself, between itself and another self that is identical. Generally speaking, an identity is always an identity of identity and difference.

Althusser argued that Hegel's concepts of negativity and contradiction were simplifications that flattened the historical and political complexity of nations into a simple matter of logical negation.[6] Althusser's own concept of negativity, however, the concept of the primacy of the swerve, is in fact quite compatible with Hegel's determination of the beginning or the origin as an "absolute negativity." Furthermore, on the very first pages of his fascinating work on *Difference and Repetition*, Deleuze wrote that the true conception of difference is only possible as anti-Hegelianism.[7] In his view, Hegel's conception of movement is nothing but a false movement, a purely abstract and logical mediation, a boring representation of concepts, a false theater.[8] The concept of contradiction, with which Hegel supposedly escaped from and successfully neutralized the menacing tentacles of identity, was in actuality, with all of the accompanying "logical perversity," just another device of the philosophy of identity.[9] In this context, Deleuze underlined Althusser's thesis from the famous paper on "Contradiction and Overdetermination," according to which the Hegelian contradiction is nothing but a simplification which serves as a necessary means by which an identity of a higher order is constituted.[10]

Yet, when Deleuze himself distinguished between two genres of repetition, between an abstract and an active repetition, he came extremely close to what in my opinion is the essential Hegelian position.

The first genre of repetition in Deleuzean typology is purely external to the concept; it is only a result of the activity of the concept, and it is therefore only a repetition in effect, completely unattached to its space and time. But the other genre of repetition is a repetition within the concept itself; it is authentic and it works as a pure movement of creation; it is *a repetition in the cause.*[11] Yet, this "authentic" repetition, as Deleuze determined it, is far from being an anti-Hegelian concept! The Hegelian critique of identity systems can be explained precisely through such a typology. The concept of production (or generation) as *emanation,* developed by Plotinus and Neoplatonism, was considered inadequate by Hegel because it presupposed that the productive principle of absolute unity is completely uninvolved in what it, as the principle, produced. It remains unaffected by it. For Hegel, in contrast to identity systems like the one presented by Plotinus, it is essential that movement itself or production itself is grasped as the absolute principle, and not simply as something that the principle does or practices while withdrawing itself from immersion in this use or practice. And so we can say that Hegel defends the position of an "original repetition" and not simply some repeatability of origin, not merely a repetition of the primary cause in a secondary effect.

This is why it is most fruitful to read Hegel in confrontation with Spinozism. As much as his reading and his explanation of Spinoza's philosophy may have been imperfect and indeed irrelevant at times, they are without a doubt extremely valuable for a productive understanding of Hegel's own philosophy. And we can make a similar claim in respect to a contemporary reading of Spinoza. It is exactly in a confrontation with Hegelianism that we can best see why it has attracted and influenced generations of thinkers, no less articulated and present in contemporary debates than their Hegelian counterparts. Spinozism admits of no imperfection, be it at the level of infinite absolute substance or at the level of finite modes. This is why it is always in danger of being read as a naive system of pure affirmation, of self-sufficient pure actuality; as a system of pantheistic utopia; as a boring, mechanical determinism; or as a system of faits accomplis: a system that cannot fail or err, because it never takes risks, and is always right, because it only articulates its truth *about* an event and *after* it. In other words, Spinozism is always in danger of being reduced to a system of pure positivity or of pure constatation (assertion), for it seems that it is unable to grasp the performative nature of truth, it seems that it is unable to grasp the very special condition where the articulation of truth is in itself an event, and where truth is produced as truth only with its articulation and through it. To read Spinozism with Hegel is precisely to ask Spinozism the question of how to think movement, change, or transformation in a system that has no imperfection, in a system which seems to hold firmly to the principle that only being is, while nonbeing is not, in a system where there is strictly speaking no falseness, where there are, just like in jazz and in any practice of improvisation, no mistakes.

Negativity at the Level of Being: Concept or Ruse?

I propose that we distinguish between two fundamentally different ways of thinking negativity at the level of being. Firstly, negativity works either as some irreducible flaw or limit of existence itself. Secondly, it is an intrinsic capability of being to transform itself, a self-transformative or self-producing capability. To make it quite clear, the idea of negativity in the sense of the finality of human existence is, in my opinion, nothing but a ruse with which traditional metaphysics turns in its grave and speaks with the ominous voice of its own resurrection. The difference with the Christian-Platonic concept of the negative is just as apparent as it is obscure. It is apparent, since negativity here inhabits being itself and there is no place for the affirmative fullness of being; it is obscure, since the hierarchical ontotheological structure remains unscathed: instead of a positive being reigning at the top, there is now the absence of it, or the void.

We are forced to include Gadamer among the thinkers of this kind of negativity. This is because his concept of how sense is produced in artistic practices, but also in language in general, is indebted to the Aristotelian and emanationist tradition of pure activity, or to use his own phrasing, to the tradition of intellectual generation, to the concept of birth where "there is no receptive part to go with a generating one."[12] In other words, truth can have its positive form only within its utterances, and cannot be, as truth, withheld from them as if existing independently of them. The original is not a complete and self-sufficient whole which is only diluted and deformed in its copies. And yet, it still operates as the sensible principle of unity. Copies or repetitions are therefore indeed the only way for the original to manifest itself. However, the distinction from naive Platonism consists only in the idea that repeatability is here inscribed in the original itself. This somehow makes repetitions themselves a necessary product and not some sort of "violence" against the principle of unity. But they are still considered as something imperfect, incomplete, insufficient, or temporary.

Gadamer's most persuasive example comes from the field of artistic production. He claimed that theater performances or poetic images are not merely secondary copies of primary essences (Platonic ideas), but rather that the very mode of being of a work of art is its presentation (*Darstellung*).[13] Works of art are therefore not only images, printed on the basis of a model or cliché (*Urbild*) that they represent. To exist as an image is an inner characteristic of the being of a work of art itself: "For strictly speaking, it is only through the picture (*Bild*) that the original (*Urbild*) becomes the original (*Urbild*)."[14] From this brilliant formulation we get the sense that the relationship between original and image is explained as a two-way relationship where none of the parties is indifferent or independent from the other. Yet, with Gadamer, the relationship explicitly remained within the framework of a renewed form of emanationism that we could call neo-emanationism.[15] This is because Gadamer, in the final analysis, remained faithful to the notion of the original as the *Unvordenkliche,* as pertaining to that abyss prior to which we cannot think. He did not understand this absolute limit of thought and language as a concept of negativity that operates only *within* language, as an intrinsic negativity *of* language, but rather as a concept of something that radically *transcends* a finite and limited human existence and understanding.[16] In order to explain the phenomenon of a work of art, however, a more radical approach than the one Gadamer allowed for is required. The image is able not only to represent the original (*Urbild*) and increase its being by bringing it to the light of day. We should go even further and claim that the image indeed *produces* the original (*Urbild*) in the strict sense of the word! There is a specific advantage of the image over the original. The original fully belongs to the realm of the *effects* of language, even though it constitutes an exception within it.

It is in this sense that we should also understand Heidegger's conception of a work of art, as he formulated it with relationship to Plato and Aristotle. The famous formula of the nature of a work of art as "the truth of being setting itself to work" (*Sich-ins-Werk-setzen der Wahrheit des Seienden*)[17] means that a work of art is an event within being itself, paradoxically producing the truth of being as its own foundation. This was especially in stark contradiction to Platonism, where a work of art could only imitate the truth (or, more precisely, it could only imitate an imitation of true being); but also to Aristotelianism, where a work of art was graciously *allowed* a decline from the truth. To make it quite clear: we should read Heidegger precisely in the sense that it is *the artistic (poetic) decline that establishes the truth in the first place.* This idea of *the primacy of the (poetic) decline* is what is lacking in the Gadamerian framework.

This outline, therefore, exhibits different conceptions of what we can understand by negativity at the level of being. But the distinction can perhaps be explained further by juxtaposing two analyses of the repetition at work in festivals, that of Gadamer and that of Deleuze. Both Gadamer and Deleuze claimed that the repetition of festivals is not merely a commemoration. But Gadamer pointed out that the repetition of a festival does not constitute a *new* festival, and concluded that the festival is temporal in its essence, that its original being already involves repeatability, so that there is no festival outside of its actual repetitions.[18] Of course, with Deleuze being the foremost philosopher of affirmation, he did not use the term "negativity" to denote the productive mechanism at work at the level of being. Nevertheless, his example is very fruitful and revelatory. The distinction with Gadamer's conception is a distinction in a detail, but this detail decides everything.

Deleuze praised Peguy's statement about the festival of Federation Day, celebrated annually in France: "As Peguy says, it is not Federation Day which commemorates or represents the fall of the Bastille, but the fall of the Bastille which celebrates and repeats in advance all Federation Days."[19] Of course, these words can be explained in a Gadamerian fashion, meaning that the original act of national constitution already involved its own repeatability, so that a celebration of the event of nationhood in a way repeats the nation itself, or even that the nation exists *only* in its celebrations, through which it exists as a nation in the strict sense of the word.[20] But it is quite clear that the Deleuzean perspective is completely different. The repetition in his conception is not a renewal or perpetuation of the symbolic order, but rather its *constitution* or *inauguration.* While a celebration of a festival for Gadamer is not a completely new festival, Deleuze seems to be interested in precisely this possibility, in an event that celebrates and repeats in advance, in an event that produces a new series of Gadamerian celebrations. While Gadamer was interested in the repeatability of the original, Deleuze developed the idea of an original repetition. This distinction might seem a mere difference of perspectives, but it is essential.[21]

Torsion or Lacuna

We can use the difference between a Gadamerian and a Deleuzean concept of repetition to distinguish between two fundamental philosophical conceptions of negativity at the level of being. In the case of a Gadamerian repetition, negativity of being operates as an ontological flaw or existential limitedness, exhibited by repetition in the relationship to the original—even though the original only exists in those repetitions. Contrary to this, the "Deleuzean concept of negativity" does not imply a deficiency or finality, but rather denotes a constitutive delay of being, that is, a decline or dilatation through which being is produced. The current most vigorous philosophical confrontations predominantly take place between these competitive conceptions of what is original. Yet, in order to fend off unashamed and indirect attempts to rehabilitate traditional metaphysical identity philosophy, we are still often forced to argue in favor of the Gadamerian repetition.[22]

What concepts of constitutive negativity have in common, generally speaking, is the idea of negativity not as something purely accidental but rather as something substantial: negativity is not some external infliction that mutilates the absolute substance; it works as its internal mechanism. There are many ways to grasp such negativity in philosophical concepts. The Aristotelian term of potentiality, understood as the actuality of potentiality, as virtuality, can be considered as a concept of constitutive negativity. It is a telos: not in the sense of an external end or an end state of a process, but rather an immanent telos of the object in question; to use Franz Brentano's ingenious term: negativity is *teleiosis*. What I refer to here as constitutive negativity in fact stretches to encompass many concepts in different systems of thought or lines of argument, such as plasticity (C. Malabou), the *Unvordenkliche* (Gadamer), ontological slime (Žižek), primordial torsion, temporal contraction, but also an accident, a surprise, an encounter—understood not as arbitrary eventualities but as coincidences that constitute the symbolic order, a kind of substantial accidents.

The distinction between the Gadamerian and Deleuzean concepts of repetition reveals two fundamental readings of the constitutive negativity: one that remains faithful to the metaphysical tradition of the finality or limitedness of human existence or understanding, and one that opens up a space for a productive negativity, following a completely different philosophical tradition. Beyond the realm of finality, we can introduce another distinction. On the one hand, the negativity within being can function as a *lacuna* within being, as proposed by the Lacanian concept of the subject, or as a *lack* or *void* pertaining to the surface of a discourse, as in the Althusserian conception of symptomal reading. On the other hand, negativity can be grasped as a constitutive *torsion* of discourse, language, or being.

This distinction proves necessary when we ask the question of how to think negativity in Spinozism and in Spinoza-inspired contemporary philosophy. That is to say: how can we avoid reducing Spinozist thought to a blindly deterministic system that is always correct since it knows no risks or surprises? Now, Spinoza's system of substance, attributes, and modes is a radically atemporal system. It can certainly account for movement, but it considers time to be, in principle, an illusion. Yet it is inappropriate to claim that a Spinozist, when explaining an event, takes a position of faits accomplis, of an already concluded combat, or that he speaks only from a temporal position of results, instead of immersing himself in the struggle as an ongoing process. In a way, it seems much more appropriate to raise the inverse objection and claim that Spinozism can never account for the end, for the result of the process. This objection expresses one of the most far-reaching differences between Spinozist and Hegelian thought. For Hegel, the questions of an absolute beginning and an absolute ending are *central* philosophical questions. Contrary to the traditional critique of Hegelianism, which unfortunately often remained within the framework of raising generalized complaints about ontological finalism and about the fascination with ideas of End Judgment and other conceptual clutter, it must be stated that the Hegelian concept of the "end" as telos is a highly productive one. It is a way to think the processual nature of the process without letting it stretch to an indefinite infinity; a way to think process not only from the viewpoint of transition, change, or movement, *but also* from the ecstatic viewpoint of its punctual result.

It may seem that we must reject Spinozism insofar as it reproduces the Aristotelian conception of movement. It is only able to comprehend the inner continuity of the process, but it can never bring this process to an end, it can never grasp it in a singular moment, in a now. A combat seems to be eternally undecided, for it never produces a winner (there is no whistle to call the game). A Spinozist sentence is never completed, it is always open to interpretations and reinterpretations: it is always in the mode of pure utterance. Now, what Hegel wanted to *add* to Spinozism was never intended to be any more than a simple full-stop to end the sentence, to bring the sentence to a definitive end and so produce its meaning. This is then the essence of Hegel's objection to Spinoza: he is incapable of formulating, producing, or thinking a break, a rupture, a clear cut. This is why it is, in the final analysis, impossible to speak about a definitive beginning or a conclusive end in Spinozism.

Yet it would be inappropriate to consider Spinozism as a system of pure affirmation. Spinoza's concept of being, if we can put it in these terms, certainly doesn't account for a lack or a rupture or a gap in being. But perhaps his concept of being as being-in-movement, as I tried to argue in chapter 4, can be explained with the idea of the primary *torsion* of being, according to which *to exist* always already means to be contorted, to be in such and such mode, to be modified, or also, to be at this or that end.

The questions of combat and result, of orientation according to intensions and setting goals, of movement and its beginning or end point help us define the relationship between the positions of Spinoza and Hegel as the relationship of *and* and *or*. The insistence of Hegelian philosophy on the problematic of an absolute beginning and absolute ending has no correlation in Spinoza. In Spinozism, one can perhaps make a Heideggerian claim that one is always already at this or that end, in the sense that one is always already modified in a determined way. But the Spinozist modification never requires a full stop as its inner goal, or to put it in different terms, whatever ending may befall a mode of the substance, it is completely external to the mode itself and can only be something that is destructive to it.

Perhaps we can grasp this distinction as a difference between the meaning of the verbs "to end" and "to stop." In Spinoza, a process on the level of finite modes can certainly be said to have stopped or ceased. It is impossible, however, to say that it has ended or that it was fulfilled, that it has reached the point of its meaningful conclusion or logical solution, the point at which, in the theater, *the curtain falls*. This is because Spinoza's philosophy is, contrary to Hegelianism, completely incompatible with the concept of telos. The thesis according to which the essence of mode is its perseverance in existence (*conatus*) must be read as precisely opposite to the concept of telos. Again, we can say that what is expressed in the concept of *conatus* is the idea that the essence of a being is precisely its being—just as we can say about the Heideggerian concept of Dasein that it is a name for that particular being that exists ontologically. In this specific sense we can perhaps even talk about telos in Spinoza: as something that is an end in itself.

But *Hegel's* concept of telos involves the idea of finalization or conclusion. This is because his dialectics conjoins the result and the process in the result itself, thus paradoxically producing the result as its own product. This self-referential character of the Hegelian telos rests upon an inner contradiction, a concept that was criticized notably by Althusser and Deleuze as enabling the persistence of the philosophy of identity. But the unity of the process and the end goal, or the combat and the result, must also be considered inversely. Not only does the process already involve its result, so that the progression in a process is in a way a self-fulfillment, but it goes the other way around, too: *the goal, once reached, still implies the tension of the combat.* It is true, therefore, that things come to their end—they don't simply stop being, but already involve the possibility of the end as fulfillment, as telos in the proper sense of the word—but at the same time this end point is not some mythical point of convergence of all possible contradictions; it is not the final judgment of

Christian metaphysics. Rather, this end point is *the turning point.* Just like a punctuation mark ends one thought and opens up the space for another. Just like one reply sparks off the reply of the other.[23]

Hence, Hegelian dialectic can be said to constitute a way to think both the combat *and* its result; either as the result already working within the combat, or as the conflict inherent to the result. It is a teleological discourse, but its telos should be understood as the turning point. On the one hand, there is the point of view of contingency: the ongoing combat is indeed an open-ended struggle and the result can only come as a surprise, as a destination that was reached after a series of contingent turns. On the other hand, there is the point of view of necessity: the retrospective gaze of the result makes clear that things could not have happened in any other way. One of the aspects of Hegelian dialectics pointed out by Catherine Malabou and explained with her temporal concept of plasticity was precisely the idea that these two processes, the process of the "becoming essential of the accident" and the process of the "becoming accidental of the essence," must be grasped in their unity.[24] To sum up: Hegel's stake is the paradoxical unity of the process and its result, of the continuous motion and an abrupt break, where the result is not the metaphysical point of the end of all things, the end of time itself, but the turning point.

But in the case of Spinozism, it seems that there are merely two options: to think *either* only the combat *or* only the result. On the one hand, we can assume the position of the logic of always-already where only the results count, or to put it in different terms, all that matters is the external appearance of things and events. In this fashion we can explain the Althusserian example for the thesis of the material existence of ideology: religion. According to Althusser, it is not important what a religious subject thinks in his head—it is only important whether he observes the rituals, goes to church, bends his knees, and prays. It is as if we must assume the gaze of a completely innocent spectator for whom this theater is acted out: the spectator anticipates nothing, assumes nothing, and understands things exactly as they appear and only insofar as they really do appear. This is how the bureaucratic State works: things only count if they are written down in ink, publicly declared, or are otherwise apparent and visible. But on the other hand, we can declare that, in Spinozism, the combat is always on, it is never resolved absolutely, we can never put a punctuation mark at the end of its "sentence." It seems that only this openness counts: there is no punctuation mark to finish the sentence, there is no judge to call the game, there is no clear set of rules that determine the rules of engagement.

These alternative objections claim that Spinozism *either* (1) has no tension of an ongoing combat but only results, only the final appearance of things, *or* (2) that in Spinozism one can never come to an ending or finalization, since movement has no telos. We can explain the relationship between the two objections by evoking the distinction (Aristotelian, in essence) between two causalities. Firstly, there is the causality of an infinite linear succession of causes and effects: one billiard ball hits another, which then hits another and so forth, to infinity. We can dub this accidental chain of events *metonymic causality*, since the causal power is transferred from one particle to another in a purely contingent yet logically consistent and determined manner. Secondly, there is what we could call *metaphorical causality*, which is traditionally known as the idea of "the great chain of being." The term "cause" here implies an ontological hierarchy. The original cause produces its effects but does not diminish in its causal (that is, ontological) power. As this causal chain progresses, the fullness and perfection of being is reduced—effects have less and less being, until at the end, there is only anamorphic mud. If we accept this distinction of horizontal and vertical causality, then we can claim that the first objection (1) declares that Spinozism doesn't recognize metonymic causality and is therefore nothing but an elaboration of the radical Eleatic position where being is immediately identical with its enunciation—contrary to the Hegelian logic where being is *produced* by its articulation and therefore involves a delay. But the second objection (2) claims that Spinozism doesn't recognize metaphorical causality and therefore reduces itself to a blind determinism, or, at best, to some sort of Kantianism where the absolute substance is nothing but an ideal of a reason for metonymic action. Both objections claim that Spinozism recognizes no tension or contradiction between the ongoing combat and the result. If Hegel demanded that being must produce its own turning point through which it is transformed, then Spinoza's being is either a complete standstill or a complete openness. The two objections agree that Spinozism is indeed capable of understanding that substance is curved, but that it fails to account for the radical event of the *turning point* where the torsion of substance itself is curved in a paradoxical yet highly productive concept of negation of negation, which, here, we can perhaps explain as torsion of torsion.

Althusser—Structuralism versus Spinozism

When discussing Spinoza's philosophy, Deleuze never forgets to point out that Spinozist ontology originated in the metaphysics of Duns Scotus.

Above all, he underlined the concept of the formal distinction as a difference that is grounded in being and therefore a real difference, while, at the same time, not manifesting itself as a numerical difference.[25] He considered the Scotist being as neutral or indifferent to the question of finite and infinite, created and uncreated. Hence, the most important contribution of Spinoza was, in his view, to understand being not as "neutral or indifferent, he makes it an object of pure affirmation."[26] Nevertheless, Deleuze believed that Spinoza did not completely follow through and that his being (substance) remained, to an extent, indifferent. The relationship between modes and substance was still only one-sided. Deleuze writes: "Nevertheless, there still remains a difference between substance and the modes: Spinoza's substance appears independent of the modes, while the modes are dependent on substance, but as though on something other than themselves."[27] In other words, and most peculiarly, Deleuze came to criticize Spinoza for a very similar reason as Hegel did: the indifference of the substance, or the one-sidedness of its relationship with modes. Just as Hegel claims that Spinoza's substance is rigid and therefore only negative, but not productively negative, that it does not comprehend the negation of negation, so Deleuze claims that Spinoza's substance is indifferent and not affirmative enough. Both Hegel and Deleuze proposed a more radical thesis, according to which the expressions of being should not be understood as its outgrowths, as a Gadamerian neo-emanationist increase of being, but rather as articulations through which being produces itself. What we have here is a rather curious case of Deleuze and Hegel allied in criticism of Spinoza!

Furthermore, Althusser stated that what he was missing in Spinozism was the concept of contradiction—as required by the idea of class struggle. This means that he, too, was missing the conception of an abrupt event, a break. Althusser's theory of ideology proposes a paradoxical relationship between the (Spinozist) thesis of the material existence of the symbolic order and the thesis of the sudden event of what he calls interpellation (which seems to be a non-Spinozist idea). The challenge is to comprehend these as both working at the same time: we are always already in an ideology and the material individual is nothing but an abstract hypothesis, but at the same time, the ideological interpellation works as an actual event where the symbolic/ideological subject and its symbolic/ideological order are mutually constituted.

Now, the traditional answer to this Althusserian paradox is the thesis that the symbolic order is constituted retroactively. The abrupt break or the turning point cannot be located in a singular event, because any such point that we posit already presumes an explanation with the symbolic order. The symbolic order is therefore always already constituted. At the same time, we must insist on the idea that such an event did in fact take place and that the whole has demonstrated itself as a logical or symbolic whole only *in retrospect.* In other words, the event of the constitution of the symbolic order really did happen, as a singular point, a breaking point; but once it has happened, we are already inside the symbolic order and we cannot articulate it in any other way than symbolically. The break between the material individual and the ideological subject, or, in other discursive practices, between nature and culture, and so on, is therefore real, but it is constituted retroactively.

But there is a trap to be avoided with this traditional structuralist response, a trap that we can perhaps call the danger of bad materialism. By this I mean the assumption that there remains, beyond the omnipresent and all-encompassing symbolic order, a monolithic or an infinitely fluid fragment of reality, some sort of primordial core of nature. Such a claim is usually presented as materialist. But it is obvious, firstly, that we must fix such a core of nature in some Beyond. We must assume the reality of a region that is radically external to the world of symbolic order and everyday experience, or to put it in perhaps suspicious terms, external to everyday "symbolic experience." Secondly, we must assume that the relationship between the rigidity or fluidity of the core, on the one hand, and the factuality of everyday symbolic experience on the other, is a strictly one-sided relationship; the symbolic experience depends upon the immediate core of nature, but this core of nature rests in its incognizable being, quite independent from representations within the symbolic order, within the world of experience, or within the world of symbolic experience. This kind of materialism differs from traditional idealism in name only: that original reality can be called matter, nature, and so on, but since it is one-sided and constitutes a Beyond, it is inseparable from what idealism calls the idea, original unity, god, and so on.[28]

The danger of falling into the trap of bad materialism forces us to underline the Spinozist, rather than the structuralist in Althusser. Hence, the thesis about the relationship between the core of the real and the symbolic order goes as follows: *The core of the real is constituted in the same instance as the symbolic order which excludes it.* The core of the real does not inhabit a positive region, demarcated from the symbolic/ideological order. It is nothing but rupture itself, included within the symbolic/ideological order. In terms of everyday life, this means that we cannot claim that first there was nature, which was later denaturalized by technology. It was one and the same event that constituted, at the same time, both nature and technology. In this sense, terms like "biologic," "organic," or any other expression of the idea of natural production are contradictory. The event of the emergence of the symbolic order is their identity, the unity of being and thought, nature and technology, truth and method. On this decisive point Hegel and Spinoza share their position: method should not be considered as something secondary in the relation to the primary, indifferent truth. Moreover, *the truth always already implies the apparatus of its demonstration.*[29] But to this we must add yet another important Hegelian warning: even the identity between truth and its demonstration should not be considered as an indifferent one! Not only is truth not indifferent to its own demonstration, since they are originally identical, but also this original identity of truth and demonstration is not an immediate given. It is only at this deeper level that Hegel criticized Spinoza's substance as being indifferent or rigid: Spinoza does understand the unity of being and thought—a unity which, for Hegel, is in fact the glorious beginning of all philosophy, of all dialectics—but he thinks this unity only as an immediate and eternal identity. The Hegelian demand for an identity which is not an indifferent identity can be formulated in the following way: a demonstration must *produce* the truth that it is demonstrating.

We have to be careful not to succumb to a naive materialist resolution of the Althusserian paradoxical conjugation of the omnipresence of the symbolic order and the turning point of the interpellation, the conjugation of the impenetrable logic of the symbolic/ideological order and the event of an accidental or surprising intrusion. We can say with Althusser that our everyday life is always already symbolized, since our actions are always actions, inscribed in the material apparatuses of the symbolic order. To use somewhat different terminology, we could also say that being itself is always an already symbolized being.

Now, one could object to this with another of Althusser's famous concepts, namely that of overdetermination. It is true that the order of economic production is not some sort of natural core of reality which determines, in concentric waves of determination, all other dependent orders, the political, the theoretical, and so on. But it still *overdetermines* them: it influences those orders without their knowledge or consent. This allows for the structuralist reading of the rapport between event and order. Even though we cannot localize the instance of the ultimate remainder of reality in a singular event (since "the lonely hour of the last instance never comes"), we must still presuppose it as the external origin of the symbolic order!

Contrary to this objection of naive materialism, I would like to make a short detour and point out an analogy between the constitution of the Althusserian subject and the question of beginning in Hegel's *Science of Logic.* In very brief terms, the beginning is formulated as a question of *uttering the unutterable.* Logic begins with *pure being* as that which is immediate and has no determination whatsoever. As such, it is absolutely negative and has therefore already passed into nothingness. But such indistinguishableness of pure being and pure nothingness can only be grasped reflexively. To think it distinctly already implies determining it and imposing on it some quality of reflection—thus, pure being is lost precisely in the attempt to grasp it. And so, at its very beginning, logic faces its own utter impossibility. But for Hegel, this impossibility of uttering (or determining) pure being does not bear the gravity of some irrevocable finality of human knowledge or ability to communicate. If this was so, Hegel could have ended his *Science of Logic* on this point—precisely at its beginning—and simply declare, like Wittgenstein, that he will keep his silence about what cannot be uttered. However, the true beginning of logic is therefore not only to acknowledge that it is impossible to express pure being in words or thoughts, but also to realize that the acknowledgment of this impossibility of uttering *is nevertheless an utterance*! This twist of words, this rhetorical trick, this primordial excess of language is precisely what sets the entire dialectical machine in motion. From this turning point onwards, pure being never stops trying (and failing) to be uttered. Pure being is a chatter-mouth.

We can find a formally analogous thesis in Althusser. In his famous article on "Ideology and Ideological Apparatuses of the State," he claimed that an ideology never sees beyond its own boundaries; moreover, it doesn't even know that it *has* boundaries—it is immersed in obviousness. Even a scientist, insofar as he or she is a subject, cannot be outside of his or her ideology. All the scientist can say is that "he or she is in ideology." The transformation of the ideological order cannot be explained as some kind of demonstrative exit from the symbolic order and a return to a natural being. A transformation is only possible as a performative action. For Althusser, a new, emerging science can establish its own region only through a (theoretical) practice within its ideology, with that symptomal reading, where the sentences of an ideology are only measured by each other, and not by some immediate, pure empiric data or any other so-called uncorrupted reality.

Even the concept of overdetermination should therefore not be confused with a determination by some positive content that remains unrecognized as a true cause. Rather, it is a determination by the force of negative cuts, breaks, and ruptures that de-form and re-form the symbolic substance. We have no reason to assume that, beyond and above (or below) the symbolic order, there lurks some affirmative instance that initiates those ruptures—at least, not if we really are materialists as well as scientific realists.

Spinoza: Negativity as Torsion

These critiques of Spinozist philosophy are densely intertwined. For the most part, they constitute different specific aspects of the same general problematic. Firstly, there is the Hegelian-Deleuzean critique—if one can indeed write these two words with a hyphen—that Spinozist substance is rigid or indifferent. Secondly, there is the question of the relationship between metaphorical and metonymical causality. Thirdly, the challenge is how to think both the continuity of the process and the singular event of the turn. And finally, there is the question of materialism.

To put it in general terms, the criticism that substance is rigid or indifferent claims that it is impossible to think determination or finality at the level of absolute substance. According to Hegel, the modifications of a Spinozist absolute substance are utterly finite and negated, contrary to substance itself, which is without determination and is therefore infinite and true. According to Deleuze, substance is indifferent to the modes and their relationship is essentially one-sided. What is at stake here, in both cases, is the well-known question of the transition from substance to modes. Hegel claimed Spinoza either didn't resolve this question at all, or resolved it only with a one-sided negation where only the modes are negated.[30]

In defense of Spinoza, perhaps one can point out the somewhat mysterious concept of infinite modes. These are movement or rest under the attribute of extension, or the absolutely infinite intellect under the attribute of thought. Alongside these immediately infinite modes, Spinoza also proposed the idea of mediated infinite modes and gave the example of "the face of the whole universe" (*facies totius universi*) under the attribute of extension. But there is no need for us to go any deeper into the analysis of such a defense; the essential stake is to claim that the transition from the infinite to the finite in Spinozism cannot be explained as a simple logical or ontological degradation from infinite substance to the relatively infinite attributes and finally to the purely finite modes, since apparently we also have *infinite modes.* But while this defense raises an interesting point, I believe it is essentially inefficient in demonstrating that Spinoza did think about determination at the level of absolute substance. Why? Both Deleuze and Macherey arranged these expressions of the attribute in a sequence, starting with the attribute itself, followed by its immediate infinite mode, then its indirect infinite mode, and lastly by singular bodies or finite, determinate modes.[31] They both declared that this does not imply a Neoplatonic ontological hierarchy;[32] but this dry declaration doesn't seem so much an attempt at a different formulation as an expression of a theoretical difficulty. The problem of the "transition from the infinite to the finite" is not resolved, because the substance is still logically superior to its modifications: first, there is substance, then there is a transition, and lastly, there are the modes.

A much better chance to solve this difficulty lies in Macherey's remark that the problematic of the infinite modes should not be considered within the context of the transition or the mediation from infinite substance to finite, determinate, singular modes.[33] In other words, Hegel's demand that Spinoza deduces his categories one from another is unjustified. This remark should be taken with the utmost earnestness and we should give it an even more affirmative meaning: *there is no ontological transition or logical mediation between the infinite and the finite.* In chapter 4, I propose an almost Heideggerian reading of the relationship between substance and its modifications, by which I mean the idea that substance only exists in the existence of its modifications. The infinite is something actual only as infinite-at-work. I believe this is a necessary thesis. For if we suppose that substance has an actual existence beyond its modifications, in other terms that substance actually exists, *but not in a determinate or defined way,* then what we propose is indeed a variant of classical onto-theological metaphysics, of the Aristotelian-Gadamerian conception of the principle of pure flowing-out. Heidegger would be right to criticize us for confusing the question of being (*Sein*) with the question of the perfect being, the being that lacks absolutely nothing and withdraws from everything and, on top of this, exists. Spinoza's ontological and other demonstrations of the existence of absolute substance would be rightfully discarded along with other metaphysical demonstrations.

In contrast to such a supposition, we should articulate the relationship between substance and its modifications not as a one-sided relationship of indifference, but as a relationship of identity-and-difference. Substance does not first exist in itself and differentiates itself only in the second place (even if this succession is purely logical and not temporal)—like Deleuze proposed. Rather, substance is to be conceived as always already modified. This is why Spinoza's demonstration a posteriori—according to which I cannot doubt the existence of substance if I do not doubt my own existence—should be understood as a thesis of the *factuality of existence* and not as proof of the anteriority of the principle of unity over any separation or difference.[34] This shows that Hegel's reading of Spinoza is not only fruitful for Hegelian philosophy proper, but also for Spinozism itself. The point is that we should take the self-determining character of absolute substance quite seriously. Even Macherey, who desperately tried to show that Hegel ascribed too much importance to the first definition of *Ethics*—the definition of *causa sui*—recognized this in the end. Moreover, he pointed out that while substance cannot be something determined in the sense of being limited or negated, it certainly is determined and can determine itself in the sense of actively transforming itself.

The second wave of criticism claims that while Hegel's paradigmatic concept of telos was an attempt to comprehend both continuity *and* rupture, both movement *and* its beginning or end, it is impossible to think both at the same time in Spinozism. You can only either take the position of the end results and dry appearances without any concept of tension or ongoing combat, without metonymical causality, or you can consider existence only as an existence-in-situation, where there is no result, no goal, no ending, and no metaphorical instance of causality to grasp the metonymical fluidity of existence and its situations in a crystallized form of a determinate being. As this may sound abstract, let me expand with the example of how a thought is articulated in a sentence. In this context, Hegelian critique claims that a Spinozist can only take one of these alternative positions: (1) he can either explain the sentence only from the point of view of the result and will thus remain blind to the instances of tension and surprise that are quite often at work in an actual process of enunciating a sentence (we are often surprised ourselves when we start speaking, thinking we are going to say one thing, but end up saying something completely different, perhaps something much bolder or much more decisive than what we actually expected of ourselves to say); or (2) he can explain the sentence only from the perspective of the immediate hermeneutical experience, where the sentence is always in the process of its enunciation and interpretation, as if it never truly ends but only stops being uttered with the pathetic openness of the three consecutive dots. In contrast, the Hegelian position cannot be thought without the "absolute punctuation mark." The fluidity of the sentence must reach the crystallized form, the definitive articulation. It has to let go and take the risk—the risk not only of being misinterpreted, but of being interpreted at all. This is the only way it can produce a true surprise: the definitive form of the sentence produces an excess, something more than what was intended.

One of the typical illustrations of the Hegelian demand to comprehend both the continuous process and a sudden rupture is the organic metamorphosis of a caterpillar into a butterfly. But let me give a perhaps somewhat mischievous "Oriental" example—the typical Japanese garden ornament that serves as an indispensable prop on the sets of many martial arts movies. The water is running down a wooden pipe and slowly fills a vessel with a weighted bottom. This vessel is not completely fixed, so when it has reached a certain level, the water outweighs the weighted bottom and the vessel turns over; the water pours out almost instantly.

However, as soon as the vessel is empty again, the weight of its bottom makes the vessel turn upright again to start the process all over. Moreover, with its upper end, the vessel hits the edge of the wooden pipe, making that characteristic, meditative, repetitive, Buddhist sound. This example is very illustrative insofar as it is an exchange of continuous flow and a sudden, abrupt event, but also because the sudden event, the turn of the vessel, is a logical result of the continuous process. However, all such illustrations share the same flaw—they can be misleading in their cyclical and organic nature. It may seem that the operation of the negation of negation reestablishes the original state of affairs *unchanged*. The point of course is, quite to the contrary, that the process or movement produces the turning point in an immanent fashion, and in return, the break establishes the process on a new foundation.

Hegel's criticism denies precisely that Spinozism is capable of such a turning point—it can perhaps explain the process, it can perhaps explain the result, but it can never explain the surprise and break that come with the result that is a necessary consequence of the process. Traditional Asian philosophies often promote the rejection of and liberation from the teleological world of desires, hopes, and fears, emphasizing the importance of the immediacy of the present moment. For Hegel, such immediacy and presence are indeed a desirable goal, but the point is that such immediacy can only be produced within the teleological process, as its own immanent product, as its inner surprise—and not by some withdrawal from it.

The shortest answer to this criticism is that Spinoza didn't overlook metaphorical causality or metonymical causality, but proposed the thesis that metonymical causality is expressed in the same way as metaphorical causality; or, to put it in Spinoza's terms: "In a word, in the same sense that God is said to be self-caused, he must also be said to be the cause of all things."[35] There is some sense in explaining Spinozism as a reductionism: there is no contradiction or competition between metaphorical and metonymical causality. This does not mean, however, that there is no difference between metaphorical and metonymical causality—if that were the case, Spinozism would indeed be reduced either to the pantheistic acosmism of mere metaphorical causality, or to a radical deterministic atheism of mere metonymical causality. It is true that causality is univocal. But this univocal causality involves a self-referential loop. The metonymical chain of causality is itself retorted in a metaphorical loop.

This is why I propose the "Heideggerian" reading of Spinoza, where infinity is understood as infinity-at-work and substance is in no way indifferent. Since the Hegelian concept of telos can be defended as the concept of the turning point that immanently turns the flow of the process, it makes sense to claim that, in Spinozism, to exist always implies the existence as the turning point. There is a popular saying, "We are the ones we have been waiting for." It expresses more than just the old practical wisdom that we are always the means of our redemption ourselves. My wager is that the point is rather that the event at the level of the universal substance (the event "we have been waiting for") is only possible as an affirmation of something utterly factual and almost absurdly concrete (ourselves, in this case). There are many Hegelian names for such a paradoxical unity of absolute universal substance and something completely determined and finite, something contingent. One of those names is the world-historical individual.[36] The point of this paradoxical concept that unites the universality of world history and the contingency of a concrete individual is not exhausted in the thesis that world history progresses at the expense of concrete individuals, sometimes even as a negation of their existence as human beings, as in the claim that Caesar had to die as a person in order to live as a necessary ideal, that is, as the idea of the empire (in German, as well as in many other languages, the word for the empire in general is derived from Caesar's contingent personal name: *Kaisertum*). Rather, the point is that world-historical events can only occur *as* an affirmation of some accidental concrete individuality, and not at their expense, not over their dead body, not as their "spiritual resurrection." To put it in more explicitly Spinozist terms: *universal substance can only produce itself as its own modification.* In Spinozism, to say that to exist means to exist as the turning point, is to say that the absolute substance is nothing beyond its modifications in which it produces and transforms itself.

We can elucidate the relationship between the process and the turning point, between the movement of universal substance and its inner negativity, which is the singular event of its transformation, by means of Althusser's train metaphor in order to distinguish between materialism and idealism. This is how the metaphor defines them: idealism gets on the train at the beginning and gets off at the last station. Materialism, however, is a "cowboy" attempt at jumping on the moving train.[37] This interesting illustration is misleading if it is meant to support the assumption that materialism typically uses the logic of always-already (in the sense that we are always already thrown on the train of existence; we never stepped on it and will never get off it), while idealism follows the logic of the turning point or the absolute break (in the sense that we are, firstly, created, then, secondly, we are, for a while, and then lastly, we are returned to eternity). The point is that jumping on the train still involves the event of the jump! And Althusser attempted to grasp both the logic of always-already *and* its transformation—just like Hegel did. Hegel's thesis that the original principle of philosophy is nothing but dialectics itself is in accordance with the image of jumping on the moving train, with regard to materialism. Did not Hegel claim precisely that affirming any kind of original principle is necessarily insufficient?

But if this is so—how do we separate Hegel from Spinoza? Their difference becomes clear again if we keep in mind that, for Hegel, proposing such principles throughout the history of philosophy was indeed inevitably fallacious and insufficient, but at the same time also productive. Hegelian dialectics is progressing precisely by boldly proposing these principles—which are never capable of expressing everything, or rather they always express a bit too much—and this is the real reason why it is possible to say that the only principle is dialectics itself, that is, the principle of the fallibility of the principle. In Spinozism, there is no such dialectics between the truth and the failed attempts to grasp it; an error can never be something that, of its own necessity, leads to the truth. It seems that Althusser was ambivalent on this question. On the one hand, his concept of symptomal reading is a Hegelian concept in that it assumes that science emerges within the ideological region, as a transformation of it. What he called *bévue* was not some accidental oversight on the part of classical economy, something that simply escaped its gaze, but was in an *essential* relationship with the scientific object of Marx's analysis. On the other hand, he claimed that an ideology can never produce scientific knowledge, can never lead to it, and is indeed organized precisely as a way to continue to be blind to it. The work of science is therefore on some awkward edge of ideology. But for Spinoza, an inadequate idea can never produce an adequate idea merely by its own affirmative power. *There is no logical relationship between the inadequate and the adequate idea.* A negation is always only a negation; there is no concept of productive negation. Moreover, one cannot override inadequate ideas by the mere presence of adequate ideas, precisely because the relationship between them is not of a logical order, but of the order of power. Adequate ideas can supersede inadequate ideas only when they produce more powerful effects.

The point of view of Spinozism is the point of view of the turning point. This is what is at stake with the famous point of view of eternity: it does not imply a perspective of some abstract and indeterminate panhistorical generality, just as it does not rely on the Gadamerian perspective of radical finality. Rather, it designates the perspective of substance in the event of its modification. If we apply this thought to the context of the Althusserian distinction between materialism and idealism, then Spinoza's materialism lies in the fact that he argued for a radical perspective of the *moment.* But not in the "Oriental" sense of the word, where the immediacy of the moment is always already there, and we must simply *withdraw* from the teleological or instrumental world of plans, hopes, and fears to *uncover* it beneath them. Rather, *to be* always implies the capability of the event or the turn. This is why, in the final analysis, Spinozism knows no dialectics between combat and result, between sentence and punctuation mark: the punctuation mark is *already at work.* This is why there is no temporal perspective: there is only the moment, the instance of the punctuation mark. In Spinoza, being is explained precisely as the fall of the punctuation mark; being *is* that fall; substance *is* its own torsion.

Notes

Foreword

1. Hegel, *TWA* 20:163–64.

2. Hegel, *TWA* 20:164.

3. Spinoza, *E*IIIP6, 283.

4. Spinoza, *E*IIIP4, 282.

5. Pierre Macherey, *Hegel or Spinoza*, trans. Susan B. Ruddick (Minneapolis: University of Minnesota Press, 2011).

Introduction

1. See Charles Taylor, *Hegel* (New York: Cambridge University Press, 1977), 16, 40–41.

2. Pierre Macherey, *Hegel or Spinoza*, trans. Susan B. Ruddick (Minneapolis: University of Minnesota Press, 2011), 195.

3. Klaus Düsing, "Von der Substanz zum Subjekt: Hegels spekulative Spinoza-Deutung," in *Spinoza und der Deutsche Idealismus*, ed. Manfred Walther (Würzburg: Königshausen und Neumann, 1992), 164.

4. Daniel Dahlstrom, "Moses Mendelssohn," in *The Stanford Encyclopedia of Philosophy, Spring 2011 Edition*, ed. E. N. Zalta, http://plato.stanford.edu/archives/spr2011/entries/mendelssohn/.

5. Hans-Georg Gadamer, in *Truth and Method*, trans. J. Weinsheimer and D. J. Marshall (London: Continuum, 2004), 273, reformulated this thesis slightly, writing that the Enlightenment was prejudiced against prejudices. Hegel himself insisted that while it is, of course, better to be led by your own judgment than to blindly follow an outside authority, this does not rid you of prejudices. In *Phenomenology of Spirit* he wrote: "The only difference between abiding by the authority of others or abiding by one's own convictions in a system of opinions and prejudices lies solely in the vanity inherent in the latter" (Georg Wilhelm Friedrich Hegel, *Phenomenology of Spirit*, trans. A. V. Miller [Oxford: Oxford University Press, 1977], 75).

6. Jacobi reports his conversations with Lessing in great detail. After reading what could be roughly understood as a Spinozist poem by Goethe that Jacobi showed to him, Lessing exclaimed that he subscribes to *hen kai pan* (One and All) and that he would not object to be called a Spinozist. Jacobi was startled,

he "blushed" and had "gone pale," for he expected a different result. The next day, Jacobi writes, they agreed on the paradigmatic example of Spinoza in philosophy. We find, phrased as a quote from Lessing, the basic formulation of what became a trademark Hegelian dictum. "[I:] In the main I had come to get help from you against Spinoza. Lessing: Oh, so you do know him? I: I think I know him as only very few can ever have known him. Lessing: Then there is no help for you. Become his friend all the way instead. There is no other philosophy than the philosophy of Spinoza. I: That might be true. For the determinist, if he wants to be consistent, must become a fatalist: the rest then follows by itself" (Friedrich Heinrich Jacobi, *The Main Philosophical Writings and the Novel "Allwill,"* trans. George di Giovanni [Montreal: McGill-Queen's University Press, 1994], 187).

7. See also Jean-Marie Vaysse, "Spinoza dans la problématique de l'idéalisme allemande," in *Spinoza au XIXe siècle,* ed. A. Tosel et al. (Paris: Publications de la Sorbonne, 2007), 65; Pierre-Henry Tavoillot, "Spinoza dans la querelle du panthéisme," in *Spinoza au XIXe siècle,* ed. A. Tosel et al. (Paris: Publications de la Sorbonne, 2007), 40.

8. Hegel, *TWA* 20:165. Hegel's alternative "entweder Spinozizmus oder keine Philosophie" is in essence very close to the alternative proposed by Jacobi (see also Adrian Johnston, *Adventures in Transcendental Materialism: Dialogues with Contemporary Thinkers* [Edinburgh: Edinburgh University Press, 2014], 34).

9. Georg Wilhelm Friedrich Hegel, *The Science of Logic,* trans. George di Giovanni (New York: Cambridge University Press, 2010), 60–61.

10. Ibid., 60.

11. Hegel, *TWA* 20:161.

12. Hegel, *TWA* 20:168: "Hätte Spinoza näher entwickelt, was in der *causa sui* liegt, so wäre seine Substanz nicht das Starre."

13. This specific way of reading philosophical texts, not taking them in as a collection of fixed statements but revealing their intrinsic dynamism, their implied, unexpressed potentiality, was an especially powerful influence on Heidegger's philosophy. The hermeneutical *structure of the question* of being is an especially important reference here, since it quite clearly states that the question itself is an integral part of being as such—which is what Heidegger underscored in the introduction to his *Being and Time* (Martin Heidegger, *Being and Time,* trans. J. Stambaugh [New York: State University of New York Press, 1996], 3–7). Moreover, Hegelian reading sets in motion all necessary aspects of Gadamerian hermeneutics, where reading is understood as religious reading, that is, as a re-reading (*re-legere*) which aims to resurrect "the dead trace of meaning" (Gadamer, *Truth and Method,* 156). And last but not least, we may cautiously suggest that there is a peculiar connection between such a notion of reading and the Althusserian concept of symptomal reading.

14. The full title of Žižek's book is *The Fragile Absolute; or, Why Is the Christian Legacy Worth Fighting For?* (New York: Verso, 2001).

15. See also Düsing, "Von der Substanz zum Subjekt," 163.

16. See Marcial Gueroult, *Spinoza I: Dieu (Ethique, I)* (Paris: Aubier-Montaigne, 1968), 223; Genevieve Lloyd, *Spinoza and the "Ethics"* (London: Routledge, 1996), 40. Negri claimed that Spinoza proposed a "strategy of constitu-

tion" against the "pantheistic utopia" (Antonio Negri, *The Savage Anomaly: The Power of Spinoza's Metaphysics and Politics,* trans. Michael Hardt [Minneapolis: University of Minnesota Press, 2000], 28–35).

17. Deleuze argued that Spinoza was fully aware that the method of mathematics is inappropriate when dealing with philosophical knowledge (Gilles Deleuze, *Expressionism in Philosophy: Spinoza,* trans. M. Joughin [New York: Zone Books, 1990], 20). Furthermore, in Deleuze's reading, the essences of the modes are not logical or mathematical structures but physical realities, *res physicae* (ibid., 192). And finally, Deleuze pointed out that the *notiones communes* (common notions) which in his judgment constituted the essential epistemological breakthrough of Spinoza's *Ethics* are to be understood as "biological, rather than physical or mathematical, ideas" (ibid., 278; see also Gilles Deleuze, *Spinoza: Practical Philosophy,* trans. R. Hurley [San Francisco: City Lights Books, 2003], 54–58). The question of Spinoza's method, *more geometrico* (or *ordine geometrico*), was explained by Macherey as a strictly anti-Cartesian concept of truth, a concept of truth that was in fact very close to Hegel's own. For both, even though they differ in what they attribute to thinking, "truth is an internal determination of thought, which excludes all relation to an exterior object" (Macherey, *Hegel or Spinoza,* 73). Lloyd warned that the sterile construction of the mathematical demonstration in Spinoza can be misleading, since the book is soaked with ironies and witty, even emotional remarks (Lloyd, *Spinoza and the "Ethics,"* 19–20).

18. Gueroult, *Spinoza I,* 41. See also Macherey, *Hegel or Spinoza,* 16.

19. Deleuze, *Expressionism in Philosophy,* 76.

20. Pierre Macherey, "Le Spinoza idéaliste de Hegel," in *Spinoza und der Deutsche Idealismus,* ed. Manfred Walther (Würzburg: Königshausen und Neumann, 1992), 149.

21. Jacobi uses the phrase in the correspondence with Mendelssohn, explaining his understanding of Spinoza: "This God therefore does not belong to any species of things; it is not a separate, individual, different, thing. Nor can any of the determinations that distinguish individual things pertain to it" (Jacobi, *Main Philosophical Writings,* 219). Further down, Jacobi quotes Spinoza's letter to Jelles from June 2, 1674, where Spinoza does in fact use the phrase "determination is negation" (Spinoza, *EPS* 50, 892). Jacobi comments: "Individual things therefore, so far as they only exist in a certain determinate mode, are *non-entia;* the indeterminate infinite being is the one single true *ens reale*" (Jacobi, *Main Philosophical Writings,* 220).

22. Hegel wrote: "Spinoza hat den großen Satz: Alle Bestimmung ist eine Negation. Das Bestimmte ist das Endliche" (Hegel, *TWA* 20:164). See also Düsing, "Von der Substanz zum Subjekt," 183.

23. Macherey, *Hegel or Spinoza,* 115.

24. See also Düsing, "Von der Substanz zum Subjekt," 169–71.

25. Deleuze, *Expressionism in Philosophy,* 171–74.

26. Spinoza, *TIE,* 9.

27. Spinoza, *TIE,* 244.

28. Hegel writes: "Meanwhile, if the fear of falling into error sets up a mistrust of Science, which in the absence of such scruples gets on with the work

itself, and actually cognizes something, it is hard to see why we should not turn round and mistrust this very mistrust. Should we not be concerned as to whether this fear of error is not just the error itself?" (Hegel, *Phenomenology of Spirit,* 47).

29. Tavoillot provided a much more measured formulation, writing that what was at stake for German Idealism in discussing Spinoza was not a faithful reconstruction of his system, but rather its philosophical value for their own time: "Savoir ce que Spinoza a vraiment dit importe alors moins que de savoir si ce qu'il a dit est vrai" (Tavoillot, "Spinoza dans la querelle du panthéisme," 36–37).

30. Throughout his oeuvre, Deleuze constantly refers to Duns Scotus and his concept of univocity of being; what is especially important in the context of Spinoza is that Deleuze argues that Scotus was the essential philosophical forerunner of Spinoza. See especially Deleuze, *Expressionism in Philosophy,* 58–67.

31. Macherey, *Hegel or Spinoza,* 75.

32. Louis Althusser, "From *Capital* to Marx's Philosophy," in *Reading "Capital,"* by Louis Althusser and Étienne Balibar, trans. Ben Brewster (London: New Left Books, 1970), 16.

33. Jacques Derrida, "A Time for Farewells: Heidegger (Read by) Hegel (Read by) Malabou," in *The Future of Hegel: Plasticity, Temporality and Dialectic,* by Catherine Malabou, trans. L. During (London: Routledge, 2005), xxvi.

34. Malabou, *Future of Hegel,* 3.

35. Hegel, *Phenomenology of Spirit,* 478.

36. Mladen Dolar, *Samozavedanje: Heglova Fenomenologija duha II* (Ljubljana: Društvo za teoretsko psihoanalizo, 1992), 9–10.

37. Ferdinand de Saussure, *Course in General Linguistics,* trans. W. Baskin (New York: McGraw-Hill, 1959), 117.

38. Jacques Derrida, *Of Grammatology,* trans. Gayatri Chakravorty Spivak (Baltimore: Johns Hopkins University Press, 1997), 44.

39. Adrian Johnston understands the category of the subject as one of the central antagonistic points in contemporary materialism: "I would go so far as to maintain that one of the primary antagonisms splitting materialism today from within is that between neo-Spinozist and neo-Hegelian tendencies, the former (incarnated by, for instance, Louis Althusser, Gilles Deleuze, and their various progeny) seeking to dissolve the figure of the subject and the latter (represented most notably by Žižek and Slovene Lacanianism) to preserve it" (Johnston, *Transcendental Materialism,* 20).

40. Mladen Dolar, "Beyond Interpellation," *Qui Parle* 6, no. 2 (1993):78.

41. Slavoj Žižek, *The Sublime Object of Ideology* (New York: Verso, 2008), 43.

Chapter 1

1. Boethius, *Consolation of Philosophy,* trans. Joel C. Relihan (Indianapolis, Ind.: Hackett, 2001), 44.

2. Jacques Lacan, *The Seminar of Jacques Lacan: On Feminine Sexuality: The Limits of Love and Knowledge, Book XX, Encore, 1972–1973,* ed. Jacques-Alain Miller, trans. Bruce Fink (New York: Norton, 1999), 94.

3. Hegel, *Science of Logic*, 59.

4. Ibid., 60.

5. Ibid.

6. Let me add that what may appear as merely a formal, accidental proximity between two concepts in two completely different philosophical projects—one from Hegel's logic, the other from Althusser's epistemology—nevertheless shares not only the formal structure, but to some extent even what is at stake. The concept of symptomal reading was a tool that Althusser developed in order to explain Marx's critique of the classics of political economy like Ricardo and Smith; its central point was that Marx did not add a positive, affirmative content to what the classics already said, nor did he separate valid points from the invalid. For Althusser, what Marx did was something altogether different: namely, Marx read classics with those very classics themselves and thus revealed in their text what their text was saying inexplicitly. The claim here is that this is basically how Hegel reads Spinoza (and all "identity systems"): by demonstrating that the Spinozist system produces its own truth in spite of itself. But what do Hegel's identity systems have *internally* in common with the classics of political economy? Is this not simply a case of structural or formal correspondence? One must, first of all, remember that what Althusser called "theoretical ideology" is not confined solely to the classics of political economy, but in fact describes every philosophy, and even the spontaneous philosophy of scientists, and in general every discourse which organizes itself in order to cover its own presuppositions. Althusser's term for this ideological procedure is to give answers without questions, that is, to produce correct answers which, however, do not correspond to any of the explicit questions of that theory. In his brilliant analysis, Robert Pfaller compares such answers without questions to the infamous Freudian concept of negation (*die Verneinung*): a patient does not know who the person in his dream is, but he claims she is "not his mother," which allows Freud to conclude that it is perhaps precisely the patient's mother (Robert Pfaller, *Althusser—Das Schweigen im Text: Epistemologie, Psychoanalyse und Nominalismus in Louis Althussers Theorie der Lektüre* [Paderborn: W. Fink Verlag, 1997], 54). This allows us to finally come back to Hegel's *Science of Logic*: the thesis is that Hegel understands the principle of Eleatic philosophy precisely as a kind of an answer without a question. In order to understand the Hegelian philosophical position, one must imagine Parmenides comfortably stretched on a couch, affirming that "being is the same as thinking . . ." We will come back to this point especially in chapter 5.

7. Hegel, *Science of Logic*, 60.

8. Dieter Henrich, *Hegel im Kontext* (Frankfurt am Main: Suhrkamp, 1971), 76.

9. Hegel, *Science of Logic*, 46.

10. Hegel, *Phenomenology of Spirit*, 47.

11. Spinoza, *TIE*, 10.

12. Louis Althusser, *Essays in Self-Criticism*, trans. Grahame Lock (New York: New Left Books, 1976), 188.

13. Hegel, *Science of Logic*, 46.

14. Ibid., 46–47.

15. Ibid., 47.

16. Stephen Houlgate, *The Opening of Hegel's Logic: From Being to Infinity* (West Lafayette, Ind.: Purdue University Press, 2005), 67.

17. Ibid., 60.

18. Houlgate is completely correct in writing: "At the start of philosophy, all we have is sheer immediacy—in the *Phenomenology*, the immediacy of sense-certainty, and in the *Logic*, the immediacy of pure being" (Houlgate, *Opening of Hegel's Logic*, 59). However—as I hope to demonstrate—it is quite problematic to interpret this immediacy of the beginning in terms of a radical "openness," even if only a hermeneutic one, as Houlgate does. It seems that Houlgate's wager on openness has found its way into the very title of his book, so it is clearly not a small matter. What is at stake for Hegel in the beginning is not simply the "free your mind" approach to the matter at hand, which is how Houlgate could be misread. What is at stake in the concept of the beginning is the acceptance of the most profound contradiction, one that runs contrary not only to Parmenides, but also to Aristotle and his principle of non-contradiction: the concept of beginning is a coincidence of "is already" and "is not yet."

19. Hegel, *Science of Logic*, 47.

20. Ibid.

21. Ibid., 65.

22. Aristotle, *Physics*, VI.5, 236a7–236b18.

23. I think Hegel's reference to Aristotle's paradox of the beginning point of change is very clear in the following passage: "But further, that which begins already *is*, but *is* also just as much *not* yet. The opposites, being and non-being, are therefore in immediate union in it; or the beginning is their *undifferentiated unity*" (Hegel, *Science of Logic*, 51). What is paradoxical for Aristotle, the position between "already is" and "is not yet," is the proper formulation of Hegel's concept of the beginning.

24. Hegel, *Science of Logic*, 51.

25. Ibid., 52.

26. Henrich, *Hegel im Kontext*, 77–79.

27. Ibid., 80.

28. While this is not the place for a polemic on this count, we must nevertheless write that the famous final proclamation of Marx from his "*Theses on Feuerbach*," namely that "philosophers have only *interpreted* the world, in various ways; the point, however, is to *change* it," hardly does him any honor (Karl Marx, "Theses on Feuerbach," in *Ludwig Feuerbach and the End of Classical German Philosophy*, by Frederick Engels [Peking: Foreign Languages, 1976], 65).

29. Gadamer, *Truth and Method*, 156.

30. Louis Althusser, *For Marx*, trans. Ben Brewster (New York: Verso, 2005), 183.

31. Mladen Dolar, *Heglova Fenomenologija duha I* (Ljubljana: Društvo za teoretsko psihoanalizo, 1990), 22.

32. Henrich, *Hegel im Kontext*, 80 (*explizieren*); 85 (*in den Blick . . . gebracht werden*); 88 (*Beweis . . . geben*); 93 (*Begründung*).

33. Andrew Cole, *The Birth of Theory* (Chicago: University of Chicago Press, 2014), 9.

34. Ibid.

35. More on Hegel's relation to Plotinus in the historical in chapter 2.

36. We will come back to the problematic of boundaries in Hegel and Aristotle in chapter 3.

37. Hegel, *Science of Logic*, 13.

38. Hegel, *Phenomenology of Spirit*, 12.

Chapter 2

1. It is probably impossible to use the word "Orient" today without at least writing a note about it. If we carry the views of the early nineteenth-century European philosopher over to the present time unmediated, without any reflection, we get a collection of quasi-intellectual racisms and shocking ethnocentrisms. However, we choose an even worse possibility if we speak from a distance and take the role of an enlightened and understanding reader who benevolently forgives the old their blunders, either correcting their philosophy according to the taste of our time or merely holding our noses shut before the worst of it, choosing to rather direct our gaze to their "relevant" theses. We thus have before us a hermeneutical contradiction *par excellence.* I propose a literal reading, a reading of Hegel with Hegel: how the concept of the Orient functions in its historical-philosophical totality. We shall simply try to see how Hegel's concept of the Orient—without an explicit analysis of how it does or does not relate to Asia, Asian philosophy, or Asian history—functions in Hegel's text.

2. Georg Wilhelm Friedrich Hegel, *Lectures on the History of Philosophy, Vol. 1,* trans. E. S. Haldane (London: Kegan Paul, 1892), 97–98; Hegel, *TWA* 18:119–20.

3. Hegel, *History of Philosophy, Vol. 1,* 117; Hegel, *TWA* 18:138.

4. Generally speaking, Roman antiquity more or less merely preserved Greek culture, while the non-German Christian nations of Europe formed only through the German ones (Hegel, *History of Philosophy, Vol. 1,* 101, 109).

5. Hegel, *History of Philosophy, Vol. 1,* 115–16.

6. Ibid., xvi.

7. Hegel, *Phenomenology of Spirit,* 22.

8. Hegel, *History of Philosophy, Vol. 1,* 116.

9. Hegel writes: "The whole of the history of Philosophy is a progression impelled by an inherent necessity . . . Contingency must vanish on the appearance of Philosophy. Its history is just as absolutely determined as the development of Notions, and the impelling force is the inner dialectic of the forms" (Hegel, *History of Philosophy, Vol. 1,* 36–37).

10. Hegel, *History of Philosophy, Vol. 1,* 40.

11. Hegel, *History of Philosophy, Vol. 1,* 97. He makes the same point in *The Science of Logic*: "With this totally abstract purity of continuity, that is, with this indeterminateness and emptiness of representation, it is indifferent whether

one names this abstraction 'space' or 'pure intuition' or 'pure thought.' It is altogether the same as what an Indian calls Brahma, when for years on end, looking only at the tip of his nose, externally motionless and equally unmoved in sensation, representation, phantasy, desire, and so on, he inwardly says only *Om, Om, Om,* or else says nothing at all. This dull, empty consciousness, taken as consciousness, is just this—*being*" (Hegel, *Science of Logic,* 73).

12. When Derrida explained Hegel's conception of the negation of negation on the basis of his concept of kenosis as *mors mortis,* he pointed out that there is always more than one farewell in a farewell, that a farewell is in a special sense always already a farewell to farewell (Derrida, "A Time for Farewells," xliii).

13. Hegel, *History of Philosophy, Vol. 1,* 240.

14. Jan Kott, *The Eating of the Gods* (Evanston, Ill.: Northwestern University Press, 1987).

15. Hegel, *History of Philosophy, Vol. 1,* 254. The translation is corrected in the last sentence to follow the original: "Dieser Anfang ist freilich noch trübe und unbestimmt; es ist nicht weiterzuerklären, was darin liegt; aber gerade dies Erklären ist die Ausbildung der Philosophie selbst, die hier noch nicht vorhanden ist" (Hegel, *TWA* 18:290). The English translator Haldane, perhaps baffled by Hegel's almost paradoxical treatment of Parmenides, assumes Hegel must still be praising Parmenides: "but to take up this position certainly is to develop Philosophy proper, which has not hitherto existed."

16. Hegel, *History of Philosophy, Vol. 1,* 278–79.

17. Ibid., 261.

18. Ibid., 279.

19. Ibid., 252.

20. Ibid.

21. Yitzhak Y. Melamed, "'Omnis Determinatio Est Negatio': Determination, Negation, and Self-Negation in Spinoza, Kant, and Hegel," in *Spinoza and German Idealism,* ed. Eckart Förster and Yitzhak Y. Melamed (Cambridge: Cambridge University Press, 2012), 177–84.

22. Aristotle, *Physics,* III.2, 202a1–2, trans. Hussay.

23. Aristotle writes (*Physics,* III.2, 202a6–8): "For to operate on this, *qua* such, is just what it is to produce change, and this it does by contact, so that it will at the same time also be acted upon."

24. Aristotle writes (*Physics,* VIII.7, 261a13–14, trans. Graham): "In general, it appears that what comes to be is incomplete and proceeds to a principle, so that what is posterior in order of generation is prior in nature."

25. This example only makes sense if we presuppose that the sequence is not related to what we can call "metonymic causality," the chain of causes and effects, in which one thing follows another in an arbitrary order, like billiard balls hitting one another. There are innumerable such chains which intertwine and take place simultaneously. The causality at stake for Aristotle here is a metaphorical causality and the question under consideration is that of causality as an ontological-causal power or fullness.

26. Deleuze, *Expressionism in Philosophy,* 169.

27. Monophysites would, of course, have a very different perspective on

the problem of incarnation, but we restrict ourselves in this account only to the most widely accepted, dyophysitic doctrine.

28. Plotinus, *The Enneads*, trans. Stephen MacKenna and B. S. Page (New York: Larson Publications, 1992), 450.

29. Ibid., 452.

30. Ibid., 425.

31. Ibid., 450.

32. See Georg Wilhelm Friedrich Hegel, *History of Philosophy, Vol. 2*, trans. E. S. Haldane and Frances H. Simson (London: Kegan Paul, 1894), 429, 413, 415.

33. Ibid., 416.

34. Ibid., 418.

35. Ibid., 421.

36. Barbara Cassin, *L'Effet sophistique* (Paris: Gallimard, 1995), 13.

37. Ibid., 27–28.

38. *Institutio oratoria*, XII, 3, 12; Quintilian, *The Orator's Education, Volume V: Books 11–12*, ed. and trans. Donald A. Russell (Cambridge, Mass.: Harvard University Press, 2002), 245.

39. Cassin, *L'Effet sophistique*, 18.

40. Ibid., 20.

41. Deleuze, *Expressionism in Philosophy*, 177.

42. Ibid., 171.

43. Spinoza, *E*IP17, 227.

44. Deleuze writes: "A cause is immanent . . . when its effect is 'immanate' in the cause, rather than emanating from it" (Deleuze, *Expressionism in Philosophy*, 172).

45. Ibid., 173.

46. Spinoza, *E*IIP10, 249.

47. See also Spinoza, *E*IIP11Cor, 250: "Hence it follows that the human mind is part of the infinite intellect of God; and therefore when we say that the human mind perceives this or that, we are saying nothing else but this: that God—not insofar as he is infinite but insofar as he is explicated through the nature of the human mind, that is, insofar as he constitutes the essence of the human mind—has this or that idea." Negri commented on these words quite unreservedly: "God lives the singularity" (Negri, *The Savage Anomaly*, 65). A bit further on, in his commentary on a problematic point in Spinoza's letter to Ludwig Meyer, in which Spinoza writes that substance exists quite differently compared to the mode, whence the difference between eternity and duration, Negri argued that such a distinction between substance and mode is merely a sign of a deep crisis in Spinoza's thought and rejected emanativism (Negri, *The Savage Anomaly*, 75–77).

48. On the question of participation in immanent causality, Deleuze writes: "Participation must be thought of in a completely positive way, not on the basis of an eminent gift, but on the basis of a formal community that allows the distinction of essences to subsist" (Deleuze, *Expressionism in Philosophy*, 174).

49. Spinoza, *E*IP25Sch, 232.

Chapter 3

1. Macherey, *Hegel or Spinoza*, 24.

2. See especially the section "*Limitation Precedes Transcendence*," in Žižek, *Tarrying with the Negative*, 35–39.

3. Žižek, *Tarrying with the Negative*, 38.

4. In *Tarrying with the Negative*, Žižek repeatedly uses the term "slime" to denote the formlessness of a substance, its lack of ontological consistency (Žižek, *Tarrying with the Negative*, 61, 186, 258).

5. See Alain Badiou, *Saint Paul: The Foundation of Universalism*, trans. Ray Brassier (Stanford, Calif.: Stanford University Press, 1997).

6. Gadamer, *Truth and Method*, 426.

7. See Žižek, *Tarrying with the Negative*, 80; Slavoj Žižek, *The Parallax View* (Cambridge, Mass.: MIT Press, 2006), 51–52.

8. Althusser, *For Marx*, 113.

9. Friedrich Nietzsche, *On the Genealogy of Morality*, trans. Carol Diethe (Cambridge: Cambridge University Press, 2006), 39.

10. Heidegger, *Being and Time*, 262.

11. Žižek, *Tarrying with the Negative*, 159.

12. But perhaps we can find an even better example where Žižek explains the Lacanian concept of castration as a circularity or loop of the subject: "Subjectivity thus involves a kind of loop, a vicious circle, an economical paradox which can be rendered in multiple ways, Hegel's, Wagner's, Lacan's. Lacan: castration means that the Thing-jouissance must be lost in order to be regained in the order of desire, i.e. the symbolic order recovers its own constitutive debt; Wagner in Parsifal: the wound is healed only by the spear that smote you; Hegel: the immediate identity of the substance must be lost in order to be regained through the work of subjective mediation" (Žižek, *Tarrying with the Negative*, 171). However, Žižek's predominant image of negativity is the gap. In the introduction to *The Parallax View*, he describes Spinoza's personal position as the eminently philosophical position, as a position of someone who was an outcast among outcasts and therefore occupied a position of the parallax (Žižek, *The Parallax View*, 8). But even more revealing is his explanation of the Christian concept of love as an introduction of a hole in the order of being through ethical violence: "Christian love is a violent passion to introduce a Difference, a gap in the order of Being, to privilege and elevate some object at the expense of others" (Žižek, *The Parallax View*, 282).

13. Spinoza, *E*IApp, 238–39.

14. Spinoza writes: "For example, those who have more often regarded with admiration the stature of men will understand by the word 'man' an animal of upright stature, while those who are wont to regard a different aspect will form a different common image of man, such as that man is a laughing animal, a featherless biped, or a rational animal. Similarly, with regard to other aspects, each will form universal images according to the conditioning of his body" (*E*IIP40Sch, 267). See also the chapter on prophets in his *Theological-Political Treatise*, where Spinoza declares that God reveals information to his prophets in a manner ac-

cording to their understanding, with images of oxen to a countryman and of armies to a soldier (*TTP*, 407). The underlying idea here is the same as in the *Ethics*: experience and habit shape abstract concepts in an accidental fashion.

15. Louis Althusser, *Lenin and Philosophy and Other Essays*, trans. Ben Brewster (New York: Monthly Review, 1971), 176.

16. As an aside let me note that it is precisely the relationship between the born and the unborn that is to my mind the most useful in explaining the somewhat obscure Heideggerian conceptual pair *Ereignis–Enteignis*, sometimes translated as appropriation–expropriation. For the purposes here, however, it is important to note that *Ereignis* can also simply mean an event, while the word *Enteignis* is Heidegger's invention and implies something that we could call the un-eventing of the event itself, its withdrawal. The birth is, of course, the happy event, *freudiges Ereignis*, but the event of the birth itself includes a withdrawal of the unborn, the *Enteignis*.

17. Spinoza, *E*IApp, 240.

18. Martin Heidegger, *Poetry, Language, Thought*, trans. A. Hofstadter (New York: Harper and Row, 1971), 144.

19. Heidegger writes: "Certainly for centuries we have acted as though the doctrine of the four causes had fallen from heaven as a truth as clear as daylight" (Martin Heidegger, *The Question Concerning Technology and Other Essays*, trans. W. Lovitt [New York: Garland, 1977], 6).

20. Ibid., 7.

21. Ibid., 8.

22. Almost everything we know about Zeno's paradoxes is from Aristotle's discussion in *Physics*.

23. Auguste Rodin, "Movement in Art," in *Rodin on Art and Artists: Conversations with Paul Gsell* (New York: Dover, 2009), 32–36.

24. Franz Brentano, *Philosophical Investigations on Space, Time, and the Continuum*, trans. Barry Smith (New York: Routledge, 1988), 8.

25. Ibid.

26. Ibid., 15.

27. Brentano writes: "However, a more careful investigation shows . . . that every boundary, because it exists only in the context of the continuum to which it belongs as boundary, must itself show up differences in reflection of differences in this continuum" (Brentano, *Philosophical Investigations*, 18).

28. Brentano does not speak explicitly about Zeno here, but he writes as if in answer to the paradox: "And thus also too, a body is not at a place with the same perfection or completeness when it is passing through it slowly or quickly as when it is at rest" (Brentano, *Philosophical Investigations*, 18).

29. Malabou, *Future of Hegel*, 163, 188.

30. Hegel, *History of Philosophy, Vol. I*, 22–23; translation modified.

31. Georg Wilhelm Friedrich Hegel, *Hegel's Philosophy of Nature: Vol. III*, trans. M. J. Petry (London: Unwin, 1970). The translation provided in the quote is modified to reflect the original; it seems that the English-language publishers, cautious as ever not to hurt the gentler souls among us, violently domesticated the harsh language of our author. See also Hegel, *TWA* 9: 538.

32. Malabou, *Future of Hegel,* 166.

33. Hegel, *Phenomenology of Spirit,* 56–57.

34. Slavoj Žižek, "Materializem in neskončnost," public lecture, Knjižnica Otona Župančiča, Ljubljana, 2007.

Chapter 4

1. Stephen Nadler, *Spinoza: A Life* (New York: Cambridge University Press, 1999), 32–37.

2. Ibid., 126.

3. Hegel, *TWA* 20:157–58: "Den Dualismus, der im Cartesischen System vorhanden ist, hob Benedikt Spinoza vollends auf, – als ein Jude. Diese tiefe Einheit seiner Philosophie . . . ist ein Nachklang des Morgenlandes."

4. Hegel, *Science of Logic,* 69.

5. Georg Wilhelm Friedrich Hegel, *Lectures on the History of Philosophy, Vol. 3,* trans. Elisabeth S. Haldane and Frances H. Simson (London: Kegan Paul, 1896), 254; see also 258–59.

6. Phil. 2:5–8 (New English Translation).

7. Georg Wilhelm Friedrich Hegel, *Faith and Knowledge,* trans. Walter Cerf and H. S. Harris (Albany: State University of New York Press, 1977), 190.

8. Luther translated the phrase "emptied himself" as *entäusserte sich selbst,* which is the only occurrence of the verb *entäussern* in his Bible (available online). In *Phenomenology of Spirit,* the term is used very often by Hegel, specifically to explain the incarnation of God in Christ, but also, and more importantly, as the power of the concept to make its way in reality (*sich verwirklichen*). Unsurprisingly, one of the clearest paragraphs is the one from the section on the beautiful soul: "It lacks the power to externalize itself [*Es fehlt ihm die Kraft der Entäußerung*], the power to make itself into a Thing, and to endure mere being [*das Sein zu ertragen*]" (Hegel, *Phenomenology of Spirit,* 399–400; Hegel, *TWA* 3:483). It is clear that for Hegel, conceptually speaking, God is nothing but a "beautiful concept" without the power to endure mere being, without making itself into a concrete being, a thing. For a discussion of the usage of the term *Entäusserung* in Feuerbach and Marx, see Andrew Chitty, "Hegel and Marx," in *A Companion to Hegel,* ed. Stephen Houlgate and Michael Baur (Oxford: Blackwell, 2011), 490–91.

9. Catherine Malabou took on herself the task of detailed argumentation against Hegel's theological critics; see especially the chapter "God without Transcendence? The Theologians contra Hegel," in Malabou, *Future of Hegel,* 91–102.

10. Malabou's defense of Hegel's reading of the concept of nous in Aristotle's *De Anima* is in principle the same as her argument against theologians who would accuse Hegel of inscribing passivity in God. For her, this is the question of what she calls "noetic plasticity," and not the passivity of nous (Malabou, *Future of Hegel,* 40–45).

11. See also Malabou, *Future of Hegel,* 56–60; Žižek, *Tarrying with the Negative,* 80.

12. Žižek renders the farthest consequences of a Hegelian reading of kenosis thusly: "Christianity . . . enacts the reflexive reversal of atheist doubt into God himself. In his 'Father, why have you forsaken me?,' Christ himself commits what is for a Christian the ultimate sin: he wavers in his Faith. While, in all other religions, there are people who do not believe in God, only in Christianity does God not believe in himself" (Slavoj Žižek, "The Fear of Four Words: A Modest Plea for the Hegelian Reading of Christianity," in *The Monstrosity of Christ: Paradox or Dialectic?* ed. Creston Davies [Cambridge, Mass.: MIT Press, 2009], 48–49).

13. See also Malabou, *Future of Hegel,* 107.

14. Gadamer, *Truth and Method,* 423.

15. Again, it may appear outlandish to readers not knowledgeable about Christianity or the philosophy of religion to talk about sexuality on the level of the utmost metaphysical conceptions of God. It may therefore be prudent to point out that the differences between Lutherans and Catholics do not only pertain to speculations on the nature of God, but also to completely practical matters of sexuality and gender with regard to priests. It is precisely because the Catholic doctrine is so profoundly Aristotelian, insisting on understanding the activity of the prime mover as a purely masculine affair, that it cannot accept that a woman could serve as a priest, or that priests could marry.

16. Malabou, *Future of Hegel,* 105.

17. Luther comments on Saint Paul's epistle to Galatians (specifically to 2:19): "Against my death I set another death, or rather life, my life in Christ. . . . For this reason was He made the law of the Law, the sin of sin, the death of death" (Martin Luther, *Commentary on the Epistle to Galatians* [Grand Rapids, Mich.: Zondervan Publishing House, 1949], 68–85).

18. Hegel, *Faith and Knowledge,* 190–91.

19. Malabou, *Future of Hegel,* 103.

20. Alenka Zupančič, *The Odd One In: On Comedy* (Cambridge, Mass.: MIT Press, 2008), 29.

21. Ibid., 27.

22. Ibid., 42–60.

23. Robert Pfaller, "The Familiar Unknown, the Uncanny, the Comic," in *Lacan: The Silent Partners,* ed. Slavoj Žižek (New York: Verso, 2006), 204.

24. *Libeled Lady* (directed by Jack Conway in 1936), for instance. See Pfaller, "The Familiar Unknown," 204.

25. Zupančič, *Odd One In,* 32.

26. Zupančič writes: "Incarnation is comedy, and comedy always involves incarnation" (*Odd One In,* 45).

27. Spinoza, *E*IVP67, 355.

28. Spinoza, *E*IIIP4, 282. This proposition has no special proof as it is supposedly quite self-evident.

29. Spinoza, *E*IIIP8–10, 283–84.

30. Spinoza writes: "The conatus with which each thing endeavors to persist in its own being is nothing but the actual essence of the thing itself" (Spinoza, *E*IIIP7, 283).

31. Spinoza, *E*IVP20Sch, 332.

32. Spinoza writes: "I shall understand by pleasure 'the passive transition of the mind to a state of greater perfection,' and by pain 'the passive transition of the mind to a state of less perfection'" (*E*IIIP11Sch, 285).

33. For a concise explanation of these relations, see Deleuze, *Spinoza: Practical Philosophy*, 48–51.

34. Spinoza, *E*IIP40Sch2, 267.

35. Spinoza, *TIE*, 7.

36. Spinoza, *E*IIP35, 264.

37. Spinoza, *E*IVP64, 354.

38. This is how Deleuze, for example, generally construed it; see Deleuze, *Spinoza: Practical Philosophy*, 71–73.

39. Spinoza, *E*IVDefI–II, 322.

40. Lloyd, *Spinoza and the "Ethics,"* 72.

41. Deleuze, *Expressionism in Philosophy*, 147.

42. Spinoza, *E*IIIIntro, 278.

43. Lorenzo Vinciguerra, *Spinoza et le signe: La genèse de l'imagination* (Paris: Vrin, 2005), 8.

44. Lloyd, *Spinoza and the "Ethics,"* 58–60.

45. See Spinoza, *E*IVP14, 328–29.

46. Negri, *Savage Anomaly*, 87–97. See also Lloyd, *Spinoza and the "Ethics,"* 63.

47. Althusser writes: "It is not their real conditions of existence, their real world, that 'men' 'represent to themselves' in ideology, but above all it is their relation to those conditions of existence which is represented to them there" (*Lenin and Philosophy*, 164).

48. Althusser, *Lenin and Philosophy*, 165.

49. Heidegger, *Being and Time*, 6 (footnote), 435.

50. Hegel, *History of Philosophy, Vol. 3*, 258.

51. Knox Peden, *Spinoza contra Phenomenology: French Rationalism from Cavaillès to Deleuze* (Stanford, Calif.: Stanford University Press, 2014), 144.

52. Negri, *Savage Anomaly*, 157.

53. Macherey, *Hegel or Spinoza*, 142.

54. Ibid., 143.

55. Spinoza, *E*IDefVII, 217. See also Macherey, *Hegel or Spinoza*, 144–45.

56. Macherey, *Hegel or Spinoza*, 91.

Chapter 5

1. Aaron Schuster, *The Trouble with Pleasure: Deleuze and Psychoanalysis* (Cambridge, Mass.: MIT Press, 2015), 38–44.

2. Althusser, *Lenin and Philosophy*, 165.

3. Louis Althusser, *Solitude de Machiavel* (Paris: Presses Universitaires de France, 1998), 184. See also Louis Althusser, "The Only Materialist Tradition, Part I: Spinoza," in *The New Spinoza*, ed. Warren Montag and Ted Stolze (Minneapolis: University of Minnesota Press, 1998), 9.

4. This is, of course, a paraphrase of the famous Proposition 7 in Part II of

the *Ethics*: "The order and connection of ideas is the same as the order and connection of things" (Spinoza, *E*IIP7, 247).

5. Blaise Pascal, *"Pensées" and Other Writings*, trans. Honor Levi (Oxford: Oxford University Press, 1995), 156.

6. Althusser, *Lenin and Philosophy*, 168.

7. Spinoza writes: "So from the fact that the power of natural things by which they exist and act is the very power of God, we can readily understand what is the right of Nature. Since God has right over all things, and God's right is nothing other than God's power insofar as that is considered as absolutely free, it follows that every natural thing has as much right from Nature as it has power to exist and to act. For the power of every natural thing by which it exists and acts is nothing other than the power of God, which is absolutely free" (Spinoza, *TP*, 683).

8. Althusser, *For Marx*, 167.

9. Althusser, "From *Capital* to Marx's Philosophy," 43.

10. Althusser, *Lenin and Philosophy*, 169.

11. Pfaller writes: "Theoretische Ideologien hängen immer von praktischen Ideologien ab (so gibt es beispielsweise keine Theologie ohne religiöse Kultformen); praktische Ideologien hingegen können selbständig existieren, sie bedürfen nicht immer einer 'theoretisierenden' Ergänzung" (Pfaller, *Althusser—Das Schweigen im Text*, 93).

12. Althusser writes: "By what right do you tell us that practice is right? says idealism to pragmatism. Your right is no more than a disguised fact, answers pragmatism. And we are back on the wheel, the closed circle of the ideological question" (Althusser, "From *Capital* to Marx's Philosophy," 57). In his writings on Machiavelli, Althusser commented on Spinoza's famous dictum "*habemus enim ideam veram*" ("for we do possess a true idea"), explaining it as a refutation of the cognitive-theoretical question on the *justification* of knowledge, since it is subordinated to the *fact* of knowledge. But the priority of knowledge over its justification has to be understood in the context of the thesis that knowledge is its own standard ("*index sui*"), in the context of the thesis about the intrinsic character of its criterion of reality. The fact of knowledge has priority only in the sense that it needs no *external* justification, unlike in pragmatism and idealism (Althusser, *Solitude de Machiavel*, 218).

13. Louis Althusser, *Philosophy and the Spontaneous Philosophy of Scientists & Other Essays*, trans. James H. Kavanagh (New York: Verso, 1990), 83.

14. Althusser, "From *Capital* to Marx's Philosophy," 58.

15. Ibid., 62.

16. The link between appropriation and conceptual grasping was made by Althusser himself. He wrote: "This clearly indicates that knowledge is concerned with the real world through its specific mode of appropriation of the real world: this poses precisely the problem of the way this function works, and therefore *of the mechanism* that ensures it: this function of the appropriation of the real world by knowledge, i.e., by the process of production of knowledges which, *despite*, or rather *because* of the fact that it takes place *entirely in thought* (in the sense we have defined), nevertheless provides that grasp (of the concept: *Begriff*) on the *real*

world called its appropriation (*Aneignung*)" (Althusser, "From *Capital* to Marx's Philosophy," 54).

17. See Althusser, *Solitude de Machiavel*, 188. In another account, Althusser understood his own addition to "Spinoza's theory of ideology" as limited to his placing, at its center, not individual subjectivity, but rather the conflictual social subjectivity of the class struggle (Althusser, "The Only Materialist Tradition," 7).

18. Hegel's exact terms are "identity of identity and non-identity" (Hegel, *Science of Logic*, 51).

19. Althusser, *Lenin and Philosophy*, 161.

20. Ibid., 170.

21. Althusser, "From *Capital* to Marx's Philosophy," 41–42.

22. See Slavoj Žižek, "Class Struggle or Postmodernism? Yes, Please!" in *Contingency, Hegemony, Universality: Contemporary Dialogues on the Left*, by Judith Butler, Ernesto Laclau, and Slavoj Žižek (London: Verso, 2000), 90–135; and Mladen Dolar, "Beyond Interpellation," 75–96.

23. Althusser, "From *Capital* to Marx's Philosophy," 18–19.

24. See Warren Montag, "Spinoza and Althusser against Hermeneutics: Interpretation or Intervention?" in *The Althusserian Legacy*, ed. E. Ann Kaplan and Michael Sprinker (New York: Verso, 1993), 51–58.

25. Robert Pfaller brilliantly elaborates on this point in his book on Althusser (*Althusser—Das Schweigen im Text*, 68).

26. Louis Althusser, *Philosophy of the Encounter: Later Writings 1978–87*, ed. Francois Matheron and Oliver Corpet, trans. G. M. Goshgarian (New York: Verso, 2006), 174.

27. Ibid., 168.

28. Ibid.

29. Ibid.

30. Ibid., 169.

31. Ibid., 175.

32. Ibid.

33. One is forced here to remember what Hegel, in one of those not particularly humble moments, declared about his own *Science of Logic*, namely that it is "*the exposition of God as he is in his eternal essence before the creation of nature and of a finite spirit*" (Hegel, *Science of Logic*, 29).

34. In this context, Althusser recalled Wittgenstein's thought that "die Welt ist alles was der Fall ist" (Althusser, *Philosophy of the Encounter*, 190, 265).

35. I must refer the reader to an excellent short essay by Heinrich von Kleist, in which he gave extremely interesting examples of such surprises that arise at the moment of utterance (Heinrich von Kleist, "On the Gradual Production of Thoughts Whilst Speaking," in *Selected Writings*, ed. and trans. David Constantine [Indianapolis, Ind.: Hackett, 1997], 405–9).

36. Althusser, *Philosophy of the Encounter*, 198.

37. Ibid., 169.

38. Ibid., 174.

Conclusion

1. Benjamin Noys, *The Persistence of the Negative: A Critique of Contemporary Continental Theory* (Edinburgh: Edinburgh University Press, 2010), 15.

2. "But modern thought is born of the failure of representation, of the loss of identities, and of the discovery of all the forces that act under the representation of the identical." Gilles Deleuze, *Difference and Repetition*, trans. P. Patton (New York: Columbia University Press, 2005), xix.

3. Heidegger, *Being and Time*, 72.

4. However, Gadamer did not completely follow through on this promise, as is discussed below.

5. Althusser, *Philosophy of the Encounter*, 163–207.

6. Althusser writes on Hegel's concept of negativity: "But [Hegelian] negativity can only contain the motor principle of the dialectic, the negation of the negation, as a strict reflection of the Hegelian theoretical presuppositions of simplicity and origin. The dialectic is negativity as an abstraction of the negation of the negation, itself an abstraction of the phenomenon of the restoration of the alienation of the original unity" (Althusser, *For Marx*, 214). And on Hegelian contradiction: "The simplicity of the Hegelian contradiction is made possible *only* by the simplicity of the *internal principle* that constitutes the essence of any historical period. If it is possible, *in principle, to reduce the totality*, the infinite diversity, of a historically given society (Greece, Rome, the Holy Roman Empire, England, and so on) to a *simple internal principle, this very simplicity* can be reflected in the *contradiction to which it thereby acquires a right*" (Althusser, *For Marx*, 103).

7. Deleuze, *Difference and Repetition*, xix.

8. Deleuze writes: "[Hegel] represents concepts instead of dramatizing Ideas: he creates a false theatre, a false drama, a false movement" (Deleuze, *Difference and Repetition*, 10).

9. "Hegelian contradiction does not deny identity or non-contradiction: on the contrary, it consists in inscribing the double negation of non-contradiction within the existent in such a way that identity, under that condition or on that basis, is sufficient to think the existent as such. Those formulae according to which 'the object denies what it is not,' or 'distinguishes itself from everything that it is not,' are logical monsters (the Whole of everything which is not the object) in the service of identity" (Deleuze, *Difference and Repetition*, 49).

10. Deleuze, *Difference and Repetition*, 311.

11. Ibid., 24.

12. Gadamer, *Truth and Method*, 423.

13. Ibid., 115.

14. Ibid., 136.

15. Ibid., 135: "By being presented it experiences, as it were, an *increase in being*. The content of the picture itself is ontologically defined as an emanation of the original."

16. See also Günter Figal, "The Doing of the Thing Itself: Gadamer's Hermeneutic Ontology of Language," in *The Cambridge Companion to Gadamer*, ed. Robert J. Dostal (New York: Cambridge University Press, 2002), 123.

17. Heidegger, *Poetry, Language, Thought*, 35.

18. Gadamer writes quite directly: "A festival exists only in being celebrated" (Gadamer, *Truth and Method*, 121).

19. Deleuze, *Difference and Repetition*, 1.

20. Perhaps we can take Gadamer literally and claim that it is not just that the state draws its real power from symbolic actions or performances like parades, celebrations, and solemn rites, but that the state exists only as its own symbolic actions, which also include the petty prosaic symbolic "actions" that we experience as bureaucratic complications—all statements and confirmations must be, in the final analysis, declared on paper, signed and stamped, otherwise they don't really count. But this would perhaps be putting Althusser's words in his mouth—the thesis of the material existence of the ideology, where the existence of the symbolic order is in its completely practical and even banal rites.

21. As far as the concept of repetition is concerned, I must refer the reader to an intelligent and extremely useful overview of the concept from Plato to Hegel, Kierkegaard, and Lacan. Bara Kolenc argues that we should distinguish four basic matrices of repetition that appear in the history of philosophy as well as in contemporary debates: (1) repetition as *deflation*, which is basically the Platonic doctrine of the infinite divide between the original and the copy; (2) repetition as *reformation*, where the repetition effectively replaces the original and becomes a new original; (3) repetition as *inflation*, which is the model of the notorious "postmodern" production where the difference between the original and repetition becomes indiscernible, so that everything is a repetition (of a repetition); and finally, (4) repetition as *production*, the idea that the repetition produces (and not only replaces) the original as well as the copy. See Bara Kolenc, "Štiri matrice ponavljanja," *Problemi* 9–10 (2016): 112–15. According to this typology, Gadamer's concept should be listed in the category of reformation, whereas what Deleuze is arguing for falls under the final category of production. It should come as no surprise that I count that which is at stake for Hegel and Spinoza in their respective concepts of the negativity at the level of the absolute itself precisely in the same category of production.

22. It is especially interesting how even Heidegger was slowly and gradually appropriated by theological discourse. His essential work, *Being and Time*, is fundamentally and openly opposed to naive affirmative theology; moreover, it demonstrates how naive or vulgar conceptions of deities, guilt, and moral actions are in fact nothing but historical obscurations of the existential character of Dasein. This did not stop, however, more subtle crypto-theologians from *inverting* Heideggerian claims to mean precisely their opposite: that the Christian metaphysical discourse is profoundly correct in its claims and that it simply needs a more contemporary interpretation for which Heidegger precisely laid the grounds. The most honest case for the theological appropriation of Heidegger was made by the great scholar John D. Caputo: "The task of theology, armed now with the Heideggerian analytic of existence, is to deconstruct and demythologize the canonical Gospels in order to retrieve their *kerygma*, the living-existential Christian message, one of existential conversion (*metanoia*), of becoming authentic in the face of our finitude and guilt, a task that faces every

human being" (John D. Caputo, "Heidegger and Theology," in *The Cambridge Companion to Heidegger*, ed. Charles B. Guignon [Cambridge: Cambridge University Press, 1993], 275).

23. The exchange of replies in a conversation, of course, is never a clearly punctuated sequence. The replies almost always overlap—except in very specific circumstances, like for instance sometimes in academic or juridical, that is to say, highly organized discourses. I am not referring here to that annoying habit of constantly interrupting one another without even listening to each other. The point is, rather, that the overlapping conversations are usually still ordered in a logical succession. This is especially clear when we report about our (everyday) conversation to a third party: this is only possible by placing the replies not only in logical, but also in temporal succession, even though they occurred as a continuous overlapping of one thought with the other.

24. Malabou, *Future of Hegel*, 178.

25. Deleuze famously wrote: "There has only ever been one ontological proposition: Being is univocal. There has only ever been one ontology, that of Duns Scotus, which gave being a single voice. We say Duns Scotus because he was the one who elevated univocal being to the highest point of subtlety, albeit at the price of abstraction. However, from Parmenides to Heidegger it is the same voice which is taken up, in an echo which itself forms the whole deployment of the univocal. A single voice raises the clamour of being" (Deleuze, *Difference and Repetition*, 35). See also Deleuze, *Expressionism in Philosophy*, 64–65; and Deleuze, *Spinoza: Practical Philosophy*, 51–52.

26. Deleuze, *Difference and Repetition*, 40. This insistence on the term "affirmative" has, of course, a polemical overtone against Hegel's privileged concept of negation. In the reading proposed here, however, the term "affirmative" designates productivity of being—which is in fact not alien to Hegel's conception at all.

27. Ibid.

28. Jure Simoniti argues that Hegel's idealism should not be interpreted as an intensification of Kant's antirealism, but precisely as a particular kind of realism. He even goes as far as to suggest that Hegel's (unrecognized) genius rests in the fact that he discovered the philosophical method of indifference to the world: while the world may be said to exist, it is bereft of truth, it simply has no truth value; by suggesting the formula of the "untruth of reality," Simoniti defends a realism which does not subscribe to the idea that truth is, for lack of a better expression, out there. For Simoniti, truth belongs specifically to language, and the subject is entitled to indifference to the outer world, just as the world itself is free to lose its meaning (Jure Simoniti, *Untruth of Reality: The Unacknowledged Realism of Modern Philosophy* [Lanham, Md.: Lexington, 2016], 33–37). In our context here, I find the usefulness of Simoniti's interpretation first in the rebuke of what I otherwise simply call naive materialism, assuming that truth is to be found at the end of a long chain of mediations, in some immediate thing; and second, in his formulation of this philosophical position, specifically attributing truth to language, nevertheless as realism of the world.

29. Their position on this point is so close that we can say that Spinoza's

rebuke of the Cartesian idea that one should first acquire a proper method in order to get to true knowledge itself is a brilliant theoretical gesture, repeated famously by Hegel's criticism of Kant's demand that we should first get to know the conditions of our possible knowledge before we can embark on the quest for knowledge itself (Hegel, *Phenomenology of Spirit,* §§73–76, and Spinoza, *TIE* 9).

30. Hegel writes: "Aber wo die Substanz zum Attribut übergeht, ist nicht gesagt. . . . Diese drei Momente [die Substanz, der Attribut, der Modus] hätte Spinoza nicht nur so als Begriffe hinstellen, sondern sie deduzieren müssen" (Hegel, *TWA* 20:169–70).

31. Macherey, *Hegel or Spinoza,* 149; Deleuze, *Expressionism in Philosophy,* 105.

32. Macherey, *Hegel or Spinoza,* 148; Deleuze, *Expressionism in Philosophy,* 184.

33. Macherey, *Hegel or Spinoza,* 147–48.

34. Spinoza's a posteriori demonstration is found in *E*IP11, 222–23.

35. Spinoza, *E*IP25Sch, 232.

36. The term "world-historical individuals" (or men, persons) features prominently in Hegel's lectures on the philosophy of world history (Georg Wilhelm Friedrich Hegel, *Lectures on the Philosophy of World History, Volume 1: Manuscripts of the Introduction and The Lectures of 1822–3,* ed. and trans. Robert F. Brown and Peter C. Hodgson [Oxford: Clarendon, 2011], 96, 172–74).

37. Althusser, *Philosophy of the Encounter,* 189. Matheron pointed out that Althusser considered Hegel by this rule as a *materialist* (François Matheron, "La Récurrence du vide chez Louis Althusser," in *Futur antérieur: Lire Althusser aujourd'hui,* ed. Jean-Marie Vincent [Paris: L'Harmattan, 1997], 32).

Bibliography

Althusser, Louis. *Essays in Self-Criticism.* Translated by Grahame Lock. New York: New Left Books, 1976.

———. *For Marx.* Translated by Ben Brewster. New York: Verso, 2005.

———. "From *Capital* to Marx's Philosophy." In *Reading "Capital,"* by Louis Althusser and Étienne Balibar, translated by Ben Brewster, 13–69. London: New Left Books, 1970.

———. *Lenin and Philosophy and Other Essays.* Translated by Ben Brewster. New York: Monthly Review, 1971.

———. "The Only Materialist Tradition, Part I: Spinoza." In *The New Spinoza,* edited by Warren Montag and Ted Stolze, 3–19. Minneapolis: University of Minnesota Press, 1998.

———. *Philosophy and the Spontaneous Philosophy of Scientists & Other Essays.* Translated by James H. Kavanagh. New York: Verso, 1990.

———. *Philosophy of the Encounter: Later Writings 1978–87.* Edited by François Matheron and Oliver Corpet, translated by G. M. Goshgarian. New York: Verso, 2006.

———. *Solitude de Machiavel.* Paris: Presses Universitaires de France, 1998.

Aristotle. *Physics: Books I and II.* Translated by William Charlton. Oxford: Oxford University Press, 2006.

———. *Physics: Books III and IV.* Translated by Edward Hussey. Oxford: Oxford University Press, 1993.

———. *Physics: Book VIII.* Translated by Daniel W. Graham. New York: Oxford University Press, 1999.

Badiou, Alain. *Saint Paul: The Foundation of Universalism.* Translated by Ray Brassier. Stanford, Calif.: Stanford University Press, 1997.

Boethius. *Consolation of Philosophy.* Translated by Joel C. Relihan. Indianapolis, Ind.: Hackett, 2001.

Brentano, Franz. *Philosophical Investigations on Space, Time, and the Continuum.* Translated by Barry Smith. New York: Routledge, 1988.

Caputo, John D. "Heidegger and Theology." In *The Cambridge Companion to Heidegger,* edited by Charles B. Guignon, 270–88. Cambridge: Cambridge University Press, 1993.

Cassin, Barbara. *L'Effet sophistique.* Paris: Gallimard, 1995.

Chitty, Andrew. "Hegel and Marx." In *A Companion to Hegel,* edited by Stephen Houlgate and Michael Baur, 477–500. Oxford: Blackwell, 2011.

Cole, Andrew. *The Birth of Theory.* Chicago: University of Chicago Press, 2014.

Dahlstrom, Daniel. "Moses Mendelssohn." In *The Stanford Encyclopedia of Philosophy,* Spring 2011 Edition, edited by E. N. Zalta. 2011. http://plato.stanford.edu/archives/spr2011/entries/mendelssohn/.

Deleuze, Gilles. *Difference and Repetition.* Translated by P. Patton. New York: Columbia University Press, 2005.

———. *Expressionism in Philosophy: Spinoza.* Translated by M. Joughin. New York: Zone Books, 1990.

———. *Spinoza: Practical Philosophy.* Translated by R. Hurley. San Francisco: City Lights Books, 2003.

Derrida, Jacques. *Of Grammatology.* Translated by Gayatri Chakravorty Spivak. Baltimore: Johns Hopkins University Press, 1997.

———. "A Time for Farewells: Heidegger (Read by) Hegel (Read by) Malabou." Translated by Joseph D. Cohen. In *The Future of Hegel: Plasticity, Temporality and Dialectic,* by Catherine Malabou, vii–xlvii. London: Routledge, 2005.

Dolar, Mladen. "Beyond Interpellation." *Qui Parle* 6, no. 2 (1993): 75–96.

———. *Heglova Fenomenologija duha I* [*Hegel's Phenomenology of Spirit, Vol. I*]. Ljubljana: Društvo za teoretsko psihoanalizo, 1990.

———. *Samozavedanje: Heglova Fenomenologija duha II* [*Self-Consciousness: Hegel's Phenomenology of Spirit. Vol. 2*]. Ljubljana: Društvo za teoretsko psihoanalizo, 1992.

Düsing, Klaus. "Von der Substanz zum Subjekt: Hegels spekulative Spinoza-Deutung." In *Spinoza und der Deutsche Idealismus,* edited by Manfred Walther, 163–80. Würzburg: Königshausen und Neumann, 1992.

Figal, Günter. "The Doing of the Thing Itself: Gadamer's Hermeneutic Ontology of Language." In *The Cambridge Companion to Gadamer,* edited by Robert J. Dostal. New York: Cambridge University Press, 2002.

Gadamer, Hans-Georg. *Truth and Method.* Translated by J. Weinsheimer and D. G. Marshall. London: Continuum, 2004.

Gueroult, Martial. *Spinoza I: Dieu (Ethique, I).* Paris: Aubier-Montaigne, 1968.

Hegel, Georg Wilhelm Friedrich. *Faith and Knowledge.* Translated by Walter Cerf and H. S. Harris. Albany: State University of New York Press, 1977.

———. *Gesamte Werkausgabe: Werke.* Volumes 1–20. Edited by E. Moldenhauer and K. M. Michel. Frankfurt am Main: Suhrkamp, 1986.

———. *Hegel's Philosophy of Nature: Vol. III.* Translated by M. J. Petry. London: Unwin, 1970.

———. *Lectures on the History of Philosophy, Vol. 1.* Translated by E. S. Haldane. London: Kegan Paul, 1892.

———. *Lectures on the History of Philosophy, Vol. 2.* Translated by E. S. Haldane and Frances H. Simson. London: Kegan Paul, 1894.

———. *Lectures on the History of Philosophy, Vol. 3.* Translated by Elisabeth S. Haldane and Frances H. Simson. London: Kegan Paul, 1896.

———. *Lectures on the Philosophy of World History, Volume 1: Manuscripts of the Introduction and The Lectures of 1822–3.* Edited and translated by Robert F. Brown and Peter C. Hodgson. Oxford: Clarendon, 2011.

———. *Phenomenology of Spirit*. Translated by A. V. Miller. Oxford: Oxford University Press, 1977.

———. *The Science of Logic*. Translated by George di Giovanni. New York: Cambridge University Press, 2010.

Heidegger, Martin. *Being and Time*. Translated by J. Stambaugh. New York: State University of New York Press, 1996.

———. *Poetry, Language, Thought*. Translated by A. Hofstadter. New York: Harper and Row, 1971.

———. *The Question Concerning Technology and Other Essays*. Translated by W. Lovitt. New York: Garland, 1977.

Henrich, Dieter. *Hegel im Kontext*. Frankfurt am Main: Suhrkamp, 1971.

Houlgate, Stephen. *The Opening of Hegel's Logic: From Being to Infinity*. West Lafayette, Ind.: Purdue University Press, 2005.

Jacobi, Friedrich Heinrich. *The Main Philosophical Writings and the Novel "Allwill."* Translated by George di Giovanni. Montreal: McGill-Queen's University Press, 1994.

Johnston, Adrian. *Adventures in Transcendental Materialism: Dialogues with Contemporary Thinkers*. Edinburgh: Edinburgh University Press, 2014.

Kleist, Heinrich von. "On the Gradual Production of Thoughts Whilst Speaking." In *Selected Writings*, edited and translated by David Constantine, 405–9. Indianapolis, Ind.: Hackett, 1997.

Kolenc, Bara. "Štiri matrice ponavljanja." *Problemi* 9–10 (2016): 105–18.

Kott, Jan. *The Eating of the Gods*. Evanston, Ill.: Northwestern University Press, 1987.

Lacan, Jacques. *The Seminar of Jacques Lacan: On Feminine Sexuality: The Limits of Love and Knowledge: Book XX, Encore, 1972–1973*. Edited by Jacques-Alain Miller, translated by Bruce Fink. New York: Norton, 1999.

Lloyd, Genevieve. *Spinoza and the "Ethics."* London: Routledge, 1996.

Luther, Martin. *Commentary on the Epistle to Galatians*. Grand Rapids, Mich.: Zondervan, 1949.

Macherey, Pierre. *Hegel or Spinoza*. Translated by Susan B. Ruddick. Minneapolis: University of Minnesota Press, 2011.

———. "Le Spinoza idéaliste de Hegel." In *Spinoza und der Deutsche Idealismus*, edited by Manfred Walther, 145–62. Würzburg: Königshausen und Neumann, 1992.

Malabou, Catherine. *The Future of Hegel: Plasticity, Temporality and Dialectic*. Translated by L. During. London: Routledge, 2005.

Marx, Karl. "Theses on Feuerbach." In *Ludwig Feuerbach and the End of Classical German Philosophy*, by Frederick Engels, 61–65. Peking: Foreign Languages, 1976.

Matheron, François. "La Récurrence du vide chez Louis Althusser." In *Futur antérieur: Lire Althusser aujourd'hui*, edited by Jean-Marie Vincent, 23–48. Paris: L'Harmattan, 1997.

Melamed, Yitzhak Y. "'Omnis Determinatio Est Negatio': Determination, Negation, and Self-Negation in Spinoza, Kant, and Hegel." In *Spinoza and*

German Idealism, edited by Eckart Förster and Yitzhak Y. Melamed, 176–96. Cambridge: Cambridge University Press, 2012.

Montag, Warren. "Spinoza and Althusser against Hermeneutics: Interpretation or Intervention?" In *The Althusserian Legacy*, edited by E. Ann Kaplan and Michael Sprinker, 51–58. New York: Verso, 1993.

Morfino, Vittorio. "The Misunderstanding of the Mode: Spinoza in Hegel's *Science of Logic* (1812–1816)." In *Between Hegel and Spinoza: A Volume of Critical Essays*, edited by Hasana Sharp and Jason E. Smith, 23–41. London: Bloomsbury Academic, 2014.

Nadler, Steven. *Spinoza: A Life*. New York: Cambridge University Press, 1999.

Negri, Antonio. *The Savage Anomaly: The Power of Spinoza's Metaphysics and Politics*. Translated by Michael Hardt. Minneapolis: University of Minnesota Press, 2000.

Nietzsche, Friedrich. *On the Genealogy of Morality*. Translated by Carol Diethe. Cambridge: Cambridge University Press, 2006.

Noys, Benjamin. *The Persistence of the Negative: A Critique of Contemporary Continental Theory*. Edinburgh: Edinburgh University Press, 2010.

Pascal, Blaise. *"Pensées" and Other Writings*. Translated by Honor Levi. Oxford: Oxford University Press, 1995.

Peden, Knox. *Spinoza contra Phenomenology: French Rationalism from Cavaillès to Deleuze*. Stanford, Calif.: Stanford University Press, 2014.

Pfaller, Robert. *Althusser—Das Schweigen im Text: Epistemologie, Psychoanalyse und Nominalismus in Louis Althussers Theorie der Lektüre*. Paderborn: W. Fink Verlag, 1997.

———. "The Familiar Unknown, the Uncanny, the Comic." In *Lacan: The Silent Partners*, edited by Slavoj Žižek, 198–216. New York: Verso, 2006.

———. *On the Pleasure Principle in Culture: Illusions without Owners*. Translated by Lisa Rosenblatt et al. New York: Verso, 2014.

Plotinus. *The Enneads*. Translated by Stephen MacKenna and B. S. Page. New York: Larson Publications, 1992.

Quintilian. *The Orator's Education, Volume V: Books 11–12*. Edited and translated by Donald A. Russell. Cambridge, Mass.: Harvard University Press, 2002.

Rodin, Auguste. "Movement in Art." In *Rodin on Art and Artists: Conversations with Paul Gsell*, 32–36. New York: Dover, 2009.

Saussure, Ferdinand de. *Course in General Linguistics*. Translated by W. Baskin. New York: McGraw-Hill, 1959.

Schuster, Aaron. *The Trouble with Pleasure: Deleuze and Psychoanalysis*. Cambridge, Mass.: MIT Press, 2015.

Simoniti, Jure. *Untruth of Reality: The Unacknowledged Realism of Modern Philosophy*. Lanham, Md.: Lexington, 2016.

Spinoza, Baruch de. *Spinoza: Complete Works*. Translated by S. Shirley et al. Indianapolis, Ind.: Hackett, 2002.

Tavoillot, Pierre-Henry. "Spinoza dans la querelle du panthéisme." In *Spinoza au XIXe siècle*, edited by A. Tosel, P.-F. Moreau, and J. Salem, 35–45. Paris: Publications de la Sorbonne, 2007.

Taylor, Charles. *Hegel*. New York: Cambridge University Press, 1977.

Vaysse, Jean-Marie. "Spinoza dans la problématique de l'idéalisme allemande." In *Spinoza au XIXe siècle*, edited by A. Tosel, P.-F. Moreau, and J. Salem, 65–74. Paris: Publications de la Sorbonne, 2007.

Vinciguerra, Lorenzo. *Spinoza et le signe: La genèse de l'imagination*. Paris: Vrin, 2005.

Žižek, Slavoj. "Class Struggle or Postmodernism? Yes, Please!" In *Contingency, Hegemony, Universality: Contemporary Dialogues on the Left*, by Judith Butler, Ernesto Laclau, and Slavoj Žižek, 90–135. London: Verso, 2000.

———. "The Fear of Four Words: A Modest Plea for the Hegelian Reading of Christianity." In Slavoj Žižek and John Milbank, *The Monstrosity of Christ: Paradox or Dialectic?* edited by Creston Davies, 24–109. Cambridge, Mass.: MIT Press, 2009.

———. *The Fragile Absolute; or, Why Is the Christian Legacy Worth Fighting For?* New York: Verso, 2001.

———. *Less Than Nothing: Hegel and the Shadow of Dialectical Materialism*. New York: Verso, 2012.

———. "Materializem in neskončnost." Knjižnica Otona Župančiča, Ljubljana, 2007. Public lecture.

———. *The Parallax View*. Cambridge, Mass.: MIT Press, 2006.

———. *The Sublime Object of Ideology*. New York: Verso, 2008.

———. *Tarrying with the Negative: Kant, Hegel and Critique of Ideology*. Durham, N.C.: Duke University Press, 1993.

Zupančič, Alenka. *The Odd One In: On Comedy*. Cambridge, Mass.: MIT Press, 2008.

Index